# FREEDOM FIGHTERS

# FREEDOM FIGHTERS

## WALES'S FORGOTTEN 'WAR', 1963–1993

John Humphries

UNIVERSITY OF WALES PRESS, CARDIFF, 2008

*www.uwp.co.uk*

*British Library Cataloguing-in-Publication Data*
A catalogue record for this book is available from the British Library.

ISBN 978-0-7083-2177-5

Typeset by the University of Wales Press
Printed on demand by CPI Group (UK) Ltd, Croydon, CR0 4YY

# CONTENTS

# FOREWORD

The maxim that one man's terrorist is another man's freedom fighter was never far from my mind in compiling this account of a period in recent history when the Welsh turned to violence to defend their cultural heritage and make a case for independence. A generation after water pipelines and government buildings were blown up, and holiday homes burned down, has the wheel finally turned against nationalist diehards in the wake of Islamic terrorism? Where there was once sympathy, even support, can the proponents of direct action in the struggle for national freedom expect short shrift if they dare to re-emerge from the shadows of a violent past?

Despite the feigned detachment of the nationalist political establishment, it is hard to deny that its cause prospered from the direct action to redress injustices, coinciding as it did with a period of unprecedented change in the way Wales was governed. While the attacks on water pipelines, second homes and the attempt to prevent the Investiture of the Prince of Wales – all symbols of Wales's cultural and economic subjugation – were loudly condemned by some, they received muted applause from others. Besides being as far as is possible an authentic record of that period, I hope that at the very least *Freedom Fighters* – by addressing what contribution, if any, direct action made towards Wales's longer term aspirations as a nation state – rehabilitates Welsh freedom fighters into the mainstream history of Wales.

A book dealing as it does with events that are still the subject of police investigation would not have been possible without the cooperation – given intentionally or without their knowledge – of a large number of persons generally regarded as being on the extremist fringes of the Welsh nationalist movement. For the assistance of those who are rarely invited into the corridors of power in Wales I am sincerely grateful. Because these are dangerous times for all who espouse nonconformist views, I doubt they would want a personal acknowledgement!

I would, however, like to acknowledge the support I received from the Freedom of Information Act in obtaining the release of documents government departments sought to suppress and the assistance of the National Archives and the National Library of Wales in helping me to delve ever deeper into events and persons from this period. A rich vein of information has also been provided by such newspapers as the *Western Mail* and *Daily Post*, which were committed to the detailed reporting of events in the period covered by *Freedom Fighters*.

Finally, I am grateful to my publishers, the University of Wales Press, for recognising as valuable to students of British history a subject that so far has been neglected by more conventional historians.

John Humphries
Tredunnoc, Gwent
September 2008

# LIST OF ILLUSTRATIONS

# 1

## THREE-MINUTE WARNING

It was just before midnight, as I left the *Western Mail*'s Cardiff newsroom for home on 6 March 1966, when the news-desk telephone rang, for what seemed like the thousandth time that day. Days on the news-desk were all much the same – long, with a pair of constantly ringing telephones primed to stop me in my tracks whenever I made a move, even if only towards the toilet. For twelve hours every day I was trapped in that great smoke-filled cavern, lined with its rows of cigarette-scarred, graffiti-engraved desks, resonating under the weight of millions of eminently forgettable words rattled out on clapped-out typewriters by equally worn-out reporters. Battered or not, desks and typewriters were assets, which the reporters, like the lost tribes of Israel, were required to hump across the road when the newspaper's new owner, Canadian press baron Lord Thomson, found a new place to pitch his tent, a 1960s-style blockhouse, Thomson House. But with the new offices came a new breed: the very first intake of university graduates, bright-eyed and bushy-tailed, flaunting their intelligence in the faces of the older hands, who regarded them as carpetbaggers committed only to their next promotion. Resented and envied in equal measure, these new kids on the journalistic block were, however, an inescapable sign that hard graft and 140-words-a-minute short-hand, fuelled by forty cigarettes a day and liquid lunches, were no longer sufficient to last the course. Every new graduate probably saw me as one of that dying breed, doomed to end its days in smoke-filled newsrooms, with no more than blind commitment and pocket dictionaries for back-up. But at least I had given up smoking that week!

'Let it ring. Leave it to the late man', I thought, spying him at the far end of the newsroom hovering around the sub-editors' desk, a large U-shaped edifice with the company sergeant major, otherwise the chief sub-editor, at its beating heart, driving his troops to catch every edition and page change, a hundred times a night, every night. The duty reporter was one of those politically astute university graduates who believed night reporting was a chore to be left to the dullards. For him, the *Western Mail* was rather like a motorway service-station: a fuel-stop before moving on to the BBC, ITV, even Westminster. As I pushed through the newsroom doors, I knew instinctively that if the night guy failed to spot the story on the end of that ringing telephone, I would carry the can while he walked away with an indifferent shrug of his shoulders. After all, it was only news, which the new breed thought that as news editor I harvested every day from some mystical orchard behind my desk.

If that were the case, then that particular day's harvest had been pretty poor. Sometimes the most memorable events are not what gets in the newspaper, but what happens in the process of putting it there. Another bad news-day sticks in my memory, for no other reason than that the 'Toasted Cheese Sandwich Affair' occurred during the years when anonymous midnight callers were writing a new chapter in the history of Wales. Because of the nature of a beast born not long after sun-up, raised in a burst of activity of cataclysmic proportions, before expiring beneath an avalanche of newsprint, a newspaper inevitably attracts a rum bunch of characters, among them fools and misfits, many whose lives are ruined by the daily rigour. Some without the mental and physical stamina resort to the bottle to escape the grinding routine that pushes them ever closer to the edge. Although I only ever encountered two with bottles secreted in their desks to get them through the day, and another with the legendary hip-flask he did his level best to empty by ten o'clock every morning, the *Western Mail* had its allocation of journalistic drifters with problems. Most gambled on escaping detection for about two years, by which time they were ready to move on anyhow.

As far as I could ascertain, the 'Toasted Cheese Sandwich Affair' had nothing whatsoever to do with anyone's drink problem. Either the pressures of newspaper work or his own inadequacies had driven 'Wally' off the precipice before he ever came to us. A new job in a new city had not saved him and, evicted from his flat, Wally was reduced to living in a battered old yellow VW car, stuffed with piles of newspapers as draught-excluders. It might have been snug, but it was certainly not hygienic, a problem he brought to the office every night, a single whiff sufficient to make Wally a social outcast throughout the building. Huddled in the same baggy grey sweater, and trailing a chunky scarf of immense length through the newsroom dust, he sat in glorious isolation at one end of the sub-editors' desk, his colleagues fighting each other to be as far away as possible at the other. I had seen something like this once before, when a copy-taker – one of those remarkable individuals who could type a news story dictated down the telephone faster than a reporter could read it – was regularly accompanied to the office by a colony of fleas. His black bowler hung menacingly on one of the newsroom's two coat-stands, the fleas playing hopscotch around the brim, while at the far end of the room the other had collapsed under a mountain of coats, jackets and hats.

It is not easy to fire someone because they smell. It is just as difficult to tell them to wash. Since no one had the bottle for this, the situation festered until the newsroom staff took unilateral action and set fire to Wally's beloved scarf, hanging in the cloakroom. Then one night, while he was on a toilet break, they stuck a toasted cheese sandwich on his seat, which he proceeded to parade upstairs and downstairs for an hour before realising he was attracting more attention than usual. At this point, the problem, together with the remains of the toasted cheese sandwich, landed on my desk, my first executive decision to manoeuvre myself into a position to deal with the furore downwind. Like most petty incidents, it was not resolved, although everyone agreed Wally had to go.

Not immediately, but later, the opportunity arose to get rid of him. As was his custom, Wally had asked, politely, if he could approach the news-desk with a query on a story. While other sub-editors would fling the copy in my face, accompanied by a tirade about incompetent reporters, Wally was always polite and differential, which was fine so long as he kept his distance.

On this occasion, he tapped the desk gently several times remarking, 'I used to fly one of these.'

'What do you mean, Wally?' I asked.

'During the War, I was in Bomber Command over Germany', he explained.

I might have agreed news editing was a bit like flying by the seat of your pants, but this was the first time I had known the news-desk described as a Flying Fortress. At the time I thought no more of the conversation, until, having cause to examine Wally's curriculum vitae, I realised that if correct he was the Second World War's only twelve-year-old bomber pilot. On the strength of this memory lapse we persuaded Wally to seek psychiatric help, from which he never returned.

That particular night in March 1966 contained no such light relief, the only thing beckoning at the end of twelve hours of jangling telephones being the Territorial Army Club, a veritable last-stop saloon for ex-soldiers and the *Western Mail*'s night staff. But there was to be no easy escape. Heading for the staff exit and freedom, I was ambushed by the night watchman.

'A call for the news desk, Mr Humphries', he said, thrusting a telephone into my hand through the window of his tiny cabin.

'Let the late-duty man take it', I snapped.

'I tried, but he said the caller wants to speak to the editor.'

Since the editor never took calls from outsiders, that meant me. As much as I felt like wringing the night reporter's neck, I had no choice but take the receiver and mumble 'news desk', two words that filled my life and dreams.

The accent of the man at the other end was nondescript, neither Welsh nor English. Whoever was calling was evidently struggling to disguise his voice. Brief, staccato and one-way, the mystery man warned the *Western Mail* that within a few minutes a bomb would explode at the Clywedog Reservoir, then being built by eleven English water companies near Llanidloes, in Montgomeryshire. There was no intention to harm anyone, he said, adding that it was a protest about the drowning of another Welsh valley to supply cheap water to England.

When completed in a year's time, the reservoir would supply six million consumers in the Midlands and counties adjacent to the English side of the river Severn with water impounded in Wales. The £4.5 million reservoir would release an additional 100 million gallons a day into the river Severn for extraction downstream, mainly during the summer months. For this, four farms and countless acres were being drowned, in return for improved flood prevention, compensation to the farmers and some new roads in one of the remotest and rarely visited parts of Wales. Montgomeryshire County Council, the only Welsh authority involved, would receive a small amount of the water from the reservoir.

The previous year, at Tryweryn, Liverpool Corporation had opened the first impounding reservoir built in Britain, in the process inundating the village of Capel Celyn, near Bala, its chapel, schoolhouse, post office and cemetery. Public outrage was of an intensity not previously experienced in Wales, this culminating in four separate attempts to sabotage the project when democratic protest failed. Despite the opposition of every Welsh Member of Parliament, Harold Macmillan's government, advised by Henry Brooke, his Minister for Welsh Affairs, ignored what was generally regarded as cultural genocide. Even the hymn-singing of seventy Capel Celyn villagers, led by Plaid Cymru President Gwynfor Evans through the streets of Liverpool, failed to move Liverpool city councillors, meeting behind closed doors to seal the fate of this remote Welsh village. The drowning of Capel Celyn, where every man, woman and child spoke Welsh, became symbolic of the cultural death-throes of a nation engulfed by processes of suppression, assimilation and exploitation.

My first thought after the midnight caller slammed the receiver back into its cradle was that it was all starting again. Scuttling back to the newsroom, I instructed the duty librarian to dig out background on 'Welsh extremism', while I rang police headquarters to alert them to the call. They knew nothing about any incident at Clywedog. This was no surprise. 'Nothing happening' was their stock answer to most press inquiries. Notoriously unhelpful, Welsh police would also prove themselves ill-equipped to deal with the bombing campaign of the 1960s, leaving the Home Office with no alternative but to dispatch a special squad to Wales, led by men experienced in counter-terrorism. A mumbled telephone conversation was precious little from which to build a story in the absence of police confirmation, although it emerged later Gwynedd police had received a warning call to their headquarters at Caernarfon fifteen minutes before the *Western Mail*. In the meantime, the most I could do for the last edition was cobble together a few paragraphs, using background from the previous sabotage attempts at Tryweryn.

Next morning, I discovered that Clywedog had indeed been bombed, the explosion bringing down a thirty-three-foot steel mast supporting an aerial cableway, known as a Blondin (after the famous French acrobat who crossed the gorge below Niagara Falls on a tightrope). The most important piece of equipment on site, the cableway carried giant buckets of concrete to build the buttresses for the highest dam in Britain. The powerful blast at 12.45 a.m. blew a seven-foot-deep hole in the rock-face anchoring the crane, in the process demolishing several thousand yards of cableway stretching across the Clywedog Valley. Despite official denials, this single act of sabotage, causing £30,000-worth of damage, would delay construction by six months.

Six men were involved in sabotaging Clywedog, two to place the bomb in position, the others acquiring the materials, building the device and providing intelligence. No one has ever been arrested. One of the saboteurs was living abroad in 2008. A Free Wales Army cap found near the seat of the explosion was planted deliberately to confuse police, because Mudiad Amddiffyn Cymru (MAC), the Movement for the Defence of Wales, the secret extremist nationalist organisation responsible for sabotaging Tryweryn in 1963, was back in business, as MAC2. The blast at Clywedog was the first of twenty incidents for which it would subsequently be held responsible.

Far from being isolated acts, Tryweryn and Clywedog were milestones in a thirty-year 'war', which had as much to do with the struggle for independence

Wreckage of the overhead cableway known as 'Blondin' used in the construction of the Clywedog Dam after being sabotaged in March 1966. Copyright: *Daily Post*, Liverpool.

as it had with saving Wales's cultural heritage. The totem around which the insurgents rallied was a concerted campaign to prevent the Investiture of the Prince of Wales in Caernarfon in July 1969. What followed Tryweryn constituted the most significant outbreak of violent protest in Wales since Owain Glyndŵr's uprising in 1400. Not even the jailing of three of the principal protagonists, Owen (later known as Owain) Williams (1963), and John Jenkins and Frederick Alders (1970), for their various parts in the sabotage campaign would break the extremist group: it retreated underground, only to re-emerge in 1979, with English-owned holiday cottages its new target. Arson attacks on about 200 holiday homes across north and west Wales, and in London and other major English cities, would continue unchecked for ten years. To this day, a young man, who was nine years of age when the first holiday home was torched, is the only person ever convicted of anything remotely connected to these attacks. His offence: sending letter-bombs through the post, for which he was sentenced to twelve years in prison.

Forty years later, the phantoms of Mudiad Amddiffyn Cymru flicker dimly. Welsh consciousness is uncomfortable with the memory of the 1960s sabotage campaign that targeted water pipelines, government offices and the Prince of Wales. Three men died, others were jailed, and Prime Minister Harold Wilson came close to advising the Palace to cancel the Investiture of the twenty-first Prince of Wales at Caernarfon Castle. If this had happened, as the insurgents intended, it would have signalled to the world that the royal writ no longer ran in Wales, a defining moment in the struggle for independence.

Who were these men who resorted to direct action in the struggle for Wales, and why did they do it? George Taylor (from Abergele, killed), Alwyn Jones (Abergele, killed), John Jenkins (Wrexham and Bargoed, jailed, ten years), Ernest Alders (Wrexham, jailed, six years), Sion Aubrey Roberts (Anglesey, jailed, twelve years), Owen Williams (Nefyn, jailed, twelve months), Emyr Llewelyn Jones (Aberystwyth, jailed, twelve months), Albert Jones (Nefyn, probation, three years), William Glyn Jones (Trearddur Bay, Anglesey, jailed, eighteen months), Dewi Jones (Porthmadoc, jailed, eighteen months), John Allan Jones (Tŷ Groes, Anglesey, jailed, six months, suspended), Cayo Evans (Lampeter, jailed, fifteen months), Dennis Coslett (Llangadog, jailed, fifteen months), Keith Griffiths (Brynteg, Anglesey, jailed, nine months), Tony Lewis (Cwmbran, jailed, eight months, suspended), Vivian Davies (Swansea, jailed, six months, suspended), William Griffiths (Lampeter, jailed, three months, suspended), Dai Pritchard (New Tredegar, fined), Dave Walters (Bargoed, fined). Others escaped imprisonment by the skin of their teeth. And there were those, like Harri Webb, the Merthyr poet and editor of Plaid Cymru's *Welsh Nation*, and Trefor Beasley, the language campaigner, whose links to the insurrection were unknown until long after their deaths.

While cultural activists were lionised, there was little place for any of these in the pantheon of Welsh heroes. They were best forgotten, as was their insurrection. According to Jenkins, jailed for ten years in 1970, 'MAC gave nationalism prison, death and blood. What more did they want? Instead, they have opted to write us out of history.'[1]

In anywhere else but Wales, the timing of the Clywedog bombing, just three weeks before the 1966 General Election, on 31 March – before even the Provisional IRA became active – might have been expected to cause some electoral ripples. As the ebullient Labour politician George Brown, soon to become Foreign Secretary in Harold Wilson's government, told me famously during the ensuing election campaign, 'Boyo, in Wales we don't count the votes, we weigh them.'

With only three weeks remaining before handing over to Cledwyn Hughes at the Welsh Office, James Griffiths, Wales's first Secretary of State, was fairly restrained in his reaction to the bombing:

> I am shocked and I know so are the overwhelming majority of my confederates by this stupid act of destruction, which can do nothing but harm to Wales and the nation. It is particularly unfortunate that it comes at a time when the Government is striving by every means to strengthen the economy of Mid-Wales.[2]

Until almost the very eve of the Investiture, by which time the sabotage campaign was into its fourth year, the official response to the escalating violence was to marginalise the saboteurs as an insignificant group of crazed nationalist fanatics. The instinctive reaction of the police to Clywedog was to blame the Welsh nationalist party Plaid Cymru, in particular those connected to the local Montgomeryshire branch. Within days of the bombing, the registration numbers of cars parked outside Plaid election rallies in the constituency were being taken and 500 people with known nationalist sympathies interviewed by police, including a headmaster within view of his school pupils. Plaid Cymru's Montgomeryshire constituency party lodged a formal complaint with the Welsh Office that police interference in the aftermath of the Clywedog bombing had destroyed its electoral chances.[3]

As it happened, Clywedog had the reverse effect four months later, when the party's president, Gwynfor Evans, won the Carmarthen by-election on 14 July 1966, following the death of the Liberal Lady Megan Lloyd George. The election of Plaid's first member of the Westminster Parliament was a seminal event in the history of Welsh nationalism. Public outrage over the drowning of Capel Celyn, followed by the building of Clywedog, not only contributed to the party's electoral triumph, but boosted its membership to a historic 30,000. The aftermath of the Clywedog bombing was one of those rare occasions when the usually pacifist nationalist leader offered succour to the saboteurs, warning that while Plaid did not support violence, the use of it was 'bound to grow and get worse if our constitutional efforts are ignored and we are continually suppressed …'.[4] He had no hesitation in blaming the exploitation of Welsh water resources by successive London governments for what had occurred. His electoral campaign received a further boost when in the middle of it the Severn River Authority revealed it was looking at even more Welsh valleys to drown. Thereafter, the new member for Carmarthen would spend much of his political career distancing himself from the direct action nationalists. Removing English-only road-signs to highlight the plight of the Welsh language was admirable; sabotage was beyond the pale. According to John Jenkins, towards the end of his life Evans regretted being the only nationalist leader never to have been imprisoned for his beliefs:

> He excused himself by saying that at the time when he should have made the ultimate sacrifice he had a growing family and a market garden to keep, and could not afford to involve himself. But there is always a good excuse for not doing anything. At the end of the day it cost me everything, my job, house, family, and liberty. This is the price you pay. Don't complain because there is never the right time to do anything. I also loved my family but I was firm with them. My eldest was ten when I went to prison and sixteen when I came out. He has not called me dad ever since. You have to be single-minded.[5]

A month after the Clywedog explosion, one of the first duties for Cledwyn Hughes, the new Secretary of State for Wales, was to meet a very worried Water Resources Board. Fearing more sabotage at the dam, the Board wanted farm-land seized compulsorily from farmers still holding out for better compensation. The process had already been complicated by a farmer having leased 2.6 acres for twenty-five years to Plaid Cymru so that the land could be subdivided into square-yard plots, rented at £12 apiece to 200 people from Wales and abroad. One of these was Sergeant John Jenkins, then serving with the Royal Army Dental Corps in Germany, the man who became chief bomb-maker for MAC2. The subdivision of the land had been a ploy to delay construction, because all landowners had a statutory right to attend any subsequent public inquiry. But this was circumvented by new government legislation.[6]

What concerned the Water Resources Board most was the 'possibility of a disaster of the first magnitude' if the dam were sabotaged once it was operational. The experience at Tryweryn in 1963 had shown that despite considerable expenditure by Liverpool Corporation to safeguard construction work, it was impossible to provide complete security. Horrified to hear from board officials of the 'fearsome possibility' of a disaster of catastrophic proportions, Cledwyn Hughes promised immediate action to protect the dam and personnel then investigating twenty other potential reservoir-sites in the Severn River basin.[7]

After the explosion halted work at the site, so concerned were the English water authorities building the reservoir that the Ministry of Defence was asked for troops and dogs to be deployed. Dismissing this as panic, the Welsh Office settled for increased policing, not that this did anything to allay the concern of the reservoir consortium, which had little confidence in the Mid Wales Police Constabulary's ability, even its willingness, to provide adequate security. The consortium would not be the first, nor the last, to express serious doubts about the competence of Welsh police-forces in dealing with extremism. Critics at the highest levels of government suspected that some officers in Wales sympathised with the extremists, to the extent of leaking information about covert police operations.[8]

Two days after his meeting with the Water Resources Board, Hughes faced questions in the House of Commons from Geoffrey Lloyd (Conservative, Sutton Coalfield) about the protection provided for the 400 construction workers, the impact the explosion had had upon recruitment and what action was being taken to prevent further delay. Hughes replied that the delay would be no longer than two months, when in fact it proved to be six. Of one thing, however, the Welsh Secretary was absolutely certain: there would be no official opening of Clywedog, whenever that might be, for fear of triggering the kind of unpleasant demonstration that had marred the opening of Tryweryn the previous year. On that occasion, hundreds of flag-waving protesters swarmed down the hillside on to the convoy of cars bringing dignitaries from Liverpool. Power cables were ripped up, the refreshment marquee collapsed and Union flags were burned in the rioting that followed. The ceremony was abandoned, and the visitors fled, incapable, it seemed from the remarks of one of the Liverpool dignitaries, Alderman David Cowley, of understanding the insensitivity of their decision to have a formal opening. 'If I had brought the Kop with me today', he told reporters, referring to the packed terraces behind the goal at Liverpool Football Club's Anfield ground, 'there wouldn't have been a murmur out of this lot. They'd have been too afraid to open their mouths. The Kop would eat them.' In the light of what had happened at Tryweryn, the security necessary ruled out the possibility of any member of the Royal Family taking part in an inauguration ceremony at Clywedog.[9]

Besides being a focus for political and cultural unrest, the significance of Clywedog and Tryweryn for the United Kingdom's water network cannot be over-estimated. Both were impounding reservoirs, collecting water in Wales for distribution at relatively little on-cost to England by using the rivers Severn and Dee as simple, inexpensive means of distribution. Experience gained from their construction was of considerable importance for the future management of the UK's water resources. Nearly fifty years later, with climate change threatening water shortages, the distribution of supplies from areas of high rainfall such as Wales to those suffering shortages by means of impounding reservoirs linked to river systems, even to canals, is seen by the industry as allowing water to be moved around and traded like any other commodity.

Initially, the government of Harold Wilson, beset by all manner of problems, made little attempt to understand what was happening in Wales. After all, had it not created a Welsh Office, to which some administrative powers had been transferred? What more could the Welsh possibly want? The threat posed by the bombings was dismissed as the work of a small bunch of fanatics, most probably with links to the self-styled Free Wales Army, which seemed to exist only in the fevered imagination of nationalist cranks and newspaper-headline writers. Only when the focus of nationalist resistance was thought to have shifted to the extremists of Mudiad Amddiffyn Cymru (MAC) was the investigation given top priority. By then both the government and bombers shared the same time-horizon: the 1969 Investiture of the Prince of Wales at Caernarfon Castle. Before that, the Prince was due to spend three months at University College of Wales, Aberystwyth, learning Welsh and something of the history of Wales in preparation for his Investiture. Much was at stake. Nothing could be left to chance.

Until the 1960s, nationalist protest had remained relatively peaceful, after Saunders Lewis, one of the founders of Plaid Cymru, accompanied by two other intellectuals, Lewis Valentine (his predecessor as party president) and the writer D. J. Williams, had set fire to parts of the Royal Air Force training base, known as the 'bombing school' at Penyberth, near Pwllheli, in September 1936. Never intended as anything other than a symbolic protest over the 'English' government's decision to turn one of the 'essential homes of Welsh culture, idiom and literature' into a site for promoting barbaric warfare, Lewis, a life-long pacifist, promptly surrendered to the police along with his two accomplices. At their trial in Caernarfon, the contemptuous attitude of the judge towards the Welsh language may have influenced the jury, which failed to agree. The retrial was at the Old Bailey, where all three were convicted, each jailed for nine months. Thousands of supporters awaited them on their release from prison. No one would be waiting at the prison gates with a hero's welcome when the 1960s bombers were released.

The Clywedog bombing may have been the first incident in a chain of explosions attributed to MAC2, but it could have been the last if the police had successfully followed up that midnight call to the *Western Mail*, because the bombers made one mistake. I cannot be certain whether it was the afternoon after the explosion, or a day later, when I was summoned suddenly to the office of the editor, John Giddings. With him were two high-ranking police officers, all three poring over a copy of the *Western Mail*. My immediate thought was that we had screwed up again and I was about to be held accountable for some incompetent reporter. But for once the police were not complaining: they wanted our help.

The newspaper apparently used to wrap the gelignite had been found beneath the wreckage of the Blondin, the steel mast supporting the aerial cableway at Clywedog. Could we identify the edition? That might give them a clue to where that particular copy was purchased and, from this, a lead on the saboteurs. I knew it was possible to relate a code used by printers to one employed by the editorial department to identify edition changes. At the foot of the back page of every copy there was a line of stars, a new star added each time a newsprint reel was changed on the presses. Since each reel printed approximately 14,500 copies of the *Western Mail*, this, taken in conjunction with content changes linked to editorial edition and page deadlines indicated by breaks in solid rules at the top of certain pages, could give a clue to where a particular copy was distributed. If the *Western Mail* had had a large enough circulation in north Wales, necessitating more frequent changes in the editorial content, we might have successfully pinpointed the very newsagent from whom the newspaper was bought. As it happened, because the north Wales edition of the *Western Mail* at that time sold fewer than 2,500 copies, the most we could say was that the newspaper used to wrap the explosives was probably sold in Gwynedd. The bombers would not make the same mistake again.

# 2

## 'COFIWN DRYWERYN' (WE WILL REMEMBER TRYWERYN)

Liverpool Corporation's construction of the reservoir at Tryweryn in the face of widespread opposition throughout Wales was the catalyst for the violent events of the 1960s, culminating in a perceived threat to the Prince of Wales if his Investiture at Caernarfon Castle was allowed to proceed. Forty years later those responsible would claim there was never any intention to harm a hair on the head of the young prince: that their aim was simply to raise Welsh political awareness to its wretched subjugation. That was not how it appeared at the time. Almost too late, the Prime Minister, Harold Wilson, and the security services woke up to the danger and the associated threat to the constitution.[1]

Tryweryn was not the first time a Welsh-speaking community like Capel Celyn had needed to be moved to make way for a new reservoir to supply England. All large towns and cities had experienced an enormous increase in demand for water during the industrial boom of the nineteenth century. Although Liverpool had previously looked towards the Lake District for water, the city corporation's attention in 1877 was drawn to Lake Vyrnwy in north Wales as a potential new source. Without any formal consultation, a parliamentary bill was introduced to build a reservoir at Vyrnwy and an aqueduct linking it to Liverpool.

The construction of the reservoir meant inundating ten farms and relocating the village of Llanwddyn, consisting of a church and two chapels, three public houses, a post office and shop, and about thirty-seven houses. The very first local people knew about the plan was from the appearance of engineers and surveyors in the area, by which time it was too late for their 331-signature petition to make any difference. After the dead were exhumed from the local cemetery and their remains re-interred on higher ground, water began flowing to Liverpool in July 1892.

At about the same time, Birmingham Corporation's decision to build a complex of reservoirs in the Elan Valley outside Rhayader meant another population transfer. While no village was affected, four hundred people were told to pack their bags, before a small church, a Baptist chapel and two large houses – one of these for a short time the home of the poet Shelley and his young wife – were submerged, along with various scattered cottages and farmhouses. The reservoir complex opened by King Edward VII in July 1904 encountered very little opposition.

Fifty years later Liverpool Corporation was running out of water again and searching for another source. At first, and without consultation, it announced in August 1955 it would build a new reservoir in the Dolanog Valley, a decision met by a storm of protest, not only because it was taking more Welsh water, but because it also threatened a national shrine – the memorial chapel to the Welsh hymn-writer Ann Griffiths. Suddenly, the plan was dropped when the corporation decided that Dolanog would not be large enough to satisfy its needs. Four months later it announced that instead it would flood the Tryweryn Valley, famed for its association with the Welsh ballad-singer Bob Roberts. More significant was the intention to submerge the village of Capel Celyn, in the process drowning a way of life. For a brief moment, this cluster of slate roofs in the shadow of the granite Arenigs, the river Tryweryn meandering lazily at their feet, became the centre of the Welsh universe. Tryweryn was the very bread and breath of heaven embracing a quality of life unique in the world, its demise an act of desecration, for some tantamount to ethnic cleansing and for nationalist leader Gwynfor Evans 'the clearest exposure in our time of Welsh political servitude'.[2]

When the *Western Mail* described Liverpool Corporation's attitude to Wales and its water resources as 'cavalier', it expressed the view of the vast majority of Welsh people, both English- and Welsh-speaking. While some saw the drowning of this tiny roadside village, with its chapel, school, post office, burial ground, eight stone cottages and railway halt, as cultural genocide, others regarded the theft of Welsh water in the same context as the exploitation of the nation's iron ore and coal reserves by largely English entrepreneurs to fuel the Industrial Revolution. Welsh nationalist sensibilities, whether dormant or suppressed, bubbled up, the ripples spreading quickly across the surface of an otherwise comatose nation. Not only was Tryweryn a defining moment for many in Wales, it was also briefly the case for the *Western Mail*, which, having begun life as an apologist for Wales's imperial masters, threw its weight behind opposition to the reservoir:

> Our view of the Dolanog scheme was that it was not permissible for representatives of English cities that needed water to roam about in North Wales, fix upon a valley and say, 'This will do'. That view holds for Ann Griffiths' valley, Bob Roberts' valley, or any other valley so long as it is in Wales.

> It is a serious business to flood our farms, homesteads, and communities, especially where they represent a surviving tradition … The handing over of large areas of land to distant cities offends local sentiment and flaunts the inhabitants' proper and natural claim to a say in the development of their own countryside … Welsh rivers are part of Wales's resources. It is only fair that the people of Wales should have a say in their control and use.[3]

Perhaps the nationalist tone of this was a step too far, but shortly afterwards the *Western Mail* published a vicious attack upon Plaid Cymru, as though seeking to reassert its position as the mouthpiece for Anglocentric conservatism.

The seventy villagers and farmers at Capel Celyn first knew about the threat to their homes from newspaper reports. Some regarded the corporation's original plan for a reservoir at Dolanog as a cynical ploy: that it had always intended to build at Tryweryn, where twice the amount of water could be impounded, allowing Liverpool to recoup its investment by selling the surplus to neighbouring English water companies.

For Liverpool Corporation and its Labour supporters in Parliament, led by the redoubtable Bessie Braddock, opposition to the council's plans was nothing less than a nationalist plot, designed to deny their thirsty constituents a free, God-given resource essential for life. In the view of the Liverpool *Daily Post* – published in England but with a substantial sale in north Wales – while there was room for debate about the export of Welsh water, it was 'more God's than Taffy's', since it dropped freely from the heavens. Standing four-square behind Liverpool was Henry Brooke, who, as Secretary of State for Housing, doubled up as Minister for Welsh Affairs or, as he became known in Wales, 'Minister for Liverpool Affairs'.

The Tryweryn Defence Committee was arrogantly shunned by Liverpool Corporation, its opposition dismissed disdainfully by Brooke, who failed to see how the preservation of the Welsh way of life had priority over slaking the thirst of Merseyside and Lancashire. For him it was incomprehensible that 'Welsh people of all people want to stand outside the brotherhood of man to that extent'.[4]

The upsurge in nationalism accompanying the struggle to save Tryweryn revived interest in self-determination by turning the spotlight on the economic and social disparities between Wales and its neighbour. Wales was one of the most needy areas of the UK, pockmarked with the scars of an industrial era, the rewards from which were hard to see. Rather than sharing the economic spoils with England, Wales had remained a frail, underdeveloped country without any of the institutional props supporting its neighbour, hence the adage: when England catches a cold, Wales catches pneumonia. While the most obvious signs of Welsh nationalism were the language, its customs, myths and memories of battles fought, what surged to the surface in the 1960s also had its roots in the uneven development of the British economy since the eighteenth century. Instead of a partnership, the Welsh were exploited by the interference and control of the imperialist powerhouse beyond its borders, leaving many with a profound sense of cultural, social and economic loss and isolation. But this feeling of deprivation was no sudden revelation on the Welsh road to Damascus. It had been a consistent process – the massive programme of pit closures throughout the 1960s and the decimation of Wales's railway network by Lord Beeching being merely the most recent consequences of the new imperialism. In the absence of any institutionalised, specifically Welsh, remedy, many turned to the Labour Party in Westminster to articulate their deep concern; others to nationalism, by invoking the past and their sense of national identity in order to subvert the present. For some, like the 1960s bombers, who looked to nationalism for the answers, it was a journey of rediscovery as they dipped into a history obscured by centuries of assimilation, the depth and extent of this defined by proximity to the English border and exposure to forces of immigration.

The insurgents of the 1960s would settle for nothing less than a complete break with the imperialist past. Even Plaid Cymru president Gwynfor Evans seemed for a time to agree. Backed by a 250,000-signature petition demanding that Wales be given control of its internal and external affairs, Evans was not afraid to tell a packed meeting of Foreign and Commonwealth journalists in London that Wales wanted complete autonomy, or dominion status, his euphemism for independence.[5] In the 1960s few in a renascent Welsh nationalist party were afraid to utter what would become the dreaded 'I' word. Before long their opponents, by portraying the English-speaking majority as second-class citizens doomed to be ruled by a Welsh-speaking elite, would drive a wedge between the languages, the implication being that no country with two spoken languages was entitled to statehood. They took care, however, not to quarrel with the patriot and his affection for his country: their fight was with nationalism's common interests and goals rooted in a common ethnicity, which they regarded as having dangerous side-effects, such as the National Socialism of fascist Germany. What is remarkable, however, is that while Plaid Cymru's ambivalence towards direct action left it vulnerable to being branded quasi-fascist, the assertion was rarely ever used to censure it or the nationalist activists responsible for the bombings and arson attacks. Was this because events as they unfolded resonated with the patriotism deep in every Welshman's soul? After all, nationalists have always been able to annex patriotism to promote their political aims. Although they considered Welsh extremism unnecessary and misguided, those at the highest levels of government never disputed the distinctive nature of the Welsh insurgency as being part of the struggle for self-determination. But while the campaign of violent direct action had its genesis in nationalist virtues and goals, it was the failure of the patriotic foot-soldiers to articulate their cause that allowed government to marginalise Welsh extremism as the action of crazed fanatics.

Tryweryn was the catalyst, exacerbated by the contempt and arrogance with which Welsh protest was usually treated. After Liverpool City Council refused to meet a deputation from Wales, Gwynfor Evans, together with David Roberts, from Caefadog, and Dr Tudur Jones, principal of Bala-Bangor College, gate-crashed a council meeting, Evans jumping up to address members the moment they reached an agenda item about Tryweryn. Drowned out by protesting councillors, led by Bessie Braddock banging the lid of her desk, Evans and the others were unceremoniously ejected by the police. Bessie Braddock was not in attendance a month later when Gwynfor Evans was permitted to address the council for fifteen minutes – she was at Westminster brokering a deal with Labour MPs, including local Members Harold Wilson and Barbara Castle, who were on a collision course with their Welsh colleagues over Tryweryn. As it happened, twenty-seven of the thirty-six Welsh MPs voted against Liverpool Corporation's Private Member's Bill promoting the construction of the reservoir, the remainder abstaining. Perversely, the Minister for Welsh Affairs, Henry Brooke, backed Liverpool, even after conceding that Tryweryn was a watershed in Wales's struggle to retain its distinctive culture and nationhood; that Wales as a separate nation faced extinction; and that for

Villagers from Capel Celyn march through the streets of Liverpool in November 1956 to oppose plans to drown their homes to build the Tryweryn Reservoir. Copyright: National Library of Wales, Geoff Charles Collection.

Plaid Cymru President Gwynfor Evans speaks to Liverpool Police during the demonstration by villagers from Capel Celyn against the building of the Tryweryn Reservoir (top). Villagers pose for photographers before boarding buses to return to Capel Celyn after Gwynfor Evans was ejected from Liverpool City Council chamber (bottom). Copyright: National Library of Wales, Geoff Charles Collection.

these reasons its people felt it absolutely essential to make a stand over Tryweryn.[6]

Several solutions were proposed to resolve the dispute, including establishing a Welsh water authority to sell water to England. Then there was Penllyn Rural District Council's suggestion to dam the river higher up the Tryweryn Valley to safeguard the economic and cultural life of the area. Wales was not refusing water to England: it simply wanted a fair price, the minimum dislocation, and concern shown for the economy and culture of the affected areas. An all-Wales conference in October 1956 convened by the Lord Mayor of Cardiff, Alderman J. H. Morgan, at the instigation of David Cole, the editor of the *Western Mail*, supported the alternative proposals, as did the Association of Welsh Local Authorities. By then, however, it was too late to prevent the enactment of the Liverpool Corporation Bill in August the following year, once it won the support of Welsh Affairs Minister Henry Brooke, who decided that keeping the Welsh way of life alive was not good enough reason to reject the proposed reservoir. Gwynfor Evans reminded a packed public meeting in Bala that Wales had failed because it had 'no self-government'. At that time, the Plaid leader's support for independence was never in doubt. But nothing, it seemed, could halt the continuing integration of Wales into England and its implications for the people of Wales.[7]

The last stand was made in the streets of Liverpool on 21 November 1956, when seventy men, women and children from Capel Celyn – just about the entire population of the doomed village – descended on the city, armed only with pathetic banners proclaiming 'Liverpool be a big city not a big bully' and singing hymns. As Liverpool City Council discussed the reservoir scheme, the strains of 'Land of My Fathers' drifting into the council chamber failed to melt the hearts of the city councillors. But there was polite applause for Gwynfor Evans when he was allowed to address the council before the final vote, members listening intently to his account of the valley's historic and cultural links – and of the need to retain the water, Wales's last natural resource, to attract industry into north Wales and halt depopulation.[8]

His impassioned plea had not the slightest affect, the council deciding by ninety-four votes to one, with three abstentions, to drown Capel Celyn. As the defeated demonstrators set off for home, the Revd Gerallt Jones, Congregational minister at Llanuwchllyn, told the *Times* reporter, 'We have achieved our aim. We have drawn the attention of the people of Liverpool to what is being done in their name.'[9]

Welsh opposition, however, would not always be this ineffective after Plaid had wrapped up its banners and moved on, leaving the bulldozers to do their job and the faded graffiti to remind future generations of a humiliating defeat. If nothing else, the government's increased fear of nationalism persuaded it to site a new integrated steel-mill at Llanwern, near Newport, Monmouthshire, rather than at Grangemouth in Scotland. Cabinet papers released in 1989 under the thirty-year rule include a memorandum to the Cabinet from the then Chancellor of the Exchequer, Heathcote Amery, warning of the political consequences if Wales did not get the project:

> There is still resentment in Wales over the support given by the Government to Liverpool's Bill for flooding part of the Tryweryn Valley in Merioneth … If the Government were now to stop the building of the strip mill in Wales, criticism of the Government would be greatly intensified and Welsh nationalist feeling aroused. The dangers of such a situation must not be underrated. [10]

Gwynfor Evans's warning to the councillors of Liverpool about Welsh determination to stop Tryweryn proved a self-fulfilling prediction, played out initially not in the language heartlands, as might have been expected, but in the south Wales valleys. Many who spoke not a word of Welsh after generations of exposure to the processes of assimilation were outraged by what they regarded as the final nail in the national coffin. Dai Pritchard, from New Tredegar, a draughtsman at the South Wales Switchgear factory in Blackwood, and Dave Walters, a miner from Bargoed, were two who decided quite independently after all else failed that direct action was all that remained.

Pritchard and Walters drove the two hundred-odd miles to the Tryweryn Reservoir construction site in September 1962. Their plan was to drain 1,000 gallons of oil from a transformer, causing it to explode when the oil ran out. All went well until the saboteurs had the bad luck to be seen by a passing police patrol-car as they left the site. Taken to Bala for questioning, Pritchard and Walters stalled, believing that if they admitted to attempting to steal tools from the site they might delay the police long enough for the oil to drain from the transformer. Unknown to them, a nightwatchman had spotted the leak and the transformer was saved. For their failed sabotage attempt, Pritchard and Walters were fined £50 each in November 1962, their fines paid immediately by nationalist supporters waiting to greet them outside the court.[11] A month later, a second attempt was made to sabotage the reservoir, when two intruders set fire to a fitters' shed. The pair escaped into the hills after grappling with a night watchman.[12]

The failure of the democratic process to stop the dam, and Gwynfor Evans's refusal to condone direct action as the only means left, came close to splitting Plaid Cymru when disaffected members formed an action group threatening sabotage.[13] But it was only talk, and for some, like the Gwynedd farmer turned café owner Owen Williams, the frustration and sense of impotency proved too much.

Williams had not long returned from Canada with his wife Irene and their two young children, Iona and Gruffydd. The couple had met on the beach at Nefyn while Irene was on holiday from Birmingham, and after living for a year in a caravan on the family farm at Gwynus, near Nefyn on the Llŷn Peninsula they decided to escape by emigrating to Vancouver – where life was even harder, working on an isolated cattle ranch with a wooden shack for a home. But the search for a better life was not the only reason Williams emigrated to Canada in 1957. By then it was evident to him that Plaid Cymru's campaign to stop Tryweryn was getting nowhere; that the future in Wales meant all talk, no action.[14]

As a youngster at Pwllheli Grammar School, Williams had ambitions to become a journalist, until, reaching the age of fifteen, he was required like so many other sons of rural Wales to swap his schoolbooks for twelve hours a day of hard labour on the family farm. A member of Plaid Cymru from an early age and keenly interested in Michael Collins and the struggle for Irish independence, Williams had followed the tragic events unfolding at Tryweryn from newspaper cuttings sent to him by his mother. After two years in Canada *hiraeth* proved irresistible and the family returned to Wales in 1959, only to discover the fate of Tryweryn sealed, the demonstrators gone.[15]

The youngest son of a tenant farmer, Owen Williams's acute awareness of Wales's journey from freedom to thraldom was rooted in the very fields his family farmed at Nefyn. Born on to the estate of the Wynn-Finches at Cefn Amlwch in August 1935 and raised on that of another absentee landlord, Williams was conscious that Gwynus was an enduring monument to the darkest day in Welsh history, the farmhouse named by its original builders after a local warrior who perished with Llywelyn, the last native Prince of Wales, in an ambush at Cilmeri near Builth Wells. Not far from what had once been summer pasture for Llywelyn's cattle, his conqueror Edward I had celebrated the defeat and subjugation of the Welsh in 1277–83 by building at Nefyn one of the most important royal palaces in the whole of Wales.

For centuries before its conquest by Edward, Wales was a country of many kings, many dynasties, many kingdoms, each a focus for communal identity and loyalty. While outsiders saw Wales as distinctive, one people 'entirely different in nation, language, laws and habits, judgements and customs', institutionalised unity, which means so much to the modern nationalist, was alien to the Welsh, the chronicler Gerald of Wales observing in his journal, 'They obstinately and proudly refuse to submit to one ruler.'[16]

Wales was a country without a centre: a collection of regions isolated by mountains, tidal estuaries, marshy lowlands, its people living along the edges of a central massif. Despite their fractured topography, the Brytaniad (later the Cymry) were bound by blood, status and nationality. Demographics may have determined the diversity of cultural, social and economic characteristics, but the Cymry's strong sense of common unity as a people was never incompatible with the absence of centralised governance. That a sense of national identity and the concept of common justice had existed in Wales from the earliest times was recognised in the very first treaty (1201), between the Norman King

John and a Welsh prince, Llywelyn ab Iorwerth, which recognised the laws of Hywel Dda (Hywel the Good) as having common currency throughout Wales.

Long before the Norman Conquest in 1066, Wales existed as an identifiable geographical unit, extending from Portskewett on the Severn to Anglesey on the shores of the Irish Sea, and from Chester in the north-east to Pembrokeshire in the south-west. Demarcated by Offa's Dyke, its border fluctuated according to the fortunes of war, colonisation and lordship. After the conquest the Normans had no immediate interest in pushing beyond Offa's Dyke, preferring to leave the security of the far west to their most loyal supporters, who were rewarded with large estates straddling the border with England. These Marcher lordships evolved into minor fiefdoms, a law unto themselves, and a sanctuary for villains and recruiting ground for private armies frequently at war with each other.

While the conquest by Edward I left the Marcher lordships untouched, the King seized the whole of Gwynedd and Ceredigion for himself, this henceforth referred to as 'the land of Wales'. Ruled over on the King's behalf by a governor general, Otto of Gronson, the new province was administered as an overseas territory, like Ireland and Aquitaine. To enforce his subjugation of the rebellious Welsh, Edward undertook the most ambitious and costly programme of castle-building ever attempted by a European monarch. The most important of these, such as Caernarfon, Conwy and Denbigh, became the focus for English settlement – at the centre of new 'plantation boroughs' reserved for English settlers, enticed to Wales by promises of substantial land grants and privileges. These hubs of civil, commercial and judicial rule, from which the Welsh were excluded, completed the process of conquest. Discrimination was legalised, and English law prevailed over Welsh law. Welsh bishoprics were reserved for royal favourites, and parochial revenues repatriated to English and French monasteries.[17]

The ruthless exploitation of the fourteenth century left the Welsh with a profound sense of disinheritance and territorial exploitation. Their precious laws and customs had been trampled upon by the incomers, leaving them with the despair and bitterness of a conquered people. Inevitably, this gave rise to racial tension, manifesting itself in anti-English sentiment. For deliverance the Welsh resorted to the past for the threads of political unity. The messiah to lead them out of enslavement would be Owain Glyndŵr.

Declaring himself Prince of Wales at his Parliament in Machynlleth in 1400, Glyndŵr embarked upon a fifteen-year guerrilla war to deliver his people from English captivity. His nation, Glyndŵr told the French king, had been 'trodden underfoot by the fury of the barbarous Saxons'.[18]

Adept at exploiting international tension, Glyndŵr struck an alliance with the French that propelled the conflict on to the world stage, where, briefly, an independent Wales was on the verge of winning international recognition. The failure of Glyndŵr's revolt led to a tightening of the colonial grip. Rural wealth was redistributed, aristocratic estates consolidated and Welsh land law replaced by English tenure. The Welsh were prohibited from buying land in English towns, whether in Wales or England, from holding major office in Wales and carrying guns on the highway and market place – and were not permitted to sue an Englishman in Wales, no matter how serious the grievance.

But the assimilation of Wales into England would not be completed until the Acts of Union or 'Acts of Assimilation', as some prefer to call Henry VIII's legislation of 1536–43. When Owain Tudor, from the royal household of Gwynedd, married into the English Royal Family, laying the foundation for the Tudor dynasty, hope flickered in Welsh hearts that a Welshman sitting on the English throne might one day restore the nation's self-respect and influence. But Owain Tudor's son, Henry VIII, had greater concerns. The Reformation and split with Rome in 1534 had exposed England to attack from France and Spain. Wales still contained pockets of potential revolt, not least the Marches, where certain lords steadfastly refused the King's writ.

The Acts of Union were presented as an expression of the King's 'singular zeal, love and favour' for his Welsh subjects, all somewhat surprising, since during the previous twenty-seven years of his reign personal pleasure had taken precedence over any expression of concern for the Welsh. Critics of the legislation regarded the 1536 Act as no less than an attempt to eradicate the native language by rooting out from Welsh society 'sinister usages and customs'. The Acts also fixed the border, in the process arbitrarily transferring Welsh-speaking areas to England for judicial and administrative purposes. This included Monmouthshire, which, though thoroughly Welsh in background and tradition, remained administratively part of England until restored to Wales in 1968. The purpose of the Acts of Union was to assimilate Wales into England, in return for which the Welsh became citizens of the realm, accountable to English custom and practice, legally and administratively. English was the only language recognised for all official purposes, and without speaking it no Welshman could hold office. The Marcher lordships were swept away, replaced by new shires similar to those in England. By completing the process of integration into England, the 1543 Act of Union was intended to crush Wales.[18] That it, and the particular forms of oppression that followed, never completely succeeded in destroying Wales's distinctive character, language and culture is not only remarkable in the annals of national survival, but meant that the building blocks have remained to create a nation state by resolving the paradox of Wales's cultural, social and economic diversity with the enduring belief in its own unity. The answer to this is that nations are not created but evolve from a psychological bond, a sense of belonging that commits people from diverse backgrounds to common values and goals. Nations are not territorial units like Britain or Germany, forged through a combination of conquest, oppression, diplomacy and dynastic ambition. The business of nation-building is, as the nineteenth-century German philosopher George Hegel asserted, a process: 'Nations may have had a long history before they finally reach their destination – that of forming themselves into states.' But like infant suns that burn themselves out, fledgling nations are not entitled to complete the process of evolution and, as in the case of Wales, remain perpetually challenged and in danger of being subsumed by their neighbours.

Owen Williams, the Gwynedd café-owner, was no different from anyone else in carrying a knapsack full of memories into later life. The big difference was that his were rooted in an enduring cultural heritage, a substantial part of which had survived the slings and arrows, unlike his kinsmen in south Wales, where the grindstone of assimilation had obliterated even memories of a noble past. Several hundred miles away, in a long line of terraced houses called Crescent Road in Newport in Monmouthshire, I had no concept of Wales as a cultural entity. The tidal wave of Anglicisation had drowned even my sense of belonging, my grammar school celebrating St George's Day with distinctly greater enthusiasm than it did St David's, leaving many contemporaries singularly unaware of the existence of any indigenous culture other than English. Those who drafted the 'Acts of Assimilation' uniting Wales with England would have been very satisfied with the outcome in Crescent Road: working-class Labour draped in the Union flag and believing that the nation's glorious history started in 1066. Neither a road nor a crescent, more of a wriggle across the side of a hill overlooking the muddy river Usk crawling wearily to the sea, Crescent Road was a monument to Anglicisation, inhabited by Joneses, Thomases and Williamses connected with Wales by name only.

When Lloyd George mobilised the 'Welsh Army' to defend the Empire from 1914 to 1918, tens of thousands rushed to die in the trenches. Not even this, or being chained to a machine-gun, as happened to my father to stop him deserting, or the shell-shock that shredded his nerves, would dent loyalty to king and country. Five years in the trenches never got Charlie Humphries, neither did the coal mine where his stepfather was crushed to death by a runaway tram, nor the workhouse where he first saw the light of day, but the heavy weight of the pennies he emptied from people's gas meters eventually did. Nevertheless, one of my most enduring memories was not the strains of 'Land of My Fathers', but pungent clouds of Digger Flake hugging the wireless set as the family sat listening intently to the Queen's Christmas sermon. For Charlie Humphries, that was the next best thing to heaven!

Owen Williams, with his innate sense of culture and heritage, might as well have been from another planet for the majority of English-speaking Welsh. That his personal crusade for a free Wales found common cause with those on the other side of the Welsh language-divide is the more surprising for someone whose first port of call might have been the respectable ranks of the middle-class, predominantly cultural nationalists of Plaid Cymru. In the 1960s Plaid was the party of preachers and teachers, having little in common with the Valleys' republican tradition. But in the same way that Tryweryn had evoked a

23

forgotten past, Williams's despair over Plaid's failure to capitalise upon the widespread support generated by the struggle struck a chord with those from a socialist republican background. All saw Tryweryn as a lost opportunity and good enough reason to join forces to salvage something from the wreckage. Frustrated by conservative nationalism's ambivalence and procrastination over independence, it was not unnatural that Williams would gravitate towards working-class patriots like John Jenkins, George Taylor and Alwyn Jones, the last two the men who would become the insurgency's principal martyrs. All had the same uncomplicated aspirations: an independent but distinctly Welsh Wales. And all agreed that violent, direct action was the only way left to achieve what democracy had failed to deliver.

On his return to Wales from Canada, Williams was helped by his father to take a mortgage on the Espresso Bar and Grill at Pwllheli, with flat above. Before long it was a successful business, on some market days serving as many as a thousand cups of coffee. The Espresso coffee-bar also became a focus for like-minded nationalists – the place where Owen Williams formed Mudiad Amddiffyn Cymru and planned the attack on Tryweryn.[19]

# 3

## THE WINKLE-PICKER SABOTEURS

Owen Williams knew hardly anything about explosives, except that to obtain them illegally a powder store at a quarry or colliery was a pretty good bet. For this he recruited the help of two local men, Robert Williams (18), from Criccieth, and Edwin Pritchard (20), from Nefyn. Both were frequent visitors to the Espresso café, where Williams, a man known for his strong militant views and passionate commitment to an independent Wales, was considered by police to exercise considerable influence over the local youth.[1]

For the raid on 15 October 1962 Williams chose Croft's granite quarry at Llithfaen, quite close to his parents' farm, and an area he knew well. It was a Saturday night, and the quarrymen would not return until after the harvest festival long weekend. Parking their car out of sight, the trio set about prising open the steel door of the powder room, a shed identified by DANGER–EXPLO-SIVES in large red letters on its side, the clatter of crowbars reverberating around the quarry walls. Once inside, they hauled out a chest marked 'Cook's Explosives', only to discover, when they opened it back at the Espresso café, that it contained enough detonators and fuse wires to start a war – if only they had the gelignite. Fifteen hundred detonators surplus to requirements were immediately buried in a sack in Pritchard's garden, others in a dump at Butlin's holiday camp at Pwllheli, some under the eaves of a shed at the back of the Espresso café. Detonators were everywhere, even hidden under a gravestone in Llanarmon churchyard at Chwilog.

Williams doubted whether Pritchard and Robert Williams had the stomach to play any further part in his plans, suspecting, correctly as it happened, that they would crack under police interrogation. For help, he turned instead to John Albert Jones (19), who was from Wrexham, but was then living with his sister at Penrhyndeudraeth after having been discharged from the Royal Air Force Police on medical grounds following a road accident. Because of the head injuries he had suffered in the accident, Jones had difficulty finding work and spent much of his time with Williams at the Espresso café. Their original plan was highly ambitious. Bombs would be planted at ten key locations, forcing the contractors to withdraw from the site entirely. A bridge carrying construction traffic on to the site would be destroyed, so would trucks, machinery and the contractors' stockpile of petrol drums. But all that changed when a third man was recruited. Emyr Llewelyn Jones, an Aberystwyth student, thought the attack on Tryweryn should be a symbolic act of defiance, in the spirit of the burning-down of the RAF bombing school on the Llŷn Peninsula. For this, said Emyr Llew (as he was generally known), they would be hailed as patriots; to go further would cast them as terrorists. Owen Williams disagreed, believing that symbolism had failed Wales in the past. The eventual compromise was that only the transformer supplying power to the site would be targeted.[2]

Unlike Williams and Jones, Emyr Llew (22), of Maesllyn, near Llandysul, was well connected. His father, also Llewelyn Jones, was twice chaired bard at the National Eisteddfod of Wales, the highest literary honour to be bestowed upon a Welsh-speaker. Although as committed as his fellow saboteurs, Emyr Llew had no real intention of avoiding retribution, unlike Owen Williams, who saw their action as the first shot in an ongoing struggle by Mudiad Amddiffyn Cymru (Movement for the Defence of Wales), the clandestine organisation the trio had formed. Despite their different objectives, Williams recognised in the younger man a commitment that went deeper than the idle boasts usually associated with students after stop-tap.[3] Besides this, the Aberystwyth student claimed to have the technical knowledge they needed. Emyr Llew wrote of his intentions in a letter to a fellow student before the raid on the transformer:

> You have heard plenty of brave words from my lips and on paper. No one is more conscious of my failure than I. I still want to commit the act and would like to meet you again for a chat … Burn everything you have ever received from me in a letter or any party literature and throw away any list of addresses you possess […] I must be careful, even letters to my parents will come to the hands of the police and it will be necessary to watch everything.[4]

The winter of 1962–3 was the coldest in England and Wales since 1740, the blizzards that swept in just before Christmas covering much of the country with deep drifts. In parts of Wales they were twenty feet deep, blocking roads and railways, isolating villages for weeks, the weight of ice bringing down overhead power cables and telephone lines. It was the year the sea froze over, the tides heaving huge blocks of ice on to foreshores around the coast. Thousands of sheep and cattle perished when farmers were unable to reach their livestock.

Farmer Owen Williams (top) and Emyr Llewelyn Jones (bottom), a student at University College, Aberystwyth, each jailed for 12 months for their part in sabotaging construction of the Tryweryn Reservoir. Copyright: Owen Williams, the author; Emyr Llewelyn Jones: National Library of Wales, Geoff Charles Collection.

By early January the freeze-up had virtually brought work to a standstill at Tryweryn, by which time the valley had already been transformed from the peaceful haven that was once Capel Celyn into a bedlam of growling bull-dozers, chewing at the rock and leaving in their wake rivers of black slime spilling across the snow-covered mountain slopes. Where sheep once grazed, across this scene of desecration drifted the all-pervasive stench of diesel fuel as Williams and Jones stumbled through waist-high snow along rocky mountain paths to reconnoitre their target. From various vantage-points, the pair filled notebooks with the registration numbers of police cars, details of shift changes, location of buildings and, most crucially, the frequency and routes of the patrols guarding the site. At one point they even entered the site, masquerading as Irish navvies after work, in order to get a closer look at their target.

The transformer was in the centre of a compound surrounded by a six-foot metal fence, at night illuminated by the glare of floodlights and patrolled by guards. Sunday 10 February 1963 was chosen as the date to plant the single bomb, timed to detonate in the early hours of the morning when the site was deserted. All three men solemnly swore the Mudiad Amddiffyn Cymru oath before embarking on their mission, this forbidding them from causing injury, or from acting independently:

> I promise to keep the activities of the movement and the names of the members secret; I promise neither to kill nor to injure any man who as part of his duty attempts to prevent me and I will do everything in my power to ensure that no one is injured or killed as a result of any act on my part. I promise not to undertake any positive act without consulting the other members of the movement.[5]

The bomb stowed in the boot of their hire car comprised about five pounds of commercial-grade gelignite, supplied by accomplices in south Wales, who had stolen it from a local colliery. The timer was a Venner switch, provided by Dai Pritchard, the mild-mannered, bespectacled South Wales Switchgear draughtsman who the previous year had been fined for trying to destroy the same transformer. Pritchard not only delivered the device to the saboteurs, but also gave them a demonstration by blowing up a rock on a beach near Pwllheli. Twenty-four hours before this second attack on the transformer, a red Vauxhall Victor hired by Emyr Llew in Aberystwyth was spotted by PC Arthur Jones passing through Fiddler's Elbow at Treharris, in the neighbouring valley to New Tredegar, where Dai Pritchard lived. Not only would Pritchard provide technical know-how for future MAC operations, he was also the organisation's link with the IRA.[6]

Shortly before the saboteurs set off, Owen Williams's wife, Irene, was rushed to hospital with pregnancy complications. By this time it was too late to cancel the operation, since Emyr Llew was already on his way in the hire car to the rendezvous point. Most roads in the vicinity of the dam site were blocked, only that from Dolgellau to Bala still being open, and this a treacherous ice-rink slithering between walls of frozen snow. After parking the car in the schoolyard at Cwmtirmynach, the three men headed along a sheep track across the snow-covered mountain, each carrying part of the bomb. None was properly equipped for the trek, Owen Williams wearing winkle-pickers, the fashion shoes popular in the 1960s.

Once off the mountain, they stopped and listened every few yards. The only sound was the rumble of a diesel engine in the distance pumping water from a tunnel the contractors had excavated in the mountainside. That Saturday night, the construction site was a ghost town. Nothing moved. The normally busy workshops were empty and still, the fleet of giant excavators slumped amongst piles of snow, as though resting before resuming their assault upon the mountain. But the site was not entirely deserted. Six guards patrolled it with dogs and walkie-talkies, every now and then one of them checking on the transformer compound, lit up like Blackpool Tower. Clambering over the last fence on the mountain, the saboteurs stepped on to the road leading to the transformer. It was a sheet of glass, every step threatening to send the trio and their explosive load tumbling into a drainage ditch. With the bomb parts held above their heads, they dropped on to their stomachs and wriggled the last few hundred yards through the snow. Frozen and soaked, they froze even more at the sound of someone crunching his way across the snow towards them; another moment, and the dogs would be on their backs. Paralysed with fear and expecting the worst, their relief was palpable when a bunch of curious sheep poked their noses out of the darkness to investigate.

A few yards from the target, Emyr Llew turned to Williams and whispered, 'I'll wire it up when I'm inside. You stand guard.' Williams the family man, his wife expecting their third child, knew what he meant, but refused to allow the young student to take any greater risk. The pair agreed to climb into the compound together and plant the bomb. Within minutes they were over the fence and squatting beside the transformer assembling the device while Jones kept watch. The biscuit tin containing the gelignite and timer was placed beneath the transformer and set to explode at 3.15 a.m. Soon they were beating a hasty retreat off the site and into the mountains – leaving in the snow a trail of footprints for the police to follow, in particular those pointed winkle-pickers!

Williams was trailing behind, a sharp stabbing pain in his leg forcing him to pull up and rest. While the others helped as best they could, he hopped most of the way back to the main road, where, as the three dragged themselves wearily across a stone wall, Emyr Llew muttered, 'Jesus Christ.' A moment later he was lying in the snow clutching the back of his leg. The barbed wire strung along the top of the wall had ripped through his trousers into his calf. With his handkerchief wrapped around the wound and his boot full of blood, he handed the driving over to Williams.

The two hours allowed for the return to Pwllheli and the sanctuary of the Espresso café was tight in the treacherous conditions, the icy stretch between Bala and Cerrigydrudion ultimately proving too much for Williams at the wheel of the Vauxhall. Revving the engine to pass a grey van stranded in a snowdrift, he skidded into one himself. In the moonlight they saw the van driver walking towards them. Close to panic, Williams could only think of passing themselves off as Englishmen returning to London. The van driver was a youngster shivering with the cold, despite his heavy overcoat and Wellington boots. Winding down the window, Williams asked, in music-hall English, 'I say, old boy, do you know if this road goes anywhere – what, what?'

Immediately suspicious of these strange 'Englishmen', the young van driver, Hugh Roberts, a butcher's assistant from Cwmtirmynach, replied, 'No it's closed. I'm stuck, too, you see.' After helping push the Vauxhall out of the snowdrift, instead of the lift he was expecting the saboteurs drove off in the opposite direction. The parting shot from Williams, intent on maintaining the masquerade, was to lean out of the car and remark, 'Blast these Welsh roads – what? I'll be glad to get back over the border, old boy! Cheerio.' But as the Vauxhall sped off into the night, firmly implanted on its bonnet was the youngster's palm-print, a vital clue in tracing the car to Emyr Llew. A handkerchief with the initial 'E' was also found lying in the trampled snow at the spot where the saboteurs' car hit the snowdrift, fuelling speculation it had been dropped deliberately. And then there were the footprints, identical to those leading from the transformer compound. These told police three men were involved, one wearing pointed shoes similar to a pair they later recovered, another wearing climbing boots and the third ordinary shoes, and that all three were the persons in the Vauxhall.

Right on time the bomb exploded, the blast alerting one of the guards, Cadwaladr Owen Jones. The site engineer and police were called immediately, but found nothing unusual. It was not until daybreak, when Cadwaladr Jones returned to switch off the floodlights, that he noticed that the snow-covered ground around the transformer was saturated with oil. A hole had been blown in it, and from near the seat of the blast police recovered parts of the timing mechanism, some red plastic material and a small torch bulb with wires attached. From fragments of greasy brown paper also recovered, police concluded the explosive was the type used in collieries. There were clues everywhere, even the shredded remains of a *Western Mail* used to wrap the explosives. But most significant were those three sets of footprints.[7]

Returning to the Espresso café without further incident, the very first thing Williams did was to telephone Dewi Sant Hospital to check his wife's condition. Irene was asleep. After thawing out and a meal, the three saboteurs also slept soundly, expecting to wake up to a BBC news bulletin about the raid. But it was not until midday on the Sunday morning that the BBC reported that they had been successful. All three jumped up excitedly, Emyr Llew shouting, 'Great, boys, great, boys!' With no power, construction would be at a standstill. Nothing could be done until the weather improved and a new transformer could be installed. Afterwards, the explosion was mentioned on every news bulletin throughout the day, television showing film of the hole in the oil tank and dozens of police officers searching the site for clues. The footprints in the snow were even mentioned. By Monday morning the *Daily Express* screamed, 'Explosion rocks valley of fear', blaming the sabotage on an unnamed 'fanatical underground movement'. The saboteurs hoped their actions would wake up Wales to the effectiveness of direct action and alert the outside world to centuries of English exploitation. Williams, in particular, believed that by resisting the combined might of England's Conservative government and Liverpool Corporation they could change the face of Welsh history, even at the cost of being reviled and persecuted by their compatriots.

At the *Western Mail* the front-page headline was 'Sabotage at Tryweryn', but inside the office the reaction of the then editor, Don Rowlands, was to pin responsibility for the outrage on Plaid Cymru. Before long, a feature writer, Peter Kane, was dispatched to prove this, in a poorly researched five-part series entitled, 'Crisis in Plaid'. To those who then ran the *Western Mail*, Tryweryn was the high-water mark of Welsh nationalist extremism. From that moment onwards Plaid and extremism became synonymous, a misrepresentation it would take years to dispel. The newspaper never had formal rules of engagement with the language, culture and national aspirations. Members of staff needed only to sniff the air to know it was dangerous to wander too far into what had become the no-man's land of nationalism. A newspaper that proclaimed its independence as the 'National Newspaper of Wales' had, since the collapse of *Cymru Fydd*, the Welsh Home Rule movement, at the end of the nineteenth century, maintained a respectable distance between itself and Wales's cultural and political ambitions. After all, had not its profits been anchored for much of its existence in the conservatism of shipowners and coalowners, who expected their newspaper to be loyal to the Union?

Not long after joining the *Western Mail* in 1954, I was reminded of this by Nye Bevan, Labour architect of the National Health Service. Bevan was expected at Newport railway station from Paddington late one Friday evening, and I was sent to extract a comment about some current live issue, the importance of which escapes me. 'Don't expect to get much, he hates the *Western Mail*', warned my chief reporter, Harry West, 'but we have to make an effort'. True to form, no sooner had I introduced myself than Bevan scoffed, 'the coalowners' newspaper', stripping off his bow-tie and dinner jacket as he stepped off the train on to platform 1; 'you'll never change it, butt, and we'll never forget', and he replaced the bow-tie with a collier's white muffler, slipping into a worn navy-blue jacket handed him by a party hack. Appropriately dressed after his

London dinner engagement, the great man could return to his Valley roots, where even Nye Bevan dared not appear among the Tredegar faithful in the enemy's uniform: the togs worn by those who read the *Western Mail*!

Perhaps if I had told the great man that my father was born in a workhouse it might have earned some brownie points. Instead, I was the enemy, a tool of the despised coalowners' newspaper. That remained more or less the case in the Valleys for the next fifty years of my journalism in Wales, even though by the time I retired only one colliery survived, Tower, at Hirwaun, saved by a workforce that proved itself as entrepreneurial as any dyed-in-the-wool capitalist quaffing brandy in the Cardiff and County Club.

The reality is that by the mid 1960s Nye Bevan's characterisation of the *Western Mail* was skewed. By then, the newspaper disliked nationalists more than miners and trade unions, because nationalists threatened the status quo in ways others never did. Reporting the Welsh cultural and political scene between 1950 and 1970 was like doing so from inside a sealed box. The enduring impression was that those brave enough to break out did so without consent and at their own risk. If it became a habit, they found themselves marginalised, 'closet nats' not to be entrusted with custody of the newspaper's soul, which was far more important than Wales's. As for the miners, the *Western Mail* had a residual guilt for the exploitation it had once excused. But it owed nothing to the nationalists and their absurd notions of self-government. The newspaper tipped its hat to St David, its essay competition for children a safe enough vehicle to introduce a few lines of harmless Welsh into its English-only columns. Even then I remember one executive screaming at me, 'What do they say? What do they say? We must have translations. Can't be trusted.' My reply was, 'But, they're only children!' Only grudgingly, and on account of the much-needed circulation boost they afforded, did editors take note of such Welsh-Welsh institutions as the National Eisteddfod. The *Western Mail* did its best to ignore Saunders Lewis, the founder of Plaid Cymu, and giant of the nationalist struggle. As for the road-sign daubing campaign of Cymdeithas yr Iaith Gymraeg (Welsh Language Society), inspired by Lewis's momentous 1962 BBC radio lecture on the desperate plight of the language, this became an irritant, preferably ignored, or dealt with as a paragraph hidden at the foot of an inside page. Paragraphs languishing at the foot of columns frequently fell victim of 'last par subbing', which meant they were likely to disappear if cuts were needed to make a story fit its allotted space.

The kindest thing to say about the *Western Mail* at that time was that, occasionally, as in the case of its opposition to Tryweryn, there were flashes of affection for Welsh aspirations. Mostly, however, the relationship was at arm's length, even the appointment of a 'Welsh Affairs Correspondent' implying distance between itself and those it professed to represent. Very simply, the newspaper's constituency was, if not part of England, certainly under its spell and within its sphere of influence. There were other ambiguities, such as claiming to be the 'National Newspaper of Wales' while insisting on describing Wales as a Principality, until I banned the word from its columns. Then there was its preference for using Anglicised place-names, much to the annoyance of Welsh-speaking readers. Fishing in choppy, confused waters, it was natural that successive editors were fearful of being sucked under by upsurges of nationalism, language and identity. To this day, the newspaper has only ever had one Welsh-speaking editor, Sir Williams Davies (1901–31), from Talley in Carmarthenshire. The in-house mood was for many years predominantly anti-Welsh, the majority of the staff monoglot English-speakers recruited from south-east Wales or England. Those Welsh-speakers who did infiltrate were watched closely for signs of having 'gone native'.

Aware that publicity was the oxygen feeding Plaid's continuing success, the *Western Mail* sought to suppress the party's rise to prominence. No edicts were necessary. Insinuation was sufficient to signal that Plaid and anything remotely connected to nationalism was most definitely not the flavour of the month. By then I was news editor, which meant every line of Welsh news passed through my hands before reaching the newspaper, including the dozens of press releases issued by Plaid Cymru. Evidently the then editor, John Giddings, or someone above him, had decided that most of these had no real substance: that the 'meetings' from which they emanated had never existed, and that I and the night editor, John Cosslett (who had a Welsh-speaking wife), had fallen prey to political spin. No instruction was ever issued, only a whisper in my ear to the effect that in future all news stories mentioning Plaid were to be delivered to the editor's office at the far end of the corridor for scrutiny. No one said as much, but Plaid was to be censored, expunged from the columns of the *Western Mail*. Few of those reports I sent in to the editor ever re-emerged from his office, those that did almost always with a red pencil scrawled across most of the words, or a scribbled note to the effect, 'Do we have to use this?' or alternatively, 'Down an inside page.' Soon it was apparent that there was little point wasting time shunting Plaid copy down the corridor. I spiked it, because that was what the company wanted. The paragraph or two that passed the censor quite often fell foul of 'last par subbing'. No one was bothered, apart from Plaid, which suspected as much but was afraid to complain too often, for fear of being barred entirely from accessing the main road to its constituents. For such reasons, the bombing campaign that accompanied Plaid's rise to political prominence rattled the bars of the establishment fortress.

Censorship did not always hover in the wings at the *Western Mail*. It stuck its nose in your face on the night of Gwynfor Evans's historic 1966 by-election victory at Carmarthen. The most important and exciting Welsh political story for heaven knows how many years laid rightful claim to lead the paper with the kind of treatment usually reserved for declarations of war. Instead, on the explicit instructions of the editor, Giddings, it was relegated to a less prominent position on page 1. Strange though it may sound, rather than douse the flames of revolt, the *Western Mail*'s inclination to jump all over those who dared raise their heads above the parapet actually persuaded some to sign up to the direct action that eventually forced its way on to front pages around the world.[8]

Tryweryn was a monumental challenge for the newspaper. That it should find itself momentarily in the same camp as nationalists was not by choice, but was unavoidable, since almost every Welsh MP agreed the dam was an act of 'autocratic high-handedness, which irritated and aroused many Welshmen of all political leanings'. But when democratic protest was followed by sabotage, the tone changed, the *Western Mail* rounding on Plaid Cymru for sitting on the fence instead of providing the enlightened leadership necessary to deal with its hotheads. It rankled that those who compared the sabotage at Tryweryn with events in Ireland pre-1916 claimed to be acting in the name of the people of Wales as a whole. Wedded for a hundred years to the idea of Wales as part of the Union, the *Western Mail* was at first amused by nationalist allegations of imperialist persecution, then incredulous. After wagging a finger reproachfully at Plaid's perceived links to violent direct action, the newspaper sought to ignore the changes taking place at the political grassroots. Commenting in the aftermath of the Tryweryn sabotage incident, the newspaper observed:

> There is a growing irritation that recent exploits are presenting a new image of Wales to the outside world, one as distorted as the old canard that Taffy was a thief, a devious peasant or belligerent miner given to saying, 'Indeed to goodness' ...

> If the Plaid is to have any coherence its leaders must say clearly that it will not dance the tune called by those who dare to go furthest in rash folly. The genuine grievances of Wales will not be given a fair hearing against a background of juvenile heroics.[9]

That these genuine grievances were failing to receive a fair and just hearing was overlooked, in the *Western Mail*'s anxiety to get back on song with its *raison d'être* as defender of the Union. Plaid Cymru facilitated this when, in response to the Tryweryn bombing, Gwynfor Evans said his opposition to violent direct action should not imply moral disapproval of those acting outside the law to achieve change. Immediately, his critics spotted the hypocrisy and fatal flaw in Evans's pacifism – one that led him to discriminate between degrees of criminality, while warning of further trouble ahead if Wales's grievances were not addressed. Language demonstrators punished by the courts after daubing road-signs or squatting on top of television masts was low-grade crime, excusable and defensible. The future activities of Mudiad Amddiffyn Cymru, however, would be disowned, the official view echoed by Dafydd Elystan Morgan, prospective Plaid Cymru candidate for Merioneth, before defecting to Labour in 1966. Efforts to achieve a Parliament for Wales would become 'well nigh impossible' if party members resorted to sabotage, said Mr Morgan, adding his 'unequivocal and absolute disapproval of the action taken by Liverpool Corporation at Tryweryn'. For those committed to independence, that sounded like surrender. [10]

In the days immediately following the Tryweryn bomb, speculation was rife as to the identity of the saboteurs, the *Western Mail* suggesting a link to a dissident group within Plaid Cymru dissatisfied with constitutional methods of protest. Also mentioned was a clandestine organisation, the Free Wales Army, which although reputed to exist had not appeared in public.

If Tryweryn was intended to be the start of an insurgency, it suffered an immediate setback with the arrest of Emyr Llew. The palm-print of the young butcher's assistant abandoned in the snow by the three saboteurs helped police trace the hired Vauxhall to the flat in Terrace Road, Aberystwyth, that Emyr Llew shared with two other students. On Monday 18 February, armed with a search warrant, detectives removed a number of articles, including the letters in which he boasted of his intentions as well as the donkey jacket worn on the night of Tryweryn. Dust samples taken from the pocket contained incriminating traces of an explosive substance. A copy of the MAC oath sworn by the three conspirators was also found.

With this, the forensic evidence and the handkerchief inscribed with the letter 'E' recovered from the spot where the hire car ploughed into the snow-drift, police were satisfied they had one of the saboteurs in the bag. Questioning Emyr Llew in Welsh at his flat, Detective Inspector Humphrey Jones particularly wanted to know what the hire car was doing at Treharris twenty-four hours before the explosion. In the week preceding the arrest of the young student there had been much media speculation that the hunt for the Tryweryn bombers was centred in Glamorgan. Resolutely, Emyr Llew stuck to the promise not to reveal the identities of his co-conspirators, insisting he had taken the car no further than Prestatyn. By the time it was returned to the Aberystwyth garage, there were 700 unexplained miles on the clock.[11]

The assize court trial was pretty much a formality. With Emyr Llew pleading guilty, attention was on the hundreds of extra police and anti-riot vans drafted in to deal with 1,200 angry supporters, who had gathered from all parts of Wales to await the verdict. Mr Justice Barry was expected to be lenient, after defence counsel, Mr Elwyn Jones QC – Prime Minister Harold Wilson's Attorney General when violent direct action escalated ahead of the Investiture – invited the judge to regard the sabotage at Tryweryn as nothing more than a symbolic act. Construction of the reservoir had aroused violent feelings and fierce opposition in Wales, leaving a legacy of disappointment, frustration and bitterness, Mr Jones told Mr Justice Barry. It was this that had motivated Emyr Llew:

For him the Tryweryn project has become a symbol of injustice and protest and his was a symbolic protest. He intended his action to be a protest against the submerging of a village, its culture and community. They are the reactions of a deeply serious young man. The evidence indicates that Jones's act was a symbolic gesture rather than an act of serious property destruction. [12]

One after another, professors and clergymen trooped into the witness box to testify to Emyr Llew's good character. The hope was that for the 'well-being and peace of the Welsh nation' the student would receive a non-custodial sentence. While accepting there was considerable sympathy for his views, Mr Justice Barry regarded what had occurred as 'most pathetic', and jailed Emyr Llew for twelve months. What no one anticipated was that the sentencing of Emyr Llew would be the signal for his two accomplices to plant another bomb, this within a few weeks of Williams's wife Irene giving birth prematurely to a daughter, Teleri Bethan.

By now the contractors had installed a new transformer at Tryweryn and tightened up security considerably. But there was one source of power supply impossible to protect – the line of high-voltage pylons snaking its way across deserted heathland from Maentwrog power station to the dam. The pylon the pair chose as their target was at Gellilydan, a village about two miles from the construction site for the new Trawsfynydd nuclear power station. There would be no timing device on this occasion, because if it misfired the occupants of nearby farms and a terraced row of stone cottages could be at risk. During the day, the lane only a short distance from the pylon was in regular use. That meant they could not risk using a timer. Instead, the bomb would be detonated by Williams flicking the ends of two wires together, and for that they needed a safe hiding-place. An old stone bridge crossing the railway line at this point was ideal, providing Williams with somewhere to shelter as he detonated the blast they hoped would bring the giant pylon, carrying 90,000 volts, crashing to the ground.

On the night of 31 March a light mist hung over the deserted heathland as the pair drove through the tiny village of Gellilydan, then along the narrowest of country lanes, sunk between rows of ancient gnarled oaks, their canopy shutting out the night sky. Parking the car on a farm track, they set off down into a valley to the nearest power pylon in a chain of masts snaking its way through the foothills. Both men had invested in a pair of army surplus Korean combat boots, reaching up to the knees and worn over normal footwear. After this explosion there would be no winkle-picker tracks to follow! One by one, the lights in the few surrounding houses were extinguished as their occupants retired for the night. Working feverishly, Williams and Jones dug holes around the four legs of the pylon so that the full force of the blast would be directed at its base, not dissipated. Five pounds of gelignite were placed against the foot of each leg, all four bombs linked together. Then the wires connecting the detonators to the firing point beneath the railway bridge were flicked together, triggering an almighty explosion.[13]

The ground shook, the pylon wobbled, the blast momentarily illuminating the night sky with a brilliant flash of blue light. Metal fragments flew everywhere, clattering into the arches of the bridge above the heads of the two saboteurs sheltering beneath. But the pylon never moved, not an inch. Not all the bombs had detonated, although the one that did was loud enough to wake the dead. Bedroom lights flicked on in the village, dogs barked. With no time to rewire the charges, the saboteurs escaped as fast as possible.

Not long afterwards, the late-night duty reporter manning the *Western Mail* news-desk in Cardiff took an anonymous telephone call from a man describing himself as being 'in charge of publicity for the organisation'. The caller said an explosion had occurred about eight miles from Tryweryn. 'It happened', he said, 'about 400 yards from the main road on the junction to Ffestiniog. The pylon is carrying electricity to the site and leads over the border into England.' The duty reporter, who immediately alerted Gwynedd police, described the caller as having a strong Welsh accent.[14] Nothing was found until the following morning a local farmer, Aneurin Jones, of Cydnarth Farm, discovered that one leg of the pylon was twisted. If the saboteurs had brought it down, supplies to a large part of north Wales would have been cut.

Newspapers were filled with accounts of this fourth sabotage attempt on Tryweryn. The situation in Wales was described as 'explosive', some commentators comparing it with the terrorist attacks then taking place in Palestine. Neither was the timing overlooked, occurring as it did just two days after one of the activists, Emyr Llew, had been jailed at Carmarthen. The pressure on Gwynedd police to catch the culprits was intense.

The game was up, after the two men involved with Williams in the earlier quarry raid were arrested and made statements implicating him. A week later, on 7 April, he was closing the Espresso café for the night when suddenly there was the sound of footsteps approaching through the kitchen at the rear. Out of the darkness stepped a line of policemen, two in uniform and five in plain-clothes, led by Inspector Cledwyn Shaw, Pwllheli's chief officer.

Told he was being arrested for breaking and entering the quarry the previous autumn and stealing detonators, Williams had only a moment to explain the situation to his wife, waiting for him before the fire in the flat above the café. At the police station just around the corner, his questioning dragged on into the early hours of the morning. The police had recovered some of the stolen detonators, and had an impression of a car tyre from a molehill at Gellilydan. The evidence was accumulating. A copy of *The Red Path of Glory*, about the IRA fight for freedom, had been recovered from his flat, which he could see from the window of the interrogation room was being searched a second time, the shadowy figures of police officers moving behind the curtains. The longer he held out, the greater the heartache for Irene and the children. Suddenly, Williams said, 'I am responsible; you can let the others go. It is possible for these things to be misunderstood. My purpose at Gellilydan also was a symbolic act. I did not intend to harm anyone.'[15]

John Albert Jones was arrested at his sister's home at Penrhyndeudraeth as he hurried down the garden path with a suitcase. Asked to open it he said, 'Do you need to see? If I open it, it is finished.' The suitcase was stuffed with incriminating evidence, including the two pairs of white canvas over-boots worn by him and Williams during the raid on the pylon at Gellilydan, also a copy in Welsh of the MAC oath. In addition, there were maps and notes of the movements of police patrol-cars, a diagram of an explosive device, and Jones's Plaid Cymru badge and membership card. Told that footprints found at Gellilydan matched the over-boots in his suitcase, Jones replied, 'Gentlemen, it is useless lying to you now. I admit my part in both explosions, but would like you to understand that I will not blame anyone else.'[16]

The pair spent the next five weeks in Shrewsbury Prison, sewing mailbags while waiting for committal proceedings to start at Blaenau Ffestiniog on 7 May. At each remand appearance, crowds packed the tiny courtroom, on one occasion pelting the magistrates with clods of earth as they left town.

# 4

## TRAGEDY

Owen Williams was not insensitive to the grief that followed in his footsteps. His elderly parents, whose lives were a celebration of their Welsh consciousness, shielded from an alien culture by the remoteness of the Llŷn Peninsula, were distraught. His wife Irene, by no means recovered from a difficult pregnancy, had suffered the trauma of a police raid, her children terrified, the flat ransacked for a collection of newspaper cuttings, a tape recorder, a home-made Free Wales Army poster and some Plaid Cymru literature. Apart from the footprints in the snow and the detonators linking the two explosions at Tryweryn, the case against Williams would have been thin, had it not been for his confession. The immediate consequence of his obsession with the destiny of Wales would be to tear his marriage apart. But for the moment his wife was at his side, arriving at Pwllheli police station the morning after his arrest with a cheerful smile and his shaving gear. No matter what happened, Irene was determined Owen Williams would present a brave, clean-shaven face to the world. But behind this a greater tragedy was unfolding.

Not long after Williams was committed for trial at Dolgellau Assizes, Irene saw that there was something seriously wrong with their daughter Teleri Bethan, then only six weeks old. An urgent brain scan confirmed the worst – the child was suffering from hydrocephalus, or 'water on the brain', which, if not surgically drained, causes extensive brain damage and is invariably fatal. The operation at Alder Hey Hospital was unsuccessful, and the parents were told that Teleri Bethan had only months to live. Although she survived for seven years, she was in a coma for much of the time.[1]

For most, a tragedy of such magnitude would extinguish all thought of political protest. Although tortured by the distress and suffering caused to his family, Williams refused to give up his struggle for a free Wales. Judged by some as having engaged in nothing more significant than a student prank, he might easily have pleaded his foolishness and left the stage to embrace his pain and personal tragedy. If he had acted 'just for kicks', as his detractors were to suggest, then it cost Williams a broken marriage, and the anguish of a child suffering a living death.

Teleri Bethan's illness cast a long shadow over her father's trial at the Dolgellau Assizes, by which time she had already lost her sense of sight and hearing. This weighed heavily on all concerned, not least Mr Justice Elwes, after a witness explained that the prognosis was extremely bad and that the child was not expected to live. Since both Williams and John Albert Jones had pleaded guilty, the case proceeded rapidly to the submission of mitigating circumstances and character references. That Jones was still suffering from the head injuries sustained in the road accident which led to his discharge from the RAF inclined the judge to the view that he might not be entirely responsible for his actions, although Jones's counsel, Mr Ronald Waterhouse, very quickly pointed out his client 'had no wish to shirk behind any medical report'.

In mitigation, the defence called the Revd Euros Bowen, vicar of the parish of Llanuwchllyn, Bala, and a member of Penllyn Rural District Council, which had opposed the Tryweryn dam since it was first announced in 1956. When he asked to take the oath in Welsh, he was applauded by the judge for 'insisting upon his rights', and also by the public gallery. The Revd Bowen told how Merioneth County Council had failed to prevent Liverpool Corporation's Private Member's Bill from becoming law, how an alternative plan to save Capel Celyn by building the dam higher up the valley was ignored, and a proposal to establish a Welsh water authority to sell water to Liverpool on more favourable terms was rejected. The deciding factor had been the decision in July 1957 by the Minister for Welsh Affairs, Henry Brooke, to support Liverpool, a case of the 'Welsh watchdog turning wolf', according to the Revd Bowen.

No attempt was made by Owen Williams to excuse Tryweryn as a symbolic act, as his accomplice Emyr Llew had done. For Williams, his was the action of a man close to despair after the democratic processes had been exhausted and failed. 'They had been heard, but they had not been heeded, and it [the sabotage] was designed to draw attention to what he believed to be a deep injustice to the causes which were dear to him, and desperate only in that sense', said Mr Philip Owen, QC, defending.

At this point the judge intervened, appearing to offer Williams a lifeline in return for an assurance he would never again resort to criminal action to ventilate what Mr Justice Elwes admitted was a 'perfectly intelligible grievance'. But first the judge needed to know whether this was just the tip of an iceberg of unrest:

> I do not know how far what he did was supported by an organisation, and how far he was connected in a representative character on the basis that it had been agreed that legitimate means of protest had been exhausted and crime was to be resorted to. If I could be assured about that position, it might go some way to help me to assess the 'iron in the soul'.[2]

Did Williams, asked the judge, have any objection to selling water to England, which had little, whereas Wales had plenty? The sale of water was welcome, replied Mr Owen on behalf of Williams, so long as it was at a fair price. What had 'eaten into the soul of the people' was that Liverpool had not only refused to negotiate a fair contract, but was intending to resell water from Tryweryn to Blackburn, Oldham and other Lancashire towns.

Clearly impressed by the arguments in mitigation, the judge admitted he was persuaded to ignore retributive punishment in any sentence, but before passing sentence would release Owen Williams on bail so that he might reconsider the position with his associates, adding,

> I cannot really deal with this case if nine-tenths of the iceberg is under the surface. I must have something, so that I do not find after I have extended the clemency, which I very much wish to do in this case, someone else goes and blows up another transformer.

After explaining that he was taking the unprecedented step of releasing Williams to calm the rising tide of unrest in Wales, the judge added,

> It is a very fine thing to be proud of your country and to be proud of your race, and it is a very fine thing to wish to be independent, but it is not a fine thing to abandon democratic processes in that laudable aim, even if those processes do not seem to work very well. It is an imperfect world in which we live, and the people who make decisions for us do not always make decisions that we like. We have to accept them whether we like them or not because that is the way democracy works. Think about it and talk about it with those people whose aims are your aims and with whom you have confidence.[3]

The courtroom erupted in a deafening cheer as Williams stepped from the dock, a free man, albeit briefly. Supporters followed him, Irene and his father to the café around the corner at Dolgellau, where over a meal the talk was of little else but the very real prospect of escaping a jail sentence.

All chance of this was swept away in a paroxysm of headlines the following morning, mostly counter-productive by implying that Mr Justice Elwes had concluded that the sabotaging of Tryweryn was a 'justifiable grievance'. The *Daily Herald* went further, its headline 'Judge hints of deal with saboteur' almost certainly killing off all hopes of leniency.[4] To make matters worse, Emyr Llew, rather than wait for his friend to be sentenced, began a hunger strike immediately the case ended, and after five days was transferred to Walton Prison, Liverpool, to be force-fed if necessary. If it had come to that, the young student would have been pinned down by warders, a block of wood with a hole drilled through the centre rammed into his mouth to keep it open while the feeding tube was pushed through into his stomach. Before that stage was reached, however, his father and a clergyman persuaded him to call off his hunger strike.

No sooner had the trial resumed, than Williams knew his fate was sealed. If Mr Justice Elwes had previously entertained thoughts of a more lenient sentence, these had been dissipated by the reaction following the trial. After defence and prosecution concluded their submissions, he turned to Williams in the dock and said:

> I wish you to understand, as I think there is some danger of you having misunderstood, that I am not concerned to consider whether your grievance was a just one; it appeared that it was an intelligible one. But it is not for me to decide whether a grievance, which arises purely from political views was a just one and it is very important that the court should not meddle with it.[5]

Saying that he had reflected on the case since the adjournment, the judge continued:

> If I were thought to have regarded the use of explosives for these purposes as something that was not very serious and blowing up installations as something that could be excused by a strong feeling of grievance for race and country, I should have insulted the people of Wales. It is an ancient civilisation and one the Welsh have right to be proud of.[6]

The MAC manifesto found at Williams's home had caused him further anxiety, added the judge. While it bound Williams and his associates together not to endanger life, the central theme of the manifesto was to conduct acts of sabotage:

> Like Mr Justice Barry who sentenced your associate Emyr Jones, I find this a very grievous task, and one I will be glad to be relieved of. I have to consider the fact that you went out to blow something else up as soon as your associate was sentenced. I have to take this into account, and you must regard as considerable leniency that I shall not impose a term of imprisonment longer than your associate's. I sentence you to twelve months' imprisonment on each of these charges … the sentences to run concurrently.[7]

Seized by the shoulders, Owen Williams was hauled off to the cells by a prison guard, first stop Shrewsbury Prison, where prisoner 287 was weighed, showered and issued with prison uniform. Name, religion and details of his sentence were noted on a card posted on the door of his cell. After three days, Williams was transferred to Drake Hall Open Prison, which was more like a wartime German POW camp, the prisoners housed in rows of prefabricated single-storey buildings. It was there that Williams spent the remainder of his twelve-month sentence. His accomplice, John Albert Jones, was placed on probation for three years. Both men gave an assurance they would not again resort to violence.[8]

Prison was a bad experience for Owen Williams. Criminalised by the media, there was always the chance of being brutalised by incarceration. Raised in the Welsh heartlands with the freedom to roam over mountain and vale, prison was stifling, depressing and harrowing for a man whom the judge agreed was a gentle, friendly individual, not insensitive to other people. Christmas in prison without his children, and knowing as he then did that Teleri Bethan would never leave hospital, not even recognise her father, was an especially bad time, relieved only by the scores of Christmas cards from supporters back home in Wales.

Five months later he was alone again in the flat above the Espresso café. His marriage had disintegrated two months after his release from prison on St David's Day 1964, wrecked by politics, imprisonment and suspicion. Alone that Christmas Day, Owen Williams picked up a letter. Not all were from supporters. This was abusive, from a person signing himself anonymously as *A Liverpool Doctor*. It read, 'I wish your baby was dead. She would be better off than having a lunatic like you for a father.'[9]

# 5

## 'I HAVE A COMMUNIQUÉ FOR MR HUMPHRIES'

As far as the police were concerned, contrary to what Mr Justice Elwes had suspected, MAC consisted only of three activists and some hangers-on, and was not the tip of an iceberg calved from the seething resentment in the aftermath of Tryweryn. Throughout the two weeks that Williams was on bail with instructions from the judge to consult with his 'associates', the Pwllheli café-owner remained under more or less constant surveillance. He contacted no one, either because no others were involved in the conspiracy, or because of more pressing personal matters. Nevertheless, Williams would live with the police at his back for much of his life, although after he and Emyr Llew were jailed nothing further was heard of MAC until the 1966 attack on the Clywedog Dam at Llanidloes.

The interregnum was filled by the Free Wales Army, following its public debut at the official opening of Tryweryn. The Lampeter horse-breeder Cayo Evans had first heard of the existence of the FWA from evidence produced at the trial of Owen Williams, who by then was widely regarded as a focus for resistance to English rule. The pair eventually met at night in 1965 on a deserted beach near Pwllheli. 'Yes, the army does exist', Williams assured him, but he was not a member, on account of being under more or less constant police surveillance. By the time the meeting ended, Cayo Evans had decided to form a unit of the FWA in west Wales. The FWA and other extremist groups, Cayo Evans claimed later, were a result of the deep sense of resentment over political attitudes towards Wales and the contemptuous disregard politicians of all parties had for Welsh public opinion.

Never formally constituted, the army very quickly established a public reputation as an extremist nationalist group committed to the violent overthrow of English rule in Wales. After plastering slogans and its emblem across the countryside to register its existence, the FWA's first appearance at Tryweryn caused a ripple of excitement, when demonstrators suddenly saw that there was some substance to what many believed was a phantom army. At first the crowd whispered, 'The Free Wales Army is here', then they hugged and cheered Cayo Evans and his two companions.[1]

For many, that was the first and last time the FWA was taken seriously. The threat it posed was almost entirely confined to newspaper headlines, among the most outrageous of these the assertion that the army received regular deliveries of arms from the IRA, landed from a Dutch coaster at Swansea Docks.

Nevertheless, a year later it seemed that Cayo Evans had recruited at least thirty-seven supporters, the number a *Daily Sketch* reporter counted on parade during the Dublin march to mark the fiftieth anniversary of the Easter Rising. The invitation to participate had come, according to the FWA, from Sinn Fein, although there is no evidence of links with the IRA or any other extremist group, whether Breton nationalists, Basque separatists or Palestine Liberation Organisation fighters, all of which were supposedly collaborating with Cayo Evans and company. The Dublin march was probably the nearest the FWA ever came to real freedom fighters. But for Cayo it was a memorable occasion. Like a

Dennis Coslett, otherwise Dafydd ap Coslett (facing) from Llangennech, Llanelli, a self-styled commander in the Free Wales Army, allegedly demonstrates how to make a bomb (left). Free Wales Army members on parade in December 1967 (right). Copyright: *Town Magazine*.

The Free Wales Army on manoeuvres at Lampeter simulate an attack using a dummy hand grenade in December 1967. Copyright: *Town Magazine*.

strolling minstrel, his accordion slung across his shoulders, Cayo entertained packed public houses with his selection of rebel songs before leading his FWA contingent through Dublin, followed by the black and white flags of the Breton Liberation Movement. Plaid Cymru had also sent a delegation, some of whose members jumped ship to join Cayo Evans's lot, which probably explains the thirty-seven members of the army counted by the *Daily Sketch*, only three of whom were decked out in the FWA's uniform.

Not long afterwards, *Daily Mail* photographer John Smart was disappointed to discover only the same three men in uniform when sent to photograph the 'army' on manoeuvres at the Evans farm. But the FWA bandwagon was rolling, and not even the truth would derail a story fuelled by exaggeration piled upon exaggeration. The FWA was backed by millionaires in Wales, the United States and England, or so the story went; and its foot-soldiers were training with the

IRA. The announcement of the opening by the Queen in September 1966 of the first Severn Bridge, linking England and Wales, elicited a threat from the FWA to blow it up. By then, this phantom army was well established in terrorist kidology.

With never more than twenty-five members, the FWA would consistently punch above its weight by allowing itself to be exploited indiscriminately by disreputable sections of the media, to whom it boasted of having 7,000 'soldiers' in the field. For anyone interested, it staged mock manoeuvres for the camera, either on Cayo Evans's farm or somewhere on the remote Abergwesyn mountain pass. At first, the police cared little for these comic opera antics, even when splashed across the media. Clipping and filing the newspaper cuttings was about the only action taken. Even the discovery of a Free Wales Army cap after the explosion at the Clywedog Dam in 1966 did not fool the police. The prosecution of these comedians for strutting their stuff around Wales was never seriously considered by the local constabulary until, like a solar eclipse, the alignment of certain events persuaded them otherwise. Or, as Mr John Mortimer, QC, aptly observed at the subsequent trial of FWA activists, the Home Office chose to use a very large British legal sledgehammer against 'a very small Welsh nut'. It was the conjuncture between the continued failure to track down the real bombers and concern for the safety of the Prince of Wales, due to be invested at Caernarfon Castle in July 1969, that caused the police, under pressure from the Wilson government, to crack down on the FWA hotheads.

William Edward Julian Cayo Evans came from a very well respected Lampeter family. When his father, a professor at St David's College, Lampeter, and former High Sheriff of Cardiganshire, died in 1958, Cayo inherited the farm at Glandennis, near Lampeter, where he bred horses and lived with his wife, Gilliane, also a committed nationalist. A mentally defective brother was admitted to the London Clinic in 1966, according to a police report.

Cayo received an expensive private education. Born in April 1937, he attended boarding school until thirteen and was briefly at Berkhamsted Public School in Hertfordshire, before completing the last two years of his studies at the prestigious Millfield Public School in Somerset. To what extent this benefited him is questionable, certainly in the light of a police report in 1966 describing Cayo as an 'undeveloped personality with the mental age of about 12', a description refuted by those who knew him as a generous, friendly, intelligent individual, although excitable.[2] According to Robat ap Steffan, who knew Cayo well, he 'was a giant of a man, a genuinely magnetic personality, the kind you don't often find in today's bland, consumerist Wales'. The same police report placed him as a habitué of public houses, dancehalls and cafés, his visits often ending in a brawl.

Not always was Cayo successful in avoiding the repercussions of a Saturday night punch-up. By the 1960s the stone memorial marking the spot at Cilmeri, near Builth Wells, where the last native Prince of Wales, Llywelyn, was ambushed and killed had become the focus for a commemorative march each year by nationalists. The commemoration usually ended in the local hostelries, in particular one appropriately named the Prince Llywelyn. Barely two months before the FWA's fantasy world crashed to earth in a police crackdown, a torch-light procession through Builth Wells erupted in a confrontation with the 'Gestapo', the word the FWA used to refer to the police. After Cayo Evans had accused one of the officers of being a 'Judas' for betraying his country, there was a general mêlée, with fists flying on both sides, before Evans was hauled into the police station and charged with assault, for which he received a four months' suspended sentence.

After completing his education, Cayo Evans had been conscripted into the South Wales Borderers as Private 23164555, one noticeable legacy of his National Service a torso almost entirely covered with tattoos. Sent to fight the communist insurgents in Malaya, he later boasted of serving as an Army Scout with the 17th Gurkha Division, engaged in flushing out Britain's jungle enemies. After National Service in 1957, he studied for a year at the Royal Agricultural College, Cirencester, before spending three months in France furthering his knowledge of farming; not that any of this counted for much in later life, Cayo preferring after his father's death to devote his energies to horse-breeding rather than farming, and his spare time to posing as a threat to the English. Partly because of the increased surveillance resulting from his political posturing, there was not a year between 1958 and 1969 when he did not fall foul of the local constabulary, mostly for trivial motoring offences and drunkenness, but also for malicious wounding and being in possession of a dangerous weapon, a knuckleduster.[3]

Owen Williams insists he had little to do with Cayo Evans and the FWA, beyond the occasional meeting and bar-room festivities following the annual march at Cilmeri. Williams would, however, become vice-president of the National Patriotic Front, an organisation regarded as a political mouthpiece for the FWA because some members had a foot in both camps. One of these, Keith Griffiths, firmly believed that if the nationalist movement in Wales ever hoped to threaten the Establishment then it needed a military wing. Born into a mining family in Merthyr, Gethin ap Iestyn, as Griffiths later styled himself, was living in Bridgend when his statutory schooling finished at Pencoed Secondary Modern. Like others in Anglicised south Wales cheated of their heritage by the Anglocentric version of history, he gravitated towards Plaid Cymru, which in the early 1960s was still regarded as a nationalist party committed to independence. But for him the language became a roadblock, separating the Welsh-speakers from activists on the English wing of Welsh nationalism. One result was the emergence of a new organisation, the Anti-Sais (English) Front, formed by Griffiths and another recruit to the FWA, Tony Lewis, the Cwmbran bus-driver responsible for designing the FWA uniform. A pressure-group offering a home to English-speaking activists cast adrift by the cosy relationship between Plaid and Welsh-speaking campaigners of Cymdeithas yr Iaith Gymraeg, the Anti-Sais Front mutated into the National Patriotic Front, with a youth wing, the Young Patriots' League, and another affiliate organisation, the Llywelyn Society, that drew upon Wales's historical past to support the struggle for independence. Although the National Patriotic Front briefly severed relations with the FWA on account of its publicity antics, members of both organisations, including Williams, were expelled by Plaid in 1966 for refusing to renounce violence. Apart from the FWA, which hogged the news pages, the other groups surfaced only occasionally, exercising little political clout, apart from the damage caused to Plaid Cymru through association.

But closest to Cayo Evans in the FWA was Dennis Coslett, otherwise Dafydd ap Coslett, self-styled commandant of the Carmarthenshire brigade. Coslett was the loosest of all the loose cannons in the FWA. As a conduit between the group and the media, he became the voice of the FWA for those eager to regurgitate the most extravagant claims as fact, when most were fiction concocted in the front room of his home at 107 Brynhyfryd, Llangennech, Llanelli, surrounded by photographs of Castro, Che Guevara, Chairman Mao and other revolutionaries. A Welsh-speaker, Coslett claimed he was not anti-English, although almost everything he said and did pointed to an individual obsessed with retribution for the damage English colonisation had caused to Wales, culturally, politically and economically. Coslett was the one who associates said would stop at nothing to reclaim Wales's independence.

At Llangennech, where Coslett was a familiar figure, decked out in his ex-army surplus, sometimes prancing up and down with his Alsatian Gelert on a leash, like a German gauleiter, villagers generally regarded him with derision, a figure of fun, an 'unbalanced personality … a crank with delusions of grandeur', according to a police report in 1965. Even his dog had been recruited into the FWA, trained, if Coslett was to be believed, to carry magnetic mines strapped to its back, which the animal would then attach to the underside of a tank on the command, 'Attack!' Not unnaturally, there was considerable consternation among pet lovers when the FWA revealed it had a pack of 'kamikaze' Alsatians. According to a police report for the Director of Public Prosecutions after the FWA paraded in a demonstration at Machynlleth, Coslett was a violent individual and was also 'cruel to his family'.[4] I only ever met him twice, and that was much later in life, by which time he had given up politics for poetry, but even then he was intimidating. Perhaps he regarded me as coming from the wrong side of the revolutionary tracks!

After losing an eye in an accident on the site of a garage in his village, Coslett had difficulty finding work. Since he was trespassing at the time, there was no compensation and, unable to return to work as a collier, he spent a great deal of his life living off social security.[5] Towards the end he did sell some of his poetry to those on the fringes of revolutionary nationalism. Like Cayo Evans, Coslett also had a string of convictions for largely petty offences.

The very first contact I had with him was during my time as news editor at the *Western Mail* from 1966 to 1972. The news-desk was the first port of call for anyone offering something of interest, Coslett always introducing himself as 'an emissary for our commandant Cayo Evans'. His voice ringing with self-importance, he invariably announced that he had 'a communiqué from our commandant for Mr Humphries', following this with some monstrous boast or threat from the FWA, far too preposterous for any responsible newspaper to touch with a bargepole. The pantomime became increasingly tedious, so much so that on one occasion, under pressure from the real news of the day, my patience snapped and I snarled back, 'For Christ's sake, Dennis, isn't it about time you moved into the real world?' Quite unfazed by my angry retort, Coslett ploughed on regardless with his press release, adding at the very end, as a sort of riposte, I imagined at the time, 'And there's a bomb in the pipeline for you, Humphries!' The FWA was so full of nonsense this could have meant anything. Not even months afterwards, when Tom Powell, a sheep farmer at Cefn Penarth, Crossgates, found gelignite strapped to a car inner-tube and stuffed inside a manhole on the aqueduct supplying Birmingham with water from the Elan Valley reservoirs, did I link the discovery with Coslett's telephone call. And it was years before I learned the real story behind the FWA's one and only attempt at sabotage.

The police and media were not the only ones irritated by the antics of the FWA. So was MAC2, which eventually decided to give Cayo Evans, Coslett and company the opportunity to prove their mettle by planting a bomb on the Elan Valley pipeline at Crossgates. The bomb MAC2 prepared for the FWA comprised forty sticks of gelignite and a detonator, strapped to an inflated car inner-tube. Told exactly where to drop it into a manhole on the pipeline, the explosion was calculated to sever water supplies to millions of consumers in the Midlands. All seemed to be going well. The FWA men found the right spot, prised open the manhole and dropped in the explosive inner-tube before fleeing – in their panic forgetting to attach the detonator! The device lay there for months, until found by the sheep farmer and destroyed by the bomb disposal squad. After this, the FWA retreated into its imaginary world of news-paper headlines. At first, the more moderate of its dispatches scraped through into the *Western Mail* in truncated form, until the editor, Giddings, hauled down the shutters on the FWA as crackpots not worthy of our consideration. Before that, however, I was given one last chance to prove to the world that the FWA was a gigantic hoax.

I had hoped to end this nonsense in May 1966 with a story headlined 'Horse breeder who runs a phantom army', published after my deputy news editor, Denis Gane, met Cayo Evans secretly at Barry Island. But the FWA publicity machine never faltered, not even momentarily, continuing to grind out press releases directed at the London-based media, which milked the story ruthlessly for its entertainment value, especially after Coslett unveiled his pack of 'kamikaze' dogs.[6]

Before long, it began to look as though the whole world believed the FWA except the *Western Mail*. The spike on my news-desk reserved for rejected stories grew thicker by the night, the FWA pronouncements binned even faster than those from the resurgent Plaid Cymru. In order to nail the lie forever, I detached Patrick Hannan, one of our most experienced investigative journalists, from normal reporting duties so that he could spend a whole month investigating the FWA's claims of a membership running into thousands. To allow someone a month to work on a single story was a massive sacrifice, a huge logistical investment for any newsroom. Hannan's brief was to go out and count them, and on 20 October 1967 the *Western Mail* devoted an entire page to the results of his investigation, under the headline: 'Welsh boys who love to play the army game'. According to Hannan, whose account was described during the FWA trial two years later as perhaps the most complete piece of research published, the 'army' had no more than twenty-five members, some of these just children. His conclusion was that it was a 'comic opera affair', best described by a written sign spotted on the windscreen of a car which said: 'FWA: gone for a drink'. The FWA were just as much in the dark as the police when, eighteen months after Clywedog, someone blew up the Liverpool Corporation pipeline at Llanrhaeadr-ym-Mochnant, following this two months later with a bomb at the Temple of Peace in Cardiff.[7]

None of this prevented Cayo Evans and company from pretending they were responsible for the most serious outbreak of violent direct action in Wales since Owain Glyndŵr's fifteenth-century rebellion. Inasmuch as their antics were a distraction for those hunting the real bombers, the FWA did play a part. From newspapers it graduated to television, the army's first big break occurring on the very day the *Western Mail* thought it had pricked the FWA bubble with its exposé by Hannan. That same evening, Evans, Coslett and their foot-soldiers paraded in battledress on ITV's *David Frost Show*. If they expected a serious discussion, they were to be hugely disappointed. After quarrelling with Frost for referring to Coslett as 'Dai Dayan' – both Israeli General Moshe Dayan and Coslett wore black eye-patches – the discussion was interrupted by a drunk walking across the stage. Other items in the programme included someone who had had a psychic vision of the Prince of Wales in bed at Cambridge and an English nationalist who wanted to raise an army to retake the colonies. Vera Lynn sang *Lily Marlene*, and an actor reminisced about growing geraniums on the bridge of a warship. For subjecting themselves to national ridicule, the FWA boys were paid £50, and reimbursed two nights' accommodation (£120) and travel expenses (£154).[8]

Nothing, however, could humiliate the FWA, its next venture a film produced by the Israeli director Gideon Haendler, starring Coslett as the bomb-maker.

Since the producers had a tight budget and could not afford to buy in archive material of pipeline explosions, Coslett volunteered to simulate one. After pouring some petrol on to a steam tank salvaged from a scrapyard, and placing two cans beside it, Coslett stepped back while Haendler lit a match and the cans exploded for the cameras. Publicity material trailing the film claimed, 'FWA training by night and also one of their members blowing up a pipeline'.

The night exercise, filmed at Pontaber in the Black Mountains, purported to show FWA members carrying guns. One of these was a car jack that looked like an automatic weapon in the dark. In another scene, shot at the home of Dafydd Rowlands in Corris, the film crew placed a copy of the book *Total Resistance* on the arm of his chair and a shotgun over the mantelpiece as props. That evening the FWA 'actors' were entertained to dinner at the Pontaber Inn, when a great deal of drink was consumed.[9]

Publicity came thicker and faster than any professional publicist could ever wish for, the FWA's next appearance a seven-page spread in *Town*, a London magazine with a dwindling circulation and on the brink of closure. The best that can be said for its headline, 'Who's at war with England?' above an article about the FWA 'on manoeuvres', is that it was tame compared with what followed. A second headline, linked to a photograph of a small group of uniformed FWA conspirators, proclaimed, 'Julian Cayo Evans and members of the Free Wales Army plot the expulsion of the English. One of these days they'd like to blow up the Severn Bridge or flood the Mersey Tunnel. Meanwhile, they have to be content with the odd water pipe.'

Much was pure fiction, in particular the FWA's claim to have planted the bomb at Clywedog in March 1966 and to the sabotaging the following year of the Liverpool water pipeline at Llanrhaeadr-ym-Mochnant. According to the author of the *Town* article, Stan Gebler Davies, and his researcher, Bryn Griffiths, the FWA had actually cut water supplies to Birmingham with its inner-tube bomb at Crossgates.

The cornerstone of *Town* magazine's account of Wales at war with England was the FWA on manoeuvres on Cayo Evans's forty-acre farm near Lampeter, described by Gebler Davies as a Welsh mountainside 'very green and very wet and liberally supplied with treacherous pools of animal dung glistening like chocolate pudding in the grass'. Bryn Griffiths, a local Welsh freelance, had set up the interview for Davies and his German freelance photographer, Jurgen Schadeberg. He had also arranged the FWA's appearance on the disastrous but hugely entertaining *David Frost Show*. Cayo Evans, he knew, would do or say anything for publicity and money.

Waiting for the journalists at Cayo's farm were four or five FWA men, including Coslett, kitted out in military-style uniform and introduced as a unit preparing to embark on a training exercise. Disappointed by the turnout, the *Town* researcher Bryn Griffiths said the story was off unless they could beef up their numbers, at which point Cayo drove into nearby Lampeter and a tour of the local hostelries, where three or four youths were persuaded to join the 'exercise' in return for £2 each. Before it started the following morning, Evans and Coslett produced 'firearms' in plastic bags, although apart from a Mauser machine pistol carried by Coslett, Griffiths could not be certain any were real.[10]

According to Stan Gebler Davies's published account, the exercise proceeded as follows:

> The guns came out of hiding wrapped in plastic, a Mauser machine pistol, a Sten gun and magazines of live ammunition, two .38 pistols, a .22 rifle, some shotguns and sundry other weapons to varying degrees lethal.
>
> The first exercise, learnt with the IRA in the Irish mountains, was to simulate a patrol along a hedge with the expectation of being shot at from the other side. 'Okay boys', whispered Cayo, 'walk slowly', and the procession crept on irregularly through the mud. 'Forward, left, right, left', said Coslett, looking in his uniform, consisting of green dyed British Army battledress, green shirt and jackboots, remarkably like an SS officer fallen on bad company. 'Don't lark about', he roared, bringing up the rear with the Sten gun, 'D'you hear?'
>
> 'In close to the hedge', said Cayo, and the white Alsatian bitch closed in wagging her tail and got in the way. 'Bitch, bitch', said Cayo, 'go home'.
>
> 'Duck, duck down', said Coslett suddenly. 'Down, down, DOWN!' They all flopped down in the grass and mud and the cow-dung, and pointed their guns over a hump through the hedge. Coslett shot his off without a magazine in it, fortunately, because one bang on the side of that mountain would have brought every CID man in Cardiganshire and his brother running.
>
> The dog, desperately interested in the proceedings, ran up close and barked. 'Bitch', said a voice pale with anxiety, 'f...off'.
>
> They all got up. 'In extended line now', said Cayo, 'zigzag, zigzag'.
>
> 'Enemy attack from the left', shouted Coslett, 'ZIGZAG, ZIGZAG!'
>
> They zigzagged. After the first bit of running around, there was a lecture on the use of weapons.
>
> 'Now the Sten gun,' said Coslett, crouching down, 'it is a very dangerous weapon. It takes a lot of practice to use it. It was cheaply manufactured in America. It was bought by the gangsters in America.'

'Ah, you're wrong, you're wrong,' said Cayo. 'You're talking about the Thomson gun.'

'No,' said Coslett, 'the Sten gun.'

'No,' said Cayo, 'the Sten gun was made for the British Army for seven and six to use captured nine millimetre ammunition.' He pointed to the gun. 'Now this,' he said, 'has been altered. Seeing as the English paid £2000 to make me an expert in guerrilla warfare I fitted this with a flash eliminator and a grip. Now a novice with a Sten gun gets his fingers nipped here, see? Also they'll catch hold of the magazine and she jams right away.'

'And that gets very hot,' said Coslett, pointing at the barrel. 'Shall we fire a burst?' They didn't. 'One burst,' said one volunteer, looking around for a potential enemy, 'and we'd be f…ed.' Coslett waved a .38 in the air. 'That,' he said, 'was used by the IRA, that gun. That won Ireland. That's the gun that won Ireland.' He shoved it in my stomach. 'Where'd you like it,' he asked. Coslett is a man notably lacking a sense of humour.

'Who's going to throw the grenade?' asked Cayo.

'I'll throw the grenade,' said Coslett.

'No,' said Cayo, 'you're trained already.'

'Let me show *how* to throw the grenade.' Coslett began to demonstrate. 'Now this is just how do you call it, a dead one for training,' he said. 'Now you have the pin here and a base plug here for cleaning or if you want to detonate it. You hold your right hand over the clip here. You pulls the pin out with your left. And this is the position of throwing the grenade. When I throw the grenade I want everyone to drop on the floor, OK?'

'Position, spread out, throw.' He threw it. Everybody hit the floor, attempting at the same time to preserve their uniforms from the natural hazards presented to them. The grenade landed with a soft thump twenty yards away. They got it back.

'Position, spread out, throw.' Everybody hit the deck again except the dog, who ran after the grenade in great excitement, a handy animal to have around. One man stayed on the floor this time because he saw no point in getting up only to lie down again.[11]

The *Town* article proceeded to attribute to the FWA some pretty wild stuff:

'We shoot to kill', said Coslett with great passion, pounding one fist into the other. 'Nothing stops us. We have dossiers on all the traitors, all of them. Cledwyn Hughes and Emlyn Hooson and all the traitors who have sold Wales out to England.'

'Sure,' said Cayo, who is not so intense, and better humoured, sipping his Guinness, 'and what about the councillor down the road?'

'I'll have him too. He's a bloody traitor, I'll shoot him,' said Coslett.[12]

Back at the pub after the 'exercise' Coslett boasted of having served his National Service in Berlin guarding Hitler's former deputy, Rudolf Hess, in Spandau prison. Hearing this, the German photographer, Schadeberg, asked whether he had read *Mein Kampf*. 'A great book', remarked Coslett. 'He had all the answers all right.' According to *Town*, Cayo Evans agreed with this, adding that it was 'a sad day for Wales when Germany lost the war', thereby reinforcing the common belief that certain Welsh nationalists had spied for Germany during the Second World War.

Of the two, Coslett was potentially the most dangerous. Given to uncontrolled outbursts of temper, especially after drinking, he was considered by the freelance Bryn Griffiths to be quite capable of violence or sabotage. *Town* magazine concluded that if a Free Wales were to have its first martyr, then it would be Coslett, who blamed the English for everything that was wrong with Wales. 'I *condemn* them all', he told the three journalists. Cayo agreed, accusing the English of destroying Welsh culture 'with their drugs and trashy music'. Coslett added recent homosexual reforms to his personal hate-list.

The more moderate of the pair, Cayo was then thirty, tall and cheerful with a disorderly disposition. Wales, he told *Town*, was only asking for the right to determine its own future, to run its own affairs without foreign (English) intervention. He thought the English would have learned their lesson when they were given 'a bloody good hiding in Aden, Cyprus, all over the world'.

Both credited the FWA and the bombing campaign with the election of Gwynfor Evans as the first Plaid Cymru MP at the Carmarthen by-election the previous year. 'We did put him there', boasted Cayo. 'We awakened the minds of the people.' As a consequence, everyone in Wales was talking about it getting its own government, Coslett insisted:

Five years ago you'd never hear a Welshman talking about nationalism but as soon as these explosions occurred the people bloody well began to talk and you can bloody well go into any pub in Wales today and you will always hear people talking about our own government, you will always hear someone arguing.[13]

Most people suspected that the only reason the FWA was not rounded up sooner was because the police genuinely considered the army harmless. The only other explanation was that the FWA 'soldiers' were allowed to strut their stuff in the hope they might help in the detection of the real bombers. But Cayo Evans and Coslett could no longer continue to be ignored when they threatened the lives of those 'traitors in the House of Commons', Cledwyn Hughes and Emlyn Hooson, QC. Hughes was Secretary of State for Wales, and Hooson, MP for Montgomeryshire, had been a serious contender for the leadership of the Liberal Party, only stepping aside at the eleventh hour for Jeremy Thorpe. After reading of the threat, Hooson immediately asked the Attorney General, another Welshman, Sir Elwyn Jones, MP QC, to investigate. It was also referred to the House of Commons Committee of Privileges as possibly constituting a prima facie breach of parliamentary privilege.

Anticipating a question in the House of Commons, Sir Elwyn sought advice from the Director of Public Prosecutions, Sir Norman Skelhorn, QC. Did the material contained in the *Town* article, published in December 1967, provide the basis for a prosecution under Section 2 of the Public Order Act 1936? The Act had been introduced to deal with Sir Oswald Mosley's British Fascists, after they were involved in extraordinarily ugly scenes during clashes with opponents on the streets of Britain's major cities prior to the Second World War. There were two sections to the Act, the first prohibiting the wearing in public of a uniform that might signify association with a political organisation or promotion of a political objective. The second part covered organising and training persons to use physical force in support of a political goal. If either aroused reasonable apprehension, then those involved were guilty of an offence.

No offence had been committed by the FWA under the first part of the Act because the uniforms were worn on private property, Cayo Evans's farm. With regard to the possible offence of organising, training or equipping the Free Wales Army, the Director of Public Prosecutions had only the statement provided to the Special Branch by freelance journalist Bryn Griffiths. While there had been numerous newspaper articles in which exaggerated claims were made by the 'army', the police at that stage had no sworn affidavits from the reporters to corroborate the published claims by Evans and Coslett that they controlled and managed the FWA. Photographs appearing in the press on various occasions usually showed the same six men posing for the cameras with what were possibly imitation weapons. The *Town* article was considered 'inaccurate and grossly exaggerated', with not a scrap of evidence implicating the FWA in any explosions. Therefore, the Director of Public Prosecutions told the Attorney General on 25 January 1968, who in turn advised the Prime Minister, Harold Wilson, that:

> The evidence disclosed as a result of the police enquiries would not at present warrant proceedings being taken in respect of the activities of this

organisation and indeed such proceedings would be undesirable [...] In the circumstances it is at least doubtful whether sufficient admissible evidence could be obtained to establish a contravention of s.2(1)(b) but even if this were possible a prosecution would in my view be taking this organisation's activities too seriously and would give it an unmerited importance and publicity which its leaders are plainly desiring.[14]

In his reply to the House of Commons, Sir Elwyn in effect dismissed the FWA as a gigantic wheeze not to be taken seriously, and said prosecution was neither necessary nor desirable. The 'army' would, however, be kept under surveillance, he promised.[15]

Twelve months later the political wheel had turned. After regarding the antics of the Free Wales Army for four years as harmless, the Home Office suddenly decided to lock them up. Not only had the bombing campaign intensified, but Welsh extremism, both real and imagined, was heading for a potentially cataclysmic collision with the most massive royal event since the Coronation of Elizabeth II – the Investiture of her eldest son, Charles, at Caernarfon Castle in July 1969. But it took another *Town*-style article, complete with mock exercise and all the trimmings, finally to prod the Home Office to take action against the FWA.

The author of the article in the *Daily Telegraph* colour supplement on 30 August 1968 was John Summers. Headlined 'Time Bomb Ticking in Wales', it was illustrated with the familiar photographs of an 'exercise', involving the same men in the same green uniforms, accompanied by explosions of sorts, detonated by a cigar-smoking commandant called 'Dai Bomber'. On cue, the participants admitted responsibility for just about everything of an extremist nature. As for the Investiture, Coslett promised something that 'would make the whole world hold its breath', adding, 'they reckon they'll be a world-wide TV audience of 400 million watching by satellite television'.

Cayo Evans was portrayed as half-French and a former Foreign Legionnaire, Coslett had won the Celtic Cross for valour in the field, and the army was collaborating with the Scottish Liberation Army, the Quebec Liberation Front and the Breton Liberation Movement, not to mention the IRA. After blowing up bridges in Pamplona, the Free Basques were now assisting the FWA. Former OAS men living in Dublin had popped across to Wales to offer instructions in bomb-making. There would be more bomb attacks on government offices and newspapers in Wales, as well as the new Severn Bridge, which seemed especially unpopular with the FWA. Consequently, Prime Minister Harold Wilson would soon be begging 'for peace talks on a coracle in the River Teifi', concluded the *Daily Telegraph* article.[16]

The *Western Mail* knew all about the author, John Summers, a freelance with the reputation of being a person prepared to do anything if it made a story. According to a confidential police report on Summers's activities, the freelance was regarded as being a thoroughly unreliable type, not held in very high esteem by his colleagues at the Bristol *Western Daily Press*, where he started his career.[17] I could certainly vouch for some of this, Summers having crossed my path in 1966, not as a result of his involvement with the FWA, but in connection with another story, the Aberfan disaster.

Within days of the coal-tip collapse at Aberfan, the *Western Mail* launched a disaster fund in aid of the village and the relatives of the 141 children and teachers buried by the mountain of slurry that had engulfed the primary school. Graphically illustrated by a photograph of a police constable carrying one of the few surviving children to safety, the tragedy touched the hearts of millions, triggering a flood of donations. Very soon the disaster fund exceeded well over £1 million, a massive amount of money in 1966. Inevitably, there were disputes about distributing the fund, how best to use the money and the timing. The *Western Mail*, having helped to organise it, sought to steer clear of what was becoming a messy situation. Summers produced a story to the effect that the FWA would resort to direct action if demands for the fund to be shared out amongst the parents by a certain deadline were not met. He repeated this claim in an Israeli-produced television film. 'A classic case of exploitation', was the conclusion of defence counsel Aubrey Myerson, QC, when Summers's involvement was mentioned during the 1969 FWA trial. Describing Summers as a 'shadowy creature', Mr Myerson added, 'What undiluted rubbish this man speaks. What nonsense.'[18]

The *Western Mail* wanted nothing to do with Summers and his stories. When he persisted, the editor, Giddings, issued the final sanction: no member of staff should speak to Summers, not even the switchboard operator. He was considered that dangerous! Such a prohibition was doomed to fail, because journalists by their very nature cannot keep their mouths shut. One evening Summers somehow persuaded the switchboard operator to put his call through to the news-desk. He was incandescent with rage, having heard of the instruction to the staff, and insisted on making a formal complaint to the editor. I picked up the direct line linking me to the editor while Summers hung on, spitting blood in my ear as he waited. John Giddings was not pleased.

'Get rid of him', he demanded. 'I want nothing to do with him. He's dangerous, unreliable. If he wants to complain, tell him to write a letter.' With that, the receiver in my other hand exploded with fury. I had failed to cover the mouthpiece and the man had heard every word. 'I heard that, the lot. And I've got it on tape', he screamed. 'I'll have you both for slander. I'll put you on the street, your wife and your children', Summers snarled into the telephone. At which point I slammed down the receiver, never to cross swords with him again, although his subsequent solicitor's letter involved me in a great deal of wasted effort in replying to his groundless accusations. Eventually he backed off and quit the scene.

If only I had known, I could have saved the editor and myself a great deal of trouble, because at that time Summers was secretly informing on the FWA. In 1966 Summers lived at Church View, Lulsgate, Somerset, and was employed by the South West News Agency. His police contact was Kenneth Clark, deputy coordinator, No. 7 Regional Crime Squad, based in Bristol. Reporters are not in the habit of informing senior regional crime squad detectives of their movements or sending them accounts of clandestine meetings with persons claiming to be engaged in extremist activities, including individual descriptions, names and addresses, as well as photographs, which is what Summers did.

In August 1966 Summers telephoned Clark to tell him that the following day he was travelling to Lampeter to interview Cayo Evans for an article for *Tit-Bits*. On his return from Lampeter, Summers told Clark that he had spent the night of 16 August at Cayo Evans's home. In the evening they were joined by about twenty-five other men, some in uniform. Later, they adjourned to the Pheasant Inn at Pont-ar-sais (Bridge on the Englishman), an appropriately named location for a hostelry described as 'a FWA pub' with a picture of Cayo on the wall. There, the men discussed blowing up the Severn Bridge by placing charges against the supporting cables. In his report to the regional crime squad officer Summers said he did not think any of those present at the meeting in the Pheasant Inn was responsible for destroying the conveyor at the Clywedog Dam that March, because they all spoke of the incident with genuine admiration. Among those present was someone called 'Mal', another named 'Llan', from Corris, and a middle-aged man referred to as 'Bont Shan', identified by Summers from a police photograph album as 'Yr Hen Bont Shan', an agitator spotted by police at Tryweryn in 1964.

Summers then proceeded to give the regional crime squad officer a detailed account of how the following morning he was taken into the mountains by a group of FWA members, who happily posed for photographs so long as their faces were hidden. Some carried 9mm Mauser-Parabellum machine pistols with wooden holsters, and one a Czechoslovakian machine-gun, although Clark thought it was more likely to have been a machine carbine. Summers handed the police officer a spent 9mm cartridge he had concealed in his shoe after finding it in the glove compartment of the car in which he was travelling.

The negatives of photographs supplied by Summers had been tampered with to disguise the identity of the participants.[19] On examination, an expert at the Home Office South Western Forensic Science Laboratory concluded they had been retouched with ink or some kind of dye to simulate debris from an explosion, while the magazines on all the weapons had also probably been produced by retouching. Only the Mauser automatic pistol photographed on the back of a man with a light-coloured jacket had not been tampered with.[20]

The Mauser would star in a number of repeat performances arranged by the FWA for the media, until it and four or five other weapons were eventually recovered by the police from a lake near Tregaron in September 1968 after a tip-off. Summers's report to the police of his encounter with the FWA was circulated to every Welsh police force and also No. 8 Regional Crime Squad, based in Cardiff, by Clark, who added:

> Summers would seem to be increasingly uneasy as to his contact with the Free Wales Army and goes to great lengths to emphasise that his only connection with the organisation is as a journalist. It is impossible to assess to what degree Cayo Evans and his henchmen have led Summers on, either with a view to publicity or simply to obtain money from him in payment for a story. Summers denies, incidentally, that he has ever paid Cayo Evans but I rather doubt that Cayo Evans has not received money from Summers himself or from his publishers.[21]

The significance of the Summers involvement is that three years before Cayo Evans and others eventually appeared in court, the police knew everything about the FWA, yet had decided they were not worth prosecuting. Although never called to give evidence when the FWA leaders were eventually charged, the shadow of John Summers hung over the proceedings, 'flitting to and fro like a phantom', according to another defence counsel, John Gower, and leaving a generally 'nasty smell'.[22]

# 6

## A DECLARATION OF WAR

The first time I rubbed shoulders with extremists with a track record for violent direct action I was squatting on the floor of a sparsely furnished apartment in Brussels drinking *pisco* sour, a Peruvian fruit drink fortified with a grape liquor that creeps up on the unsuspecting like a revolutionary. The Belgian capital has long been a sanctuary for political refugees, among my companions that particular evening three Marxists from Pinochet's Chile and two Argentines on the wrong side of the military junta. Radiating ownership of our little soirée was the Argentine-born Marxist revolutionary Che Guevara, his iconic image plastered around the walls as well as replicated on the T-shirt worn by my host. The conversation dragged on, firstly in English for my benefit, before reverting to rapid-fire Spanish fuelled by jugs of *pisco*. No one picked up a guitar to strum nostalgically at some cherished Chilean melody, or hum a patriotic song, as I had expected. The evening was about political creed and the class war, and how oppression was a manifestation of the competing dogma. National consciousness and cultural pride were never mentioned by the protagonists, whose instinctive regard for such matters as intrinsic and incontestable was a painful reminder of how far Wales still had to travel in resolving its own predicament.

The violence in Wales in the 1960s was incomprehensible to those accustomed to manning the traditional political barricades, because it had nothing whatsoever to do with class conflict. The motivation for a chain of events that threatened the status quo was a profound sense of national loss, for which revolution seemed the antidote. The iron in the soul of Welsh-speaking Owen Williams when Capel Celyn was drowned was the product of a determined process of cultural dispossession. John Jenkins, the Valleys boy, like so many born on the wrong side of the Anglo-Welsh blanket, had been expelled into the mists swirling about Mother Wales, robbed of his language, his cultural ties, his roots. But embedded in the psyches of both men was a common national ethos that not even an alien culture could displace. For such reasons the insurgents rejected further assimilation into England, their insurgency, in effect, a declaration of war against a regime they held responsible for the erosion of national esteem.

Jenkins first saw the light of day at St David's Hospital, Cardiff, afterwards returning with his parents to their terraced home at Aberfan. He spent only three years in the village, but the disaster that eventually engulfed it was a crucial influence in his life, epitomising for him English neglect and exploitation. According to the *Western Mail* he embarked upon his life of terrorism because he was 'insensate with grief' over the loss of so many young lives beneath that avalanche of black coal slurry.[1] Naturally shy and retiring, rather than the 'clever, ruthless fanatical' leader of a terrorist group, Jenkins in later years resembled a slightly crumpled, world-weary grandfather, his predilection for wearing black T-shirts and trousers the only visible sign of the sinister ambience with which he was endowed.[2] A little intimidating, perhaps, when squinting at you, but that probably explained by his being blind in one eye!

It was a youthful interest in history that led Jenkins to rediscover his roots. Walking on Gelligaer Mountain one day he stumbled upon the ruined walls of what was once a chapel of rest dedicated to the Celtic St Gwladus. The memorial plaque dated 428 AD puzzled him, since he had always been taught that St Augustine had converted the pagan Welsh almost two hundred years later, in 597 AD.

> From the very earliest, the policy was to rubbish the older Celtic Church and replace it with an English-centric one. After that the anomalies struck me thick and fast, including Owain Glyndŵr's depiction as a rebel not a patriot, or freedom fighter. Soon I saw there were two histories, the official and the real one, and that at school I was being taught something that was simply untrue.[3]

After the family moved to Penybryn, school was Bargoed Grammar, his English teacher Fred Evans, the former Caerphilly Labour MP. One of his classmates was Allan Rogers, a member of the European Parliament in Strasbourg when I was there as a journalist, Rogers later representing the Rhondda at Westminster. As youngsters, both played in the local jazz (kazoo) band, in which Jenkins was taught the drums by Rogers's brother Clem. At that time, every town in the Valleys had a kazoo band, which for many was the start of a lifelong interest in music.

Leaving school at fifteen without any qualifications, Jenkins became an apprentice blacksmith, before enlisting in the Royal Army Dental Corps in 1951 for five years. Military discipline and organisation would help him escape detection when later he embarked on his bombing campaign. The Army also reminded him that he had enlisted in 'England UK', the Army an Anglocentric institution with a thousand ways to remind a young soldier that the Welsh were second-class citizens. Like a constant pinprick, the irritation followed

Former Army Dental Corps sergeant John Jenkins, originally from Treharris in South Wales – the mastermind behind the bombing of water pipelines and public buildings in Wales by Mudiad Amddiffyn Cymru (Movement for Defence of Wales) (top). In 1970 Jenkins was jailed for ten years. Celtic artwork by Jenkins (bottom). Copyright: John Jenkins, the author; Celtic artwork, John Jenkins.

Jenkins's 19-year-old accomplice Frederick Ernest Alders, who was sent to prison for six years after admitting his part in a bombing campaign widely regarded as the most violent since Owain Glyndŵr's fifteenth-century uprising.

Jenkins to Germany, where the sign outside his billet proclaimed *Englisch Kaserne* (English Barracks). Not that any of this was especially unusual. I became a lot more anti-English when during my National Service I was locked in a cupboard by a bunch of cockney bullies!

The campaign to save Tryweryn had not long started when Jenkins was demobbed for the first time. By then, his personal journey of rediscovery was leading in the direction of nationalism via the Valleys' republican tradition. After a year underground, he was briefly a steelworker before training as a male nurse at East Glamorgan Hospital. There he met and married Thelma, another trainee nurse. The pay was poor and the hours long, the only way to provide a reasonable quality of life to re-enlist in the Dental Corps, which he did in 1958. Posted to Cyprus before the troubles between Greeks and Turks led to the island's partition, the inevitability of conflict was plain to him from watching the Turkish fleet on manoeuvres a few miles offshore from the walled city of Famagusta.

Like so many who venture abroad, the tug of Welsh consciousness grew stronger the longer his absence. When his first son, Vaughan, was born at Dhekelia Military Hospital (on the British sovereign base now straddling the Green Line between Greek and Turkish Cypriots) Jenkins resolved that his children would be raised in a Welsh-speaking environment. After being posted to Germany for a second tour of duty and the birth of a second son, Rhodri, he asked for a transfer back to Wales so that the boys could attend a Welsh-medium school. For the Army such a request 'blotted his copybook', for it revealed that 'England UK' no longer had first call on his loyalty, which is how Jenkins arrived at Saighton Camp, Chester, where under their very noses he assembled bombs for Mudiad Amddiffyn Cymru (MAC2).

The sentiments that persuaded John Jenkins to go to war can sound banal with the passage of time.[4] People ambivalent about the processes of assimilation have little inclination or incentive to understand the nationalist aspirations of a drowning man, having themselves jettisoned the desire for Home Rule, along with striped flannel petticoats, shawls and funny hats. No matter what the cost in national esteem, the concept of independence becomes increasingly incomprehensible for those wedded to economic and social dependency on 'England UK'. But in the 1960s, when nationalism was enjoying a revival in the wake of the anti-colonial movements in Africa and Asia, the failure of Wales to join this rush of nations into independence remains for many the great tragedy of the post-war period. For their part, Jenkins and Owen Williams tried to reignite the national consciousness, but Wales needed a much greater eruption of national sentiment to create an appetite for independence, because in the final analysis nations are self-defined, not defined by others.

Mudiad Amddiffyn Cymru had first surfaced as an extremist group committed to violent direct action during the struggle over Tryweryn. Afterwards driven underground, it was resurrected by persons unknown to organise the sabotaging of the Clywedog Dam in 1965. Jenkins was recruited into Mudiad Amddiffyn Cymru (MAC2) by Dai Pritchard from New Tredegar, then left to build and run the organisation, Pritchard playing no further part beyond providing material support for activists, including timing devices for some of the first bombs. Once installed as 'Director of Operations' with a 'Supreme Council' of five, Jenkins made it absolutely clear he wanted nothing whatsoever to do with the FWA, which he described as 'top of the shit parade'.[5] Anyone joining MAC2 was told to sever links with all other organisations, although some would retain a foot in both camps. On his return from Germany in 1966, Jenkins had at first become involved only at the margins, at meetings in smoky bars full of 'Saturday night talk'. His decision to take a lead in the insurgency was born from frustration with those Saturday nights, filled with nothing more than vast amounts of bluster and bravado:

> I just wanted to lead an ordinary life but it soon became clear no one was going to do anything, apart from shout and bawl. I didn't relish the idea but I could see that if I didn't do something about the democratic deficit no one else would.

> Everywhere it was British, British – time to show that contrary to what might have happened in the past we could still successfully draw attention to the colonial approach of the establishment.[6]

According to Jenkins, some hotheads boasted of 'driving the English into the sea' and of their willingness to carry out assassinations. Those, like Dennis Coslett, regarded as unsuitable and unstable took their crackpot ideas and outrageous pronouncements back to the FWA. Paranoid about security, the army sergeant set about restructuring MAC2 so that instead of a loosely knit group of loose cannons it became a network of tightly controlled cells, with Jenkins as the only person with knowledge of the entire organisation:

> In each cell only the cell leader knew me, and then only by sight, not my name, where I lived or anything else. I vetted every recruit personally and trained each cell leader personally. They were then left to recruit their own people. If there was a job, I would call unannounced, give the leader the target and the stuff, leaving him to organise the rest. [7]

It was not entirely coincidental that this cell system was eventually employed by the Provisional IRA. Sean MacStiofain, the founder of the breakaway Provisionals, adopted the cell system in 1968, at about the time he gave sanctuary to the Welsh activist Owen Williams, who, after jumping bail on an explosives charge, had fled to Ireland.[8]

MacStiofain was born John Edward Drayton Stephenson in Leytonstone, east London, of an English father and an Irish mother from Belfast. After a spell in the Royal Air Force, Stephenson married a girl from Cork, changed his name to MacStiofain and led his first IRA raid in 1953, on the armoury at the British officers' training corps at Felsted, Essex, for which he was sentenced to eight years in Pentonville. A firm believer in the armed struggle for a united Ireland, MacStiofain learned Irish while in prison and also acquired a detailed knowledge of guerrilla warfare. On his release he moved to Ireland to re-engage in the struggle, and in 1968, when Owen Williams arrived at his bungalow at Navan in County Meath, MacStiofain was at the centre of a right–left split then tearing the IRA apart. Traditionalists like MacStiofain were fiercely opposed to those on the Marxist-influenced wing seeking to replace the armed struggle with revolutionary social and economic objectives. When Owen Williams fled to Ireland, MacStiofain's breakaway group was within months of forming the Provisional IRA – and he had been impressed with what he heard about MAC2's cell system.

Before MAC2 embarked on its campaign of violent direct action, Jenkins the south Walian needed the support of activists in north-west Wales, where opposition to the imminent Investiture of the Prince of Wales was centred. During six months devoted to compiling a list of people and resources, one of Jenkins's first contacts was Owen Williams, 'a good bloke, go-between and well-established person in the northwest':

> People knew that unless I was trustworthy Owen wouldn't have introduced me. But I couldn't use him. He was too well known. MAC2 was a bit

like working in a colliery: one or two at the coalface, a lot of others in support. I was the only one who knew everything and everybody. The cells were independent, totally unaware of each other's existence. That is why it came as such a shock to the police. They had no record of my people because they never got involved in parades and banner waving. Neither did the police have public support. No one saw anything. If they did, nothing was said. The police and authorities tried to isolate us but this was an all-Wales campaign of direct action.[9]

Only Jenkins knew how many activist cells were formed, and he has refused to say. For one reason, a number of the participants remain at large, some involving themselves in the Cottage Arson Campaign a decade later, much of which remains shrouded in mystery because it was also organised as a network of unconnected cells. My researches, however, suggest that during the 1960s bombing campaign there were at least five cells across north Wales, another in south-east Wales, responsible for the attacks in Cardiff, and a further cell based in south-west Wales. Usually small – never more than three members – these 'active units' had the support of more than fifty people for munitions, food, a bed for the night and alibis, if needed. In the week preceding the Investiture in 1969 four bombs were planted by separate MAC2 groups: two at Caernarfon, one at Holyhead and the other at Abergele, the last exploding prematurely and killing the saboteurs George Taylor and Alwyn Jones. The fifth north Wales cell comprised Jenkins and his young accomplice, the television-aerial rigger Ernest Alders, who together were implicated in several attacks on water pipelines and government offices in north Wales and across the border in England. The only contact Jenkins had with active units was when he delivered a bomb in a shoebox together with instructions about the target, leaving the cell leader to organise the rest. By controlling the explosives and bomb-making, Jenkins dictated policy.

Far from being an isolated bunch of fanatics, as the government wanted the world to believe, MAC2 was relatively well organised. It even had its designated 'Quartermasters'. One was the language campaigner Trefor Beasley from Llangennech, whose links with the organisation were not suspected until Jenkins appeared as a pallbearer at his funeral in accordance with his last wishes. Beasley is best remembered for campaigning for eight years for bilingual rate demand notices from Llanelli Rural District Council. On six occasions bailiffs entered his home to seize property for non-payment. A disaffected member of Plaid Cymru, Beasley was recruited to assist insurgents active in south Wales. 'He was only one of our quartermasters. There were others. It made sense to have key supporters in various parts of Wales', said Jenkins.

Beasley's wife Eileen, a widely respected Welsh civil rights campaigner known as the 'Welsh Rosa Parks' (after the black civil rights campaigner who refused to surrender her seat to a white on a bus in Alabama), was quite unaware of her husband's connections to MAC2 but had taught at Rhydfelen Welsh school, where both Jenkins's sons were educated during his imprisonment.[10]

Beasley was not the only one whose involvement with MAC2 was unknown. Another was the Anglo-Welsh poet Harri Webb, prominent member of Plaid Cymru and editor of its weekly newspaper *Welsh Nation*. Webb was recruited by MAC2 for his links with the Breton nationalists and to provide political advice to the insurgents. His flat at the top of a rickety staircase at Garth Newydd, a rambling old house in Merthyr Tydfil, was a meeting place for nationalists frustrated by Plaid's attitude towards independence and its leader's rejection of direct action. Webb always had a bed and bacon sandwich for anyone of a similar persuasion. When first Owen Williams, then later John Jenkins, knocked at his door looking for help it was he who pointed them towards Dai Pritchard. A man with nationalist contacts throughout Europe, Webb arranged for a leader of the underground Breton National Army to visit Merthyr to discuss a possible rapprochement, including an offer of training facilities, even safe houses for Welsh extremists hiding out in Brittany. But it was not pursued.[11]

> I realised very early on that we could not operate in a political vacuum. We needed someone like Harri Webb who could keep us informed about what was happening. Webb was recommended by a trusted member of the organisation as someone, a political adviser we could bounce ideas off. He moved in respectable circles whereas we couldn't. The important thing for me was to delegate certain things. His function was one of those. He was not the only one. There were others affiliated to MAC2.[12]

According to a police statement made by Ernest Alders – Jenkins's apprentice bomber – MAC2 had a financial backer, a millionaire south Wales businessman only ever referred to as 'Mac'. Alders claimed that 'Mac' had promised to provide financial support for the families and dependants of those killed or imprisoned in the struggle for Welsh independence. While admitting having said this, Jenkins insists it was untrue, a smokescreen to confuse Special Branch and MI5. Apart from the occasional donation, MAC2 never had a financial backer.[13]

It had, however, patriotic supporters like Trefor Morgan, the millionaire founder of Cwmni Undeb, the Aberdare-based insurance company. A self-educated Valleys boy born into poverty at Tonyrefail, Morgan was capable of arguing the case for Home Rule with eloquence and conviction. But Plaid's insistence on placing the language and interests of the rural heartlands above all else led to an early clash with Gwynfor Evans, ending when Morgan quit to form the Welsh Republican Movement with Cliff Bere and Gwilym Prys-Davies. Years later, Morgan emerged from the shadows to fund Owen Williams's defence on an explosives charge. And for seven years, Morgan's daughter Lowri lived with Jenkins, while his wife Gwyneth provided support for the Jenkins family during his imprisonment.

Unafraid to advocate militancy in the pursuit of independence, the Welsh Republican Movement published its own newspaper, *Y Gweriniaethwr* (The Republican), its columns awash with patriotic fervour. One of its editors was none other than the Merthyr poet-politician Harri Webb, now known to have been on the fringes of MAC2's direct action campaign. An organisation with a very similar name – The Republicans (Y Gweriniaethwyr) – claimed responsibility in 1952 for an unsuccessful attempt to blow up a pipeline at Claerwen, then the latest reservoir built by Birmingham as part of its Elan Valley complex and opened by Queen Elizabeth II on her accession to the throne. Coincidentally, that same year there was some recognition of Welsh aspirations when Prime Minister Winston Churchill gave his new Home Secretary, Sir David Maxwell Fyffe, additional responsibility for representing Wales at government level, as the very first Minister for Welsh Affairs. Visiting Wales to familiarise himself with his new brief, Sir David was greeted by a slogan painted on the wall of Caernarfon Castle urging him to 'Fight for a Welsh republic'. Another frequent contributor to *Y Gweriniaethwr* at that time, and also briefly its editor, was Cliff Bere, a lifelong opponent of English rule and the first person to set fire publicly to the Union flag, before it became a national pastime among activists. A prolific letter-writer, Bere's correspondence, now deposited in the National Library of Wales, testifies to a rich seam of nationalist sentiment on which the likes of Jenkins and Owen Williams could draw, explaining why the 1960s became a high-water mark in the struggle for Welsh independence. Those not prepared to raise their heads above the parapet did, however, provide safe houses, beds for the night, even money. Bere was a campaigner to the very last, fighting for the early release of Jenkins from prison, and at the age of sixty-five one of forty nationalists indiscriminately rounded up by police hunting the cottage arsonists of the 1980s. Even the ill-fated Free Wales Army could count on Cliff Bere's support.[14]

Gwynfor Evans's repudiation of militant nationalism meant that many activists disaffected by Plaid's increasingly slavish commitment to the ballot box felt they had nowhere to go but the extremist fringe. Accused by some of cowardice for failing to capitalise upon Tryweryn, the Plaid leader aggravated the division in nationalist sentiment by prohibiting party members from even accepting Trefor Morgan's generous offer of cheap insurance!

Evans steered clear of the militants congregating in smoke-filled public houses like the Red Cow at Treorchy, refusing to share the same platform with the likes of Owen Williams and Trefor Morgan. To venture from his pacifist redoubt risked his rubbing shoulders with Dave Walters and Dai Pritchard, the pair from the Valleys convicted for releasing oil from a transformer at Tryweryn while Plaid were waving banners. Gwynfor might even have shaken hands with the unassuming Alf Williams from Maesycwmer, quite unaware that, having been taught how to make bombs by the British Army, Williams was actively passing on that expertise. Around the margins of those conspiratorial gatherings, the Plaid leader would have been surprised to see Trefor Beasley and shocked at the sight of Harri Webb, editor of his party's newspaper. One person he would never have seen was John Jenkins, who avoided public appearances like the plague.

No one was more disappointed by Plaid's failure to provide leadership than Huw T. Edwards, one of the most influential Welsh political figures in the 1950s and 1960s. The north Wales secretary of the powerful Transport and General Workers' Union, 'Huw T.' was regarded as the 'unofficial Prime Minister of Wales'. Corresponding regularly with prime ministers, cabinet ministers and high-ranking civil servants, he enjoyed a close friendship with Nye Bevan and James Griffiths, and previously Ernest Bevin, before his dramatic resignation from the Labour Party to join Plaid Cymru, in protest at the government's failure to stop Tryweryn. Perhaps as a sign of his anger, Huw T. stood bail for Owen Williams after he was arrested for blowing up the transformer. His admiration for Gwynfor Evans did not prevent Huw T. from observing, 'The Plaid has a terrifically strong weapon in Welsh self-government but one is driven to weep almost by this slavish idea of seeking this through contesting for seats at Westminster.' In another letter he reminded his correspondent that he, a man with socialism in his blood, was prepared to abandon it to prepare Welsh public opinion for revolution. Contesting elections was anathema to this diehard socialist, who believed his first responsibility to the nation was to achieve its freedom. 'The weakness of Plaid is that it attempts to imitate the popular parties rather than going into the wilderness to search for the nation's soul', he wrote.[15] The violent direct action campaign initiated by Mudiad Amddiffyn Cymru in the 1960s was all about igniting that same national consciousness. John Jenkins, Owen Williams and Huw T. Edwards were marching to the same tune. According to Jenkins: 'Energy needed for other things has been dissipated. Plaid might feel they have the moral high ground but who owns Wales? It's still the English. Plaid's peaceful approach has cost Wales everything. In my view we are still cleaning out the stables.'[16]

The year following the sabotage at Clywedog, Jenkins claimed control of MAC2 by demonstrating to his accomplices that he had more to offer than talk and bluster. Believing the smaller the active unit the safer it was, he recruited Frederick Ernest Alders (21), a television-aerial fitter from Rhos, near Wrexham. Alders had joined the Territorial Army unit of the Royal Welch Fusiliers in 1967 and very soon became a member of the Drum and Fife Band at Wrexham, to which Sergeant Jenkins was attached as drum instructor. The band was on its way by coach to Rhyl for a performance when a heated discussion developed between four or five members about Welsh nationalism, Jenkins declaring, 'time bombs were the means by which most propaganda could be delivered'.

At that moment Alders sensed that his drum instructor had possibly some-thing to do with the Free Wales Army. 'There were subsequent discussions between Jenkins and myself about Welsh nationalism', he later told police. 'These discussions culminated in me joining the organisation called MAC, which Jenkins told me about.'[17]

The recruitment of Alders did not happen quite like that, according to Jenkins. Rather, it was Alders who shouted the odds about nationalism, while Jenkins, playing devil's advocate, criticised what had occurred at Tryweryn and Clywedog as pointless. 'He was always jumping up and shouting out on behalf of Wales. It soon became clear that he was sincere and his feelings ran deep. He bit at my bait beautifully', explained Jenkins. [18]

The moment of truth came at the end of September 1967, by which time Jenkins was ready for his first bombing mission. The gelignite came from a colliery in south Wales, and the timing device, a Venner switch commonly found in streetlights, was provided by Dai Pritchard. The target was one of four huge Liverpool Corporation pipelines at Llanrhaeadr-ym-Mochnant, trans-porting water to Liverpool from the new reservoir at Tryweryn. Close by was Pistyll Rhaeadr, the 200ft waterfall regarded as one of the seven wonders of Wales. A famous tourist attraction, the road to the waterfall was generally quite busy at weekends, so the saboteurs were unlikely to attract attention.

Although prepared, Jenkins was still not entirely sure of Alders. One evening they were drinking with others in the all ranks' mess at the Royal Welch Fusiliers Hightown Barracks in Wrexham when Jenkins casually asked whether Alders still wanted to do something for Wales. Alders nodded, and the pair moved to another table so as not to be overheard. After a few moments, Jenkins invited Alders to swear an oath of allegiance to MAC2 on pain of death, which Alders agreed to do. But it was only after Jenkins threw open the boot of his car to reveal twenty half-pound sticks of gelignite that the young television rigger knew it was for real, and that their first target would be the pipeline at Llanrhaeadr-ym-Mochnant.

A few days later Jenkins joined his army buddies in the sergeants' mess at the barracks. After settling down with his pint in the corner and taking a couple of sips, he got up and left. Alders was waiting outside at the wheel of his black Austin A30 when Jenkins appeared, carrying a holdall with the bomb. During the drive to Llanrhaeadr-ym-Mochnant, Jenkins explained that the explosives had been supplied by 'men in MAC' who worked in the mines:

> I asked who was head of the organisation and he said a man in South Wales known as 'Mac'. When I asked how many were in the organisation Jenkins replied it was just a handful of people who were actually doing something but there were hundreds who got explosives and helped in that direction. Jenkins also told me on the way that he had done a course in explosives.[19]

Llanrhaeadr-ym-Mochnant was chosen with the help of a MAC2 contact, who assured them the house nearest to the pipeline was empty that weekend. As darkness fell, Alders parked the car on a wide grass verge, near a gateway leading to the pipelines and the spot where they were to plant the bomb. Jenkins led the way across a field, carrying the timing device and a pair of pliers. Alders, wearing surgical gloves, followed, the bundle of gelignite taped together and held tightly between both hands. For the explosion to be most effective the gelignite was wedged between a concrete support pillar and one of the three-foot-diameter steel pipes, and then attached to the detonator and the clock. After testing the timer, Jenkins set the explosion for 2 a.m. The entire operation took only five minutes and by 9.30 p.m. Jenkins was back at the sergeants' mess, finishing his pint. By then, most of his army mates were too drunk to have noticed his absence. Next morning Wales woke to the news that a huge hole had been blown in the pipeline – and the start of a sabotage campaign that continued beyond the Investiture in July 1969.

Alders's evening had ended in a blazing row with his girlfriend, Anne Woodgate, after he told her what he had done, despite a warning from Jenkins to say nothing unless absolutely sure of the young woman. But unable to resist boasting, Alders even took his girlfriend for a driving lesson up to the waterfall, where he pointed to the very spot. Miss Woodgate tried to reason with him, but he refused to listen:

> I asked him why he did it and what he thought he would get out of it. I told him that if anybody found out what he had done he would go to prison. But he was very persistent that it was for the good of Wales and that in time Wales might be a nation of its own.[20]

Although she was concerned about Alders's involvement with Jenkins, the couple's relationship survived Llanrhaeadr-ym-Mochnant and they were engaged not long afterwards. Soon they were visiting Jenkins and his wife in their army quarters on Range Road, Wrexham, on a regular basis, sometimes babysitting, at other times the women chatting while the men read books about Wales and studied maps. On one occasion Jenkins spoke about the need to stop the Investiture, indicating that plans were being prepared for this, and that others were also involved. Both were openly critical of the export of water from Wales to England.

One Sunday Alders took his fiancée for another driving lesson – a spin around Liverpool Corporation's reservoir at Lake Vyrnwy in the Berwyn Mountains, about forty miles from Wrexham. After practising some three-point turns they were about to head home when Alders spotted some large water pipes running across the ground below the dam wall, remarking that they were probably carrying water to some English city and that he should mention this to Jenkins. A little later, while the young couple were babysitting, Miss

Woodgate heard the pair talking about Vyrnwy. Shortly afterwards there was an explosion at the dam. When she asked Alders if he was involved, all he would say was that he regretted so little damage was caused. The engagement did not last much longer after that. But no sooner was it broken off than Alders struck up a relationship with another woman, and was very quickly married.[21] Miss Woodgate is suspected by some, including Owen Williams, to have been instrumental in the unmasking of MAC2 when she told her father what she knew. Whoever was responsible did not blow the whistle on the insurgents until three years after the blast at Llanrhaeadr-ym-Mochnant. One thing is certain – it was an informer that eventually led police to Jenkins and Alders, rather than a smart piece of detective work.

# 7

## SPOOKS AND MANDARINS

The stakes were raised dramatically when, two months after Llanrhaeadr-ym-Mochnant, there was another bomb. The target was not a pipeline but the Temple of Peace in Cardiff, a fine Gothic building given to the people of Wales by the wealthy industrialist Lord David Davies of Llandinam as a memorial to those killed in the Great War, the 'war to end all wars'. The explosive device was placed above the entrance to the Portland stone building in Cathays Park on 17 November 1967, on the eve of the first meeting of the committee comprising the good and the great to prepare for the Investiture of the Prince of Wales in 1969.[1] It was a clear signal that if the Investiture went ahead, the life of the Prince could be at risk.

Bomb disposal experts estimated that twenty pounds of gelignite were used, the force of the blast causing extensive external and internal damage. Metal fragments from a shattered bronze window-frame flew like missiles in all directions, smashing every pane of glass in the front of the Welsh Board of Health 60 yards away across King Edward VII Avenue, which bisects Cathays Park. Windows in nearby University College, Cardiff, and the National Museum of Wales, 600 yards from the seat of the explosion, were also shattered, and marble walls in the Temple of Peace cracked and holed as if peppered by machine-gun fire.[2]

The bomb, hidden in a canvas bag placed on the lintel above the main entrance, would have killed and maimed scores if the timing device, a Venner switch identical to those used at Clywedog and Llanrhaeadr-ym-Mochnant, had been set to coincide with the arrival of VIPs for the Investiture committee meeting. It had, however, been timed to explode at 4 a.m., when the area was expected to be deserted.

According to John Jenkins, a 'lot of rubbish' was published afterwards about the threat to the life of Lord Snowdon – who had responsibility for staging the Investiture at Caernarfon – and the other VIPs, because to avoid injuring anyone the saboteurs had kept the Temple of Peace under surveillance for several days before deciding on the precise moment to detonate their bomb. The explosion was also intended as a reminder to Cymdeithas yr Iaith Cymraeg (Welsh Language Society), who were planning a protest to coincide with the arrival of VIPs the following morning, that the Establishment would not be shamed into bowing to opposition to the Investiture by their members staging a sing-song outside the Temple of Peace. 'This was the Welsh national shrine commemorating our war dead', Jenkins said later.

> These people, perhaps misguidedly, were using the building as a political forum to preserve English rule in Wales. They threw the gauntlet down; we were picking it up … It wasn't so much English rule we were against as English misrule, which was killing us from the social and economic point of view …[3]

Only the week before, Sir Goronwy Daniel, Permanent Under-Secretary of State at the Welsh Office, had received an alarming assessment of the Welsh extremist threat, prepared by Dick Thistlethwaite, Director of F Branch, the counter-subversion division of MI5.[4] Thistlethwaite was at the very centre of the web of counter-subversion operations, run by a tightly knit group who, having earned their spurs in military intelligence during the Second World War, now commanded the heights of Britain's security services. Cast in the James Bond mould, the clandestine activities of men like Thistlethwaite, his boss, Sir Martin Furnival Jones, the anonymous head of MI5 and Sir Burke Trend, Secretary to the Cabinet Office, never registered on the public radar. As personal adviser to the Prime Minister, Burke Trend was a more important spoke in the security wheel than even George Wigg, Paymaster-General and Harold Wilson's Downing Street security confidant. Paranoid about reds under the bed, Wilson had ordered Thistlethwaite to bug the National Union of Seamen headquarters, believing it to have been infiltrated by the Communist Party. Two years later his Home Secretary, James Callaghan, would authorise Thistlethwaite to tap the telephones of fourteen Welsh terrorist suspects.[5]

Thistlethwaite was an intelligence officer of considerable experience. As MI5's liaison with the FBI, he was involved in the investigation of Burgess and Maclean, the spies who supplied the Soviet Union with nuclear secrets before fleeing to Moscow in 1956. He was also responsible for briefing newly appointed Cabinet ministers on the security risks, for which purpose he produced a 59-page classified guide, warning that: 'KGB spies are with us all the time … interested in everything, defence secrets, scientific secrets, political decisions, economic facts, even people's characters.' After Thistlethwaite had briefed Tony Benn on security on joining Wilson's 1964 government, Benn noted in his diary having spent a very unpleasant hour and a half with a man who, 'though very intelligent was deep in the heart of the James Bond world'.[6]

Convinced that the left wing was plotting against him, Wilson instructed Thistlethwaite to conduct an urgent assessment of the threat of subversion.

The wrecked entrance to Cardiff's Temple of Peace in Cathays Park in November 1967 after Welsh extremists exploded a bomb on the eve of a conference to prepare for the Investiture of the Prince of Wales at Caernarfon Castle. Copyright: *Western Mail*, Cardiff.

While his main focus was communist infiltration, three pages of his 29-page report, *Subversion in the United Kingdom*, dealt exclusively with Welsh extremists.[7] Despite the Freedom of Information Act, the document remains classified, although a copy of the section referring to Wales did arrive on Sir Goronwy

Martin Furnival Jones (top), the head of MI5 when it was asked by Home Secretary James Callaghan to help track down the Welsh bombers. The Secretary of State for Wales, Cledwyn Hughes (bottom), was concerned there would be a disaster 'of the first magnitude' if the Clywedog Dam was sabotaged once it was operational.

Daniel's Welsh Office desk a few days before the Temple of Peace bomb. From the ensuing correspondence it is possible to deduce that the report came as a wake-up call for a Welsh Office in denial over the seriousness of the extremist situation on its doorstep. By drawing a sharp distinction between the dangerous men behind MAC2 and the Free Wales Army comedians parading in their ex-army surplus, Thistlethwaite debunked the notion that the bombers were an insignificant bunch of fanatics best ignored.

Immediately on the Monday morning following the Temple of Peace bomb, Sir Goronwy wrote to Burke Trend in the Cabinet Office, expressing his Secretary of State's deep concern about security in Wales:

> If the timing mechanism of that bomb had functioned a few hours in arrears there would have been very serious loss of life. Moreover, the fact that a bomb was used to protest against a meeting arranged to prepare for the Investiture of the Prince of Wales carries with it the threat that the same means of protest will be used again as arrangements for the Investiture proceed and there is the danger that the consequences of this could be very serious indeed.
>
> The Secretary of State has asked me to express his hope that every effort will be made by the security and police services to arrest those who were responsible. They would appear to be a small group with expert (perhaps ex-Army) knowledge of bombs and access to explosives. They are also likely to be Welsh speaking and to have links with extreme nationalist and Welsh language movements. They were probably responsible for all four recent sabotage incidents.
>
> The overwhelming majority of Welshmen would welcome news of the arrest, prosecution and imprisonment of these men and the Secretary of State sincerely hopes they will not still be left at large during the period leading up to and including the Investiture.[8]

For the Secretary of State, Cledwyn Hughes, the explosion at the Temple of Peace provoked 'deep distress throughout Wales'. Not so for the crowd of language supporters besieging VIPs arriving for the Investiture conference the following day. 'Republic not Royalty', the banners demanded, and 'Wales pays £2.5 million for English prince' proclaimed others. Among the demonstrators was National Patriotic Front organiser Keith Griffiths armed with eggs, these discharging their contents in his pockets when he was snatched by the police and carried away. After watching the demonstrators chanting, banging on cars and struggling with the police, Welsh Secretary Hughes observed sadly: 'I hope they will soon see the error of their ways.' That same evening there was a bomb scare at City Hall, where James Callaghan was attending his last official dinner as Chancellor of the Exchequer.[9]

As Chancellor from 1964 to 1967, Callaghan had presided over a turbulent period for the British economy, wrestling unsuccessfully with a balance of payments deficit and speculative attacks on the pound that ended in sterling's devaluation. Instead of resigning from the Cabinet for having failed to prevent near meltdown in the economy, 'Lucky Jim' would swap the Treasury for the Home Office, where one of his most important decisions was to deploy British troops to Northern Ireland after rioting in Derry's Catholic Bogside. Before that, however, the new Home Secretary faced violent unrest on his home patch in Wales, which he attributed to the rise of Plaid Cymru, following Gwynfor Evans's historic victory in the Carmarthen by-election. Callaghan vigorously opposed devolution as having any part to play in confronting Britain's social and economic turmoil. New government machinery was unnecessary, because the people were bound together by history, tradition and migration, according to Callaghan. It was absurd, he told the City Merchant Company in Edinburgh, to try to deal with Britain's problems separately. Although representing a Cardiff constituency, Callaghan was not Welsh and at no time in his career expressed any sympathy or support for Welsh sentiment.

No matter how much the bombing campaign was publicly condemned, it was undoubtedly providing sustenance for nationalists, both political and cultural. Language campaigners fed off the nationalist sympathies and covert admiration excited by the upsurge in extremism. While most took care not to dip their toes too deeply into these dangerous waters, language activists and their movement drew momentum from the destabilising effects of extremist activities.

Meanwhile, the *Western Mail* focused on denouncing the 'wild men of Welsh politics' for deliberately creating 'a climate of thought in which it was quite possible to imagine some individual as unbalanced as President Kennedy's assassin Oswald being driven to do murder'.[10] On the day following the Temple of Peace bomb and the Investiture conference, which went ahead despite the damage, Plaid Cymru held its annual Christmas Fayre in the same building, this proving, according to its General Secretary, Elwyn Roberts, it could not possibly have had anything to do with the outrage.[11]

All this coincided with the results of an opinion poll commissioned by the *Western Mail* that found that six out of every ten Welsh voters backed a Welsh Parliament and that there was widespread disillusionment with the government in Wales. The editor, John Giddings, was away that day, leaving the field open to those suspected of being closet nationalists to persuade his deputy, a Jerseyman who knew little about Wales, to publish an editorial advocating an elected Welsh Parliament with revenue-raising powers.[12] When the editor read what his paper had signed up to in his absence he was furious, thereafter clamping down on even the smallest expression of nationalist sentiment. I declared myself firmly part of the anti-nationalist brigade, fearing, like most Anglicised Welsh persons at that time, that the Welsh-speaking bandwagon was about to overwhelm us.

Even though the Temple of Peace explosion confirmed that something more serious was afoot than the Free Wales Army, it remained convenient to regard the FWA as the culprits. Little if anything was known of the perpetrators,

Mudiad Amddiffyn Cymru (MAC), if indeed such an organisation existed. The general public were quite unaware of those behind this resurgence in violent direct action, because MAC2 was never mentioned in the media. Whatever the world thought of Cayo Evans and his confused, sometimes comic, articulation of the nationalist cause, his Free Wales Army continued to provide a major distraction for those hunting the real bombers. Notwithstanding this, MI5 and Special Branch believed their best chance of tracking down the mystery sabo-teurs was to leave Cayo Evans and company to play their army games, in the hope they might eventually lead to MAC2.

The year 1968 was one of violent dissent in a decade of global unrest. John F. Kennedy's brother Robert and the human rights leader Martin Luther King both fell to assassins' bullets. The Soviet Union invaded Czechoslovakia to quash the 'Prague Spring'. Social and political disturbances over the Vietnam War and the draft rocked the United States, with tens of thousands demon-strating on university campuses throughout the country. In London 250,000 marched on the US Embassy in Grosvenor Square. Richard Nixon's promise to bring US troops home won him the Republican nomination and presidency after he narrowly defeated the Democratic contender Hubert Humphrey, whose Democratic National Convention in Chicago was marred by several nights of street violence.

In Europe, ETA, Euskadi Ta Askatasuma (Basque Homeland and Freedom), murdered the San Sebastian police chief, the first victim in its struggle for a separate Basque state. When thousands of students took to the barricades in France, President de Gaulle sent in the troops to deal with the revolutionary fervour. West Germany, too, was in the grip of left-wing anarchist turmoil. Student revolt had spawned the Baader–Meinhof Gang, responsible for unleashing a maelstrom of death and destruction. Incredibly, MAC2 could have been sucked into this had it listened to 'Red' Rudi Dutschke, the left-wing German student leader.

After escaping an assassination attempt in Berlin in April 1968, Dutschke fled to Britain, where he seized upon the bombings in Wales as an opportunity to forment leftist revolution. Somehow, Dutschke contacted MAC2, with a view to holding a meeting with Welsh extremists at Swansea. Ever since arriving in Britain, Dutschke had been under more or less constant police surveillance, but after succeeding in losing his 'minders' while attending a London conference he caught a train to Swansea. The meeting never took place, Jenkins and other members of MAC2 having decided beforehand they had nothing in common with the German revolutionary. Not long afterwards, Dutschke was expelled from Britain for his subversive activities.[13]

In Britain, as the economic crisis deepened, Wilson's siege mentality inten-sified, not helped by divisions in his Cabinet and suspicions that the unions were plotting against him. With barely a year to go before the Investiture, and no sign that the Welsh police were any closer to catching the insurgents, he faced the very real prospect of having to advise the Palace to cancel the event at Caernarfon Castle. Most agreed this would be a massive constitutional setback. The Investiture could be held outside Wales, but like cancellation that would also have signalled to the world that the Monarch's writ no longer extended to Wales: that it was another British colony whose concerns and aspirations could not be ignored, which was exactly what the insurgents intended.[14]

Meanwhile, there was no pause in the bombing campaign. After the widespread publicity generated by the large bomb planted at the Temple of Peace, the next was small by comparison, involving at the most four pounds of explosives, placed on a lintel above a ground-floor window at the Snowdonia Country Club at Penisarwaun, a village five miles from Caernarfon. The explosion, in the early hours of 5 January 1968, was again triggered by a Venner time-switch. The switches were easy enough to obtain through advertisements in *Exchange and Mart* and *Poultry World*, although this would be the last occasion a Venner was used by the saboteurs, who afterwards adapted Smiths clocks, bought from Woolworths, as timing devices.[15]

The club, recently built by retired Manchester businessman Jack Nix, was unpopular in the area, in addition to which Nix had upset the locals by selling square-yard plots of Snowdonia to tourists at £5 a time. The blast blew a four-foot hole in the brick and breeze-block wall, with sufficient force to lift the roof and destroy furniture and other fittings. A door from the club was found fifty yards away.

During their investigation police were told of a man known only as the 'receiver', whose role was to acquire explosives, the gelignite for the club explosion having been obtained from a quarryman. Much of what the police knew came from Robert Griffith Jones (37), of Groeslon, and Edward Hope Wilkinson (43), of Llanllyfni, two former members of the Free Wales Army, who admitted being in unlawful possession of explosives when their homes were searched following the club bombing. At the time, Wilkinson considered himself the leader of the FWA in the Caernarfon district, but both he and Jones denied planting the bomb at the club. The fuse wire found at their homes was used either to poach salmon or smoke out rats, they said. Considered minor players, Jones and Wilkinson declared they had renounced violence and were each given a year's suspended sentence when they appeared before Mr Justice Lane at Caernarfonshire Assizes on 28 February 1968. Jones, in particular, was filled with remorse, and according to his lawyer was convinced he had been manipulated. While he and Wilkinson gave police another name and undertook to identify the man if called upon, they referred to him only as the 'receiver' in their witness statements, because, they said, of the Free Wales Army oath, initiated at the point of a dagger held to their throats, in which they swore, 'In the name of God and of our dead patriots, I swear that I shall never reveal any secrets of our organisation even if I am captured and tortured.' Originally, the police did not want to prosecute either Jones or Wilkinson, in return for their

Rudi Dutschke, the left wing German subversive, tried to arrange a meeting with the leaders of Mudiad Amddiffyn Cymru (MAC) before he was expelled from Britain for subversion. Copyright: Deutsches Historisches Museum, Berlin.

evidence against the 'receiver', who was considered a much bigger fish and 'a member of a small group of men behind the explosions in different parts of Wales'. This individual might have had connections with the FWA, but never paraded in uniform for fear of compromising his clandestine activities, according to a police report to the Department for Public Prosecutions.[16] The not-infrequent references to the FWA in statements taken by the police, especially during the earliest months of the sabotage campaign, testifies to the confusion at the highest levels as to the identity of the insurgents. For some, the FWA and MAC were synonymous, and while activists around the fringes might have had a foot in both camps, Jenkins was generally successful in maintaining clear blue water between the two.

A third man was arrested after the Snowdonia Country Club explosion. Gwynedd farmer Owen Williams was in London buying a car when he heard that police wanted to question him. On returning to the family farm at Gwynus, near Nefyn, he was told traces of nitroglycerine had been found on parts of his father's Vauxhall Cresta, which Williams had parked outside Rhyl railway station before catching the train to London. Despite claiming this had been planted during his absence, he was, nevertheless, charged with unlawful possession of explosives and remanded in custody on five separate occasions, until eventually granted bail. But instead of answering to it on 6 March, Williams fled to Ireland, although the first place the police looked for him was in Colombia in South America, where he was rumoured to be hiding out on the ranch of the eccentric Welsh millionaire cattle-rancher Howell Hughes. Interpol were also asked to search the home of Cayo Evans's mother, then living in Marbella, Spain.

But Williams was much nearer home, in Ireland, hiding behind a pair of sunglasses and a ginger beard, first at Sean MacStiofain's bungalow at Navan before heading to Kinsale, a small fishing village nestling at the mouth of the Bandon River in West Cork, land of his childhood hero Michael Collins. His Irish accent was passable; his cover story, if pressed, that he was a fugitive from Rhodesia wanted by the British for supporting Ian Smith's Unilateral Declaration of Independence. Inside his rucksack was a codebook containing details of his contacts back in Wales.

In the seventeenth and eighteenth centuries, the harbour at Kinsale was an important British naval base, strategically located behind narrow straits guarded by the twin forts of Charles and James. A garrison town for several centuries, Kinsale was noted for its Georgian architecture and narrow winding streets, set amongst green trees and surrounded by fine beaches. Williams camped on one adjacent to Old Head, a rugged peninsula jutting into the Atlantic and scene of the sinking of the liner *Lusitania* by a German U-boat in 1915, with the loss of 1,195 lives.

For the next six weeks he lived on the beach off chips, bread and cheese, until he struck up a relationship with Catherine Quaid, an assistant manager at Kinsale's Trident Hotel. Afterwards there were chicken sandwiches and champagne from the hotel kitchen, a small Welsh Dragon flag fluttering above the tent Williams acquired from some English tourists. Before he fled to Ireland, Williams had secretly met John Jenkins and Ernest Alders in the village of Loggerheads, between Mold and Ruthin in north Wales.

It was St David's Day, and Jenkins's Territorial Army Drum and Fife Band was in great demand to celebrate Wales's patron saint. After its first function, in the village hall at Llanferres, the band had an hour to spare before the next engagement, so Jenkins used the time for a pre-arranged meeting with Owen Williams. Both he and Alders were resplendent in their scarlet uniforms and bearskins as they waited for Williams, who arrived in the company of a fair-haired young woman. She joined Alders in one car, while the others stood talking beside his van. Jenkins believes it was those scarlet uniforms, illuminated by the beam of the car headlights, that ultimately led to his detection when Williams's female companion, distraught at the news of the death of two MAC2 saboteurs on the eve of the Investiture, contacted the police. What no one knew was that George Taylor and Alwyn Jones, the two who blew themselves up with the bomb they intended planting on the route of the Royal Train at Abergele, had also carried out the Snowdonia Country Club bombing eighteen months earlier.[17]

After the Country Club explosion MAC2's supply of explosives and timers was running low. While security had been tightened at quarries to prevent workmen from trafficking in gelignite, Jenkins obtained a map from a contact showing the location of the explosives magazine at Hafod Colliery, Wrexham. A sturdy brick-built building inside a walled compound, it stood in the middle of a field and was surrounded by a high earth bank. Scaling the wall, Jenkins and Alders forced the heavy steel door with a crowbar, hammer and chisel, the high protective wall muffling the racket. When the door burst open the pair froze on the threshold. Winking at them was an alarm. Had they triggered it? After waiting for half an hour, when no one appeared, they stepped inside the explosives store to discover that Jenkins's accomplice had thoughtfully wedged a small piece of rubber inside the alarm to prevent it from ringing. With the coast clear, Alders drove his Austin A30 into the field, and together they loaded five or six boxes of gelignite into the boot, probably nearer 300 pounds of explosives than the 150 pounds later reported stolen. The haul was driven immediately to Saighton Army Camp and stored in the dental centre's darkroom, used only by Jenkins.[18] By controlling the explosives and making the bombs, Jenkins was from then on able to dictate the course of the insurrection, confident that so long as he was in charge they would not be detected.

With their supply of Venner time-switches exhausted, the pair improvised by adapting a Smiths alarm clock bought from Woolworths. Alders planned the electrical circuit, using the clock, a battery, bell-push and bulb. All that was needed was to devise a means of breaking the circuit, using a time delay. After the second hand was removed, wires were threaded through holes drilled in the clock face with an army dental drill, so that the explosion could be triggered when the hour hand struck the detonator wire. After experimenting under the very noses of the Army at the dental centre, they believed they had a timing device that was foolproof and safe. It would prove not to be the case for poor George Taylor and Alwyn Jones, who blew themselves up with one of the eight or nine time-switches Alders and Jenkins subsequently built. What is thought to have happened in their case is that the two were killed because they tested the circuit *after* connecting it.[19]

The new timer was used for the first time in a bomb at the Inland Revenue offices, Llanishen, Cardiff, on 24 March 1968. Ten pounds of explosive knocked down four walls inside the building and blew sheets off the roof. Parts of a Smiths alarm clock were recovered by Home Office forensic experts from near the scene of the blast. Jenkins and Alders had reconnoitred the tax offices some weeks previously, but it was a south Wales member of MAC2 who broke in to plant the bomb against the doorpost of an internal wall. Afterwards, he escaped by mixing with the crowds streaming from Cardiff Arms Park at the end of a rugby international.[20]

The continued failure of the Welsh police to crack the conspiracy caused a breakdown in confidence with the Home Office. The focus for this was the Chief Constable of Gwynedd, Lieutenant Colonel William Jones Williams, on whose patch much of the extremist activity was centred. Even when a bomb exploded at the bottom of his garden in Caernarfon, Lt. Col. Williams still resented, to the point of obstruction, investigations by the outsiders the Home Office ultimately felt it necessary to send to Wales.

By the end of 1967 the perceived threat to the Prince of Wales was serious enough for Sir Eric St Johnston, HM Chief Inspector of Constabulary, to alert the Earl Marshall, the Duke of Norfolk, who had oversight of the Investiture, to the possible implications for the Prince's safety.[21] Without proper intelligence from Wales, those at the highest levels of government were unable to differentiate between the antics of the FWA and the real bombers, whoever they might be. After discussing the situation at length with a senior aide, Sir Philip Allen, Permanent Secretary at the Home Office, asked the Attorney General, Sir Elwyn Jones, for an assurance that the necessary steps were being taken to ensure an effective organisation was in place in Wales to collect and sift intelligence. Sir Philip wrote:

> These matters have been giving us a great deal of concern in the particular context of the investiture of the Prince of Wales; and the Prime Minister has asked to be assured that the Security Service and the police are fully alive to the risk of violence and are taking all possible steps to anticipate it
> …
>
> We do not in any way under-rate the importance of these matters, and are giving every possible encouragement to the police to pursue their enquiries with diligence. [22]

Not long after the bombing of the Snowdonia Country Club, all the Welsh chief constables, together with senior agents from the security services, were called to a meeting in London to discuss arrangements for the Investiture and the coordination of security in the meantime. Emphasising the scale of the operation, Sir Philip reminded those present that 20,000 troops and 2,000 police officers had been deployed for the last Investiture, of Edward VIII in 1911. The immediate objective was to increase the intelligence effort necessary for rounding up the extremists. By the end of the meeting it was agreed the investigation would be coordinated by John Parkman, Head of the Regional Crime Squad in Cardiff. He would form a special unit to collect and collate intelligence, supported by Special Branch officers to be appointed by each of the Welsh police forces. MI5 and the Metropolitan Special Branch were also to become more actively involved.[23]

Reporting to the Prime Minister on the outcome, Burke Trend, his Cabinet Secretary, said the bombing of the Temple of Peace and the most recent attack on the Snowdonia Country Club meant they 'must take seriously the possibility that the Nationalists may try deliberately to wreck the Investiture': 'I do not think that we can do any more for the time being; but I propose, if you agree, to have another look at the position in a few months' time and I will report to you

again in light of the results.'[24] Despite all the promises of improved cooperation, the Welsh police forces, jealous of their independence, continued more or
less as they had previously. Rather than acting as conduits feeding every scrap
of information bearing on extremist activity to Parkman at the Regional Crime
Squad, some never even bothered to appoint a dedicated liaison officer. The
reluctance to cooperate was contagious, extending to MI5 and the Special
Branch, neither of which was prepared to share intelligence relating directly to
Investiture security with the Welsh, for fear of their sources being compro-
mised.[25] Neil Galbraith, HM Inspector of Constabulary in Wales, thought he
knew exactly where the problem lay: with Col. Williams, the reactionary Chief
Constable of Gwynedd. According to Galbraith, 'the old man of the Welsh
mountains' was inordinately conscious of any apparent attempt to 'subordinate
the autonomy of the Chief Constable to external influence, Home Office or
otherwise'.[26]

Minds became more sharply focused when MAC2 tried to blow up the Welsh
Office in Cathays Park in May 1968. Although only windows were damaged,
this seventh attack since Tryweryn was on the very heart of government,
raising the spectre of real fatalities unless stopped. Given the dismal record of
the Welsh police, Sir James Waddell, Deputy Under-Secretary at the Home
Office, saw no alternative but for the Home Office to put its own man into
Wales, reporting directly to the Home Secretary. Waddell called another top-
level meeting with MI5 and Special Branch operatives in London on 7 June to
review the investigation, by which time Liverpool's huge Vyrnwy Reservoir had
been sabotaged. The bomb placed by Jenkins and Alders under the main water
outlet from the dam lifted and fractured a four-foot diameter, one-and-a-half-
inch-thick steel pipe. Luckily, there was no water flowing through it at the time.
But with this latest outrage ringing in their ears, the Security Services told
Waddell that what they needed in Wales was someone they could trust.[27]

Waddell advised Callaghan to impose a solution on the recalcitrant Welsh
police forces, even if it 'touches on a number of delicate relationships and
arouses the susceptibilities of some of the Welsh chief constables'. Matters had
to be taken 'effectively in hand'. Callaghan agreed, insisting on being updated
on the extent of the threat to the Prince of Wales ahead of the Labour Party
Conference that September.[28]

A leaflet received by the Home Secretary a few days later reinforced his
concern. Distributed by the Anti-Investiture Campaign Committee, of which
Owen Williams – on the run in Ireland since the beginning of March – was
president *in absentia*, the leaflet called for a mass protest outside the blitzed
Welsh Office in Cardiff to coincide with a visit by Prince Charles on 28 June. A
rallying call to all activists for a show of strength, the leaflet dubbed the Prince
as 'The Pretender, Charles Windsor':

> The Pretender will be accompanied by the Quisling-in-Chief 'Fuehrer'
> Thomas, for a look over the 'slightly damaged' Welsh Office. We ask you to

attend and organise transport etc to make sure this is a really good show, and give the Pretender a fitting welcome to our homeland. Prepare posters, banners and placards. Also bring as many flags as you can. Arrive if possible before 3pm. The Pretender will also be visiting Llanelli (10am), Abertawe (12 noon), Port Talbot (2pm). We ask fellow Welshmen at these places to organise protests at this visit. Please take care that the timetable for this tour may be changed – so listen carefully to all news reports to enable you to keep up to date of the visit and tour timetable.

REMEMBER LLYWELYN EYN LEYW OLAF – REMEMBER CILMERI
REMEMBER IRFON BRIDGE AND THE DEATH OF THE GLORIOUS 18

CHARLEY WINDSOR SHALL NOT PASS

Anti-Investiture Campaign Committee [29]

Chief constables exercise extraordinary independence over criminal investigations, and Whitehall bureaucrats know to tread carefully if they are to avoid being accused of interference. If Waddell was to parachute a Home Office specialist into the extremist investigation, then first he needed the support of the autocratic Chief Constable of Gwynedd, Colonel William Williams, who was intensely suspicious of any attempt to usurp his authority. Dipping his pen deep into the professional civil servant's inkpot, Waddell began his letter to the colonel in the most conciliatory fashion by inquiring whether he was likely to be in London soon:

> I would like your help about a matter affecting Welsh extremism and I think this may call for a talk rather than a letter. But we can judge this better when you have seen what is troubling me.

> The nub of the matter is that in the special circumstances created by recent outrages and with the Investiture looming, the Home Secretary is anxious to keep himself fully informed about the criminal activities of extremists in Wales and the action being taken to deal with them. I have told him about the energetic work being done by the police both in the forces and through the Regional Crime Squad and by the Security Service and Special Branch. But ordinary means of communication with all these elements are not sufficient and he has decided that exceptional arrangements are necessary.[30]

Waddell then proceeded to explain that Frank Williamson, HM Inspector of Constabulary (Crime), had been given a special assignment to liaise with the regional crime squads, constabularies and security services. While Col. Williams was assured that Williamson would have no operational responsibilities, this was said only to appease the old man of the hills. Waddell's instruction to Williamson was to take charge: find out what needed to be done to catch the saboteurs before the Investiture. Wales was getting a supremo, this to be followed soon by another crucial appointment.

The letter from Waddell dropped on to the Gwynedd Chief Constable's desk on 28 June 1968, the same day as the anti-Investiture demonstration in Cardiff, and also a massive explosion on the Liverpool Corporation pipeline at Hapsford, near Chester. The river Dee aqueduct was a symbolically important target for the saboteurs Jenkins and Alders, carrying as it did water from Tryweryn, where the insurgency had started. A huge hole blown in the sixty-inch-diameter pipe where it crossed the Chester–Warrington railway line at Hapsford cut Liverpool's water supply by half, flooding the railway line and an adjacent road. The embankment on either side of the rail cutting was under-mined, and the track closed in the nick of time when a security officer from a nearby factory pointed out that the rail signal was set on green.

Timed to coincide with the Cardiff demonstration at the end of the Prince of Wales's first royal tour of Wales, the Hapsford explosion caused a major security alert, with Lancashire police posting round-the-clock patrols along fourteen other lengths of pipeline considered vulnerable to terrorist attack. Back in Cardiff smoke bombs were exploding around the Prince, who bravely broke away from his security escort outside the Welsh Office to confront about two dozen booing demonstrators waving anti-royalist banners. 'We admire your guts but not your position', shouted a demonstrator as the young Prince approached. Pointing to one banner recalling the killing of Llywelyn, the last native Prince of Wales, Charles asked, 'What does it mean?' Murray Jenkins, a member of Cymdeithas yr Iaith Gymraeg, replied, 'It says remember Llywelyn who was massacred by the English.' The Prince said he did not know about that as he was 'not too well up on Welsh history'. Jenkins, a labourer, retorted, 'I will accept that – you are not very brilliant.' Welsh Secretary George Thomas, who had followed Charles as he approached the crowd, interjected, 'He is, you know.' The next day the *Western Mail* said the whole of Wales applauded the Prince for 'his disarming courage in confronting his critics at close quarters'.[31]

Meanwhile, the Home Office had still not received a reply from the Chief Constable of Gwynedd to its plan to insert its own man, Williamson, into the hunt for the Welsh extremists. Waddell wrote again to Col. Williams, this time receiving a reply to the effect the first letter had probably been lost, on account of the go-slow on the railways! Of course, said Col. Williams, he would meet Williamson; in fact, he had written that very day inviting him to Caernarfon for a briefing, regarding 'what really is an old problem as far as we are concerned, as we have had a few explosions by extremists in this area over the past five years', adding, 'Personally, I feel rather sore that the Assize Courts in this area have dealt so leniently with the people brought before them for these grave crimes and I am sure that had they adopted much sterner measures, we would not have this trouble today.'[32] When the Home Office man finally met the Chief Constable of Gwynedd he was promised police cooperation – but reminded this did not permit him to usurp the Chief Constable's paramount role in criminal investigations.[33] By this time, however, Williamson had decided the only way to crack the conspiracy was to form a special unit, led by officers from the Met experienced in counter-terrorism. This he proposed a fortnight later to a summit of chief constables, Scotland Yard Special Branch, MI5 and Ministry of Defence, held at Hayes House, Cardiff, on 16 July. All the big guns concerned with counter-subversion were present – Ferguson Smith (Commander, Metropolitan Police Special Branch), Tom Roberts (MI5), Charles Simkins (Ministry of Defence, Security Division) and E. Brampton (F2, Home Office Police Division).

Immediately afterwards, Williamson drove down to the Cliff Hotel, Gwbert-on-Sea, Cardigan, for a few days' leave and a round of golf. From there, he scribbled a handwritten note to his boss, Sir Eric St Johnston, HM Chief Inspector of Constabulary, admitting the situation remained unsatisfactory. Nothing was working: Parkman's regional crime squad in Cardiff had failed, Special Branch and Box 500 (code for MI5) did not trust the Welsh to collect, evaluate and circulate intelligence, and there was a flagrant lack of liaison between the various police forces and the regional crime squad. Invited to face up to their failure, the Welsh chief constables were chastened by their lack of success. Everyone agreed a fresh approach was needed, at which point Williamson proposed the setting-up of a Special Unit, accountable directly to himself, located just across the border in England and headed by a Detective Chief Superintendent seconded from the Metropolitan Police.[34] The direct consequence of this humiliating defeat for Welsh policing was that in future the security services would be primarily responsible for the surveillance of nationalist activity in Wales.

# 8

## LAST POST FOR THE ARMY

The man chosen to run the Welsh bombers to ground was John 'Jock' Wilson, a 46-year-old Special Branch veteran from the Metropolitan Police, steeped in Cold War intelligence matters. Wilson was the high-profile officer sent to interview Mrs Blake when her husband, George Blake (born Georg Behar, a former Dutch/British spy and Soviet double agent), fled to Moscow after escaping over the wall at Wormwood Scrubs, where he was serving forty-two years, then the longest sentence imposed on anyone in Britain. Wilson's Number Two, Chief Inspector John Bryan, arrived directly from MI5 to join what became known as the Shrewsbury Unit, on account of its being based deliberately just across the border, away from the frustrating influences of the Welsh police. Apart from Wilson and Bryan, the other seven members were all Welsh and hand-picked for their experience of extremist activity, which was not great. From August 1968 the unit ran the investigation in partnership with Frank Williamson, the Home Secretary's eyes and ears in Wales.[1] Uppermost in everyone's mind was whether the situation could at the very least be brought under control for the Investiture to take place safely. But that was not the squad's only concern. The insurgency had created security issues for the Royal Mint, then in the process of relocating from London to Llantrisant in south Glamorgan.[2]

Shortly before Jock Wilson's special squad began operations, the Welsh police were able to register at least one success: the arrest of Owen Williams on his arrival at Birmingham Airport from Dublin, accompanied by his dark-haired Irish girlfriend, Catherine Quaid.[3] Landing on 27 August en route to Wales, Williams was immediately aware of increased police activity in the baggage reclaim area. Other officers were loitering near the customs desk as the pair handed over for examination their only piece of luggage, a carrier bag, at which point two detectives from Warwickshire stepped forward, one of whom said, 'It is Owen Williams?' Told they had a warrant for his arrest, Williams replied, 'I am not guilty morally. I was going to the police after I had seen my children.' As they were hustled from the airport into patrol cars and on to Ladywell police station, he slipped his precious codebook filled with the names of contacts to Catherine Quaid, who was spotted by Detective Sergeant James Cuthbert stuffing it into her handbag. It was confiscated before she was released to continue her journey to Caernarfon.[4]

The following day Detective Sergeant Gwyn Owen arrived from Caernarfon to collect Williams. 'Six months are up on Sunday', Williams told him. 'I was going to come to Caernarfon and give myself up to take what is coming. I would rather face what is to come than be persecuted all the time. I wanted to see my children first.' Williams and Detective Sergeant Owen had known each other ever since the protests over Tryweryn placed the Gwynedd farmer at the centre of police radar. Owen considered Williams 'a man of strong militant views who passionately believes in establishing a Welsh republic … A man who had stated openly he believes in the use of force to gain this end.'[5]

The trial of Owen Williams opened at Caernarfon Assizes on 5 November 1968, when he pleaded not guilty to having in his possession thirteen sticks of gelignite in suspicious circumstances. His defence costs were paid by Trefor Morgan, the millionaire founder of Undeb Insurance. At the committal proceedings the magistrates had found no case to answer on two other charges of possessing explosives. The prosecution centred on the explosion at the Snowdonia Country Club, Sir Alun Talfan-Davies, QC, alleging that a month before this Williams had been handed a packet of explosives in a public-house car park. The explosives, obtained from a slate quarryman, passed through several pairs of hands before allegedly being delivered to Williams by a Free Wales Army member, John Gwilym Jones. Two of those who handled the explosives before this were Eddy Wilkinson and Robert Griffith Jones, both of whom had already been given suspended sentences after admitting possessing explosives. The other crucial piece of prosecution evidence was the minute traces of nitroglycerine found in Williams's car, parked outside Rhyl railway station, which he claimed had been planted during his absence in London.

Much of the evidence was circumstantial, based largely on conversations between Williams and others, including the allegation of a plan to raid Saighton Barracks, Chester, for arms for an uprising in Caernarfon, to coincide with the Investiture. A plan to seize Caernarfon Castle five days before the inauguration ceremony was also mentioned in court, as was the suggestion that a marksman positioned behind rocks near Cledwyn Hughes's home would fire a shot through his car window to 'scare him into resigning as Secretary of State for Wales'. A photograph of the new Severn Bridge marked with an X was produced as evidence against Williams, who, it was claimed, had administered the Free Wales Army oath of allegiance to John Gwilym Jones at the point of a dagger.

Asked by Mr Alun Talfan Davies, QC, for the Crown, whether he agreed with such slogans as 'Death to Prince Charles', and 'Go home English bastards',

Williams replied, 'I would disagree with that completely.' But when shown a newspaper photograph of a damaged water pipeline on the Denbighshire–Merioneth border and asked if he condoned such action, he answered, 'The only way I can answer that is to say I don't condemn it.' Cross-examined about the traces of nitroglycerine found in his car, and whether he had associated with anyone who might have handled it, he parried, 'It has been suggested that certain people have not only carried but admitted possession of it, so it is not for me to make any suggestion of this.' As for failing to answer to his bail and fleeing to Ireland, Williams explained that the case was a delicate one, as other men were involved, and he needed time to 'think it over' and to prepare his defence. All that he said about the IRA was that he had met a man in a Dublin pub.

The prosecution case fell apart when Andrew Rankin, QC, defending Williams, called Robert Griffith Jones, of Llanllynfi, one of the two previously convicted of possessing explosives. The prosecution case was that Griffith Jones passed the parcel of explosives to John Gwilym Jones, who handed it on to Williams in a hotel car park. Asked about this by Mr Rankin, Griffith Jones said the parcel contained not gelignite but a pistol. The prosecutor Alun Talfan-Davies was stunned, able only to nod his head in disbelief. All that remained was for Owen Williams's barrister to remind the jury that his client was not

Commander Jock Wilson (centre), the top Special Branch officer drafted in from Scotland Yard to lead the hunt for the Welsh bombers, arrives at RAF Pembrey after a warrant officer was seriously injured by a shoebox bomb. MAC has always denied it planted the device in September 1968. Copyright: *Western Mail*, Cardiff.

charged with being a Welsh nationalist or holding any particular viewpoint. The case stood or fell on whether the jury were convinced Williams had been passed a packet of explosives. After deliberating for one and a half hours the jury found him not guilty. The case had lasted barely five days. At an impromptu press conference afterwards Williams talked about standing for Parliament as a candidate for the National Patriotic Front. Catherine Quaid was not in court to hear the verdict. A few days into the trial, Miss Quaid had been ordered to stay away by the judge, after she asked two women jurors she met in the toilet to treat Williams leniently.[6]

By this time Jock Wilson's special squad was up and running, and its attention occupied by the most recent incident. From all appearances the saboteurs

Some of the Free Wales Army weapons recovered by the 'Shrewsbury Unit' headed by Commander Jock Wilson. Copyright: *Western Mail*, Cardiff.

A frogman finds the Free Wales Army's arms cache at the bottom of Maes Llyn, a shallow lake near Tregaron, in September 1968. Copyright: *Western Mail*, Cardiff.

had stepped up a gear, exploding a shoebox bomb inside the RAF control tower at Pembrey in Carmarthenshire on 9 September 1968, seriously injuring Warrant Officer William Houghman (42). An important airfield during the Second World War, Pembrey had since become a security station for a bombing range behind the dunes, dive-bombers being directed on their practice runs from the control tower. Also nearby was the Pembrey Munitions Factory, once Britain's largest producer of TNT, but then in the process of being dismantled. Because of the implications for national security and the injuries caused to the Warrant Officer, who lost fingers on both hands and was partially blinded when the shoebox exploded in his face, the Pembrey bomb caused great alarm in Wales and Westminster.[7]

Although John Jenkins has said MAC2 was not involved in this particular incident, the whole of Wales was convinced Welsh extremists were responsible. The police theory was that a man and woman posing as a courting couple carried the shoebox through the perimeter fence, the woman waiting while her accomplice planted the bomb in the control tower and set the timing device. Significantly, the timing device was a clock similar to that used to blow up the Liverpool Corporation water aqueduct at Hapsford, near Chester, three months previously.

Warrant Officer Houghman was called to the control tower after the radio operator, Senior Aircraftsman Marshall Gray (21), discovered the shoebox

After the bombing of the control tower at RAF Pembrey, Secretary of State for Wales George Thomas described those responsible as a 'cowardly bunch who creep up in the dark', and that the spate of extremist attacks had earned Wales notoriety as 'a land of violence'.

containing eight sticks of gelignite and timer on a table in the ground-floor radio room. Houghman had handled explosives before in Aden, where he had served before being posted to Pembrey. But as he carried the shoebox to safety it exploded, leaving him sprawled in a pool of blood, his clothes in ribbons and suffering from severe face, hand and chest injuries, eventually requiring plastic surgery. Police had no doubt it was the work of political extremists, who had crept into the control tower after approaching across the sand-dunes from the direction of Cefn Sidan beach. Secretary of State for Wales George Thomas telephoned the Prime Minister with news of this latest outrage before flying immediately to Pembrey from RAF St Athan. A 'cowardly bunch who creep up in the dark to do their dirty work' was Thomas's comment to the waiting media. If anyone thought violence would bring about a change of policy in Wales, they were underestimating the will of the Welsh people, he added. It was 'as clear as daylight' someone would lose their life if a halt were not called to the violence.[8]

His savage condemnation of the bombers was endorsed by the *Western Mail*, which added for good measure:

> It is sad that just when Wales is attempting to present the world with a true image of itself it should now achieve notoriety as a land of violence. It is deplorable that earnest efforts to achieve greater devolution of power

to Wales should be made more difficult by crass acts of extremism by fanatics who represent no one but themselves.[9]

Just about the entire political class joined the stampede to put distance between themselves and the extremists, Dr Gareth Morgan Jones, assistant general of Plaid Cymru, 'deploring the subversive attacks … for the irreparable damage they do to the image of Wales'. Edward Millward, soon to retire as vice-president of Plaid to teach Prince Charles Welsh during his three months at University College, Aberystwyth, suggested raising a fund for the injured RAF man. A week later Plaid decided at its annual conference not to vote on a reso-lution to boycott the Investiture of the Prince at Caernarfon Castle, for fear this might threaten its electoral chances.

Ironically, one of the few politicians who dared to suggest that the latest act of sabotage might be linked to the campaign for a free and independent Wales was Wales's first Secretary of State, Jim Griffiths, in whose constituency the bombing occurred. After making clear his 'detestation at this horrible outrage', Griffiths, in a letter published by the *Western Mail*, reminded readers that such acts of violence did not occur in a vacuum:

> They are the products directly or indirectly of the political climate resulting from the political controversies of our days. It is already evident that from now on, to the time of the next general election, and at the elec-tion, the major controversy in Wales will be the future constitutional position of our country. The question as to whether Wales should seek to become independent of the rest of the United Kingdom is a vitally import-ant one.[10]

Griffiths wanted a reasonable debate about Welsh aspirations without its degenerating into an anti-English squabble. There had already been signs, he said, at the recent Carmarthen, Rhondda West and Caerphilly by-elections (where Plaid had pushed Labour hard) of an anti-Welsh backlash. Bert Pearce, leader of the Welsh Communist Party, another brave enough to suggest a connection between the bombings and the struggle for freedom, thought the main political parties, rather than wringing their hands, would be better employed considering how best to set up a Welsh parliament. Meanwhile, Home Secretary James Callaghan was supposedly hatching a secret plan, according to George Thomas, to catch the bombers before Prince Charles presented himself at Aberystwyth for the spring term immediately preceding his Investiture.

A week later there seemed to be a breakthrough in the hunt for the Pembrey saboteurs when explosives were discovered stuffed up the chimney of a derelict terraced house on the main Llanelli–Swansea road at Yspitty Road, Bynea, near Loughor Bridge, twelve miles from Pembrey. Found by a tramp sheltering in the house, the gelignite was wrapped in a copy of the west edition of the *Western Mail* dated 5 September, four days before the control-tower explosion. Ten of the fourteen pages of that day's issue were recovered by police and the printing ink tested by forensic experts to see if they could match it to one of the 10,000 papers on the west Wales edition run. Although the *Western Mail* provided lists of newsagents, it was not possible to pin down the one who had sold it. Police were able to confirm, however, from testing powder traces that the same gelignite was used in the Pembrey bomb. Despite having more clues than ever they had previously, no one would be charged, and the case remains open.

Despite John Jenkins's boasts that only he had his finger on the pulse of the organisation, MAC2 could have had a rogue operator. Such a possibility is supported by another incident occurring three months later in Cardiff, when the city police headquarters were bombed. More immediately, Pembrey precipitated a crackdown on the Free Wales Army. The day afterwards, police frogmen started searching Maes Llyn, a shallow lake near Tregaron, after an anonymous tip-off that the Free Wales Army weapons featuring in their manoeuvres for the media were hidden there. Since known FWA members and prominent nationalists were all questioned in the aftermath of Pembrey, it is possible someone panicked and tipped off police about the weapons cache. The discovery of the weapons coincided with the Prime Minister's increasing concern for the safety of the Prince of Wales, exacerbated on reading John Summers's article in the *Daily Telegraph* colour magazine showing the FWA on manoeuvres in the Welsh mountains. In the corridors of power, the FWA and the sabotage of water pipelines and government offices, for which the army often claimed responsibility, were synonymous. Earlier that year Wilson was advised not to prosecute, for fear of creating martyrs, but after the Summers article, followed almost immediately by the Pembrey bomb, he demanded to know why the Director of Public Prosecutions had not taken action under the 1936 Public Order Act proscribing the wearing of uniforms and the carrying of firearms, as pictured in the *Daily Telegraph*.[11]

The discovery of the arms persuaded the Director of Public Prosecutions, now under intense political pressure, to begin proceedings against the FWA. The anonymous caller was thought to have been Cayo Evans, responding to a deal the FWA claimed it was offered by Jock Wilson, after the Pembrey explosion, that if it surrendered its weapons within 48 hours no action would be taken. Whether or not this was true, the sequence of events cannot be ignored: the Pembrey bomb, questioning of known activists and discovery of the weapons, all within the space of a few days. The discovery of the weapons provided the missing link needed to make a prima facie case against the FWA. The four weapons recovered from the lake were all in working order, although parts were missing from some. The most powerful was a semi-automatic Sten gun made in Germany in 1945. A self-loading Mauser, which Coslett carried, dated from 1930. The Smith and Wesson .455 British military revolver was even older, a relic of the First World War, but still serviceable, as was the British military Luger.[12]

Four months after this discovery the FWA ringleaders were rounded up in pre-dawn swoops. The arrests were no surprise to one of the group, Keith Griffiths (Gethyn ap Iestyn), who had warned Cayo Evans repeatedly 'the past will catch up with us' unless Coslett were told to stop wearing his uniform in public and to refuse all TV and press interviews. In a letter found during a search of Cayo Evans's farmhouse, Griffiths, described as 'Director General of the National Patriotic Front', told the FWA leader that those opposing the Investiture could face heavy fines, even jail, and that, personally, he was ashamed of *Y Fyddin* (The Army):

> The trouble is Cayo, you out in the west are totally out of touch with things, not only in the south but outside nationalist circles. I have nothing against Coslett as a nationalist or a man but when it comes to FWA affairs it is a different matter. He is making the Army look stupid, Cayo; wake up to the fact. Without the uniforms and Press and TV dancing around him, would Coslett still be in this game? Probably, yes, he's that much of a patriot but that does not get us away from the fact he is still fucking things up … We must remember, the FWA is living on a legend of newspaper cuttings …[13]

From a second letter recovered by police it is clear the FWA had no idea who was behind the bombings. Speculating about their possible identity, Griffiths wrote:

> Let's face it, pal. There's nothing substantial behind us at all. Even I am having second thoughts on recent bomb attacks and I am wondering whether or not it is the Secret Service [security services] or an unknown quantity. One thing I know, without these attacks now and again, the FWA would not be worth tuppence. If it's the Army then we are OK. But if it's the SS [security services] or unknown quantity, then, pal, the past will catch up with us one day and then we are going to look like complete idiots and the army will be once and for all shattered without the authorities lifting one iron glove to put us down. They will leave it to the jackals of the television and Press who will claw us apart and I for one don't want to see this happen to the army.[14]

For the *Western Mail* and much of the media the FWA was the lunatic fringe of nationalism. As early as 1966, Griffiths and seven others tried to sever their links with an organisation whose antics were increasingly embarrassing. After celebrating Gwynfor Evans's by-election victory at Carmarthen, they handed a signed declaration to the police at Maesteg, to the effect that they were no longer members of the group and had never possessed arms, ammunition or explosives.[15] Griffiths then formed the National Patriotic Front out of the Anti-Sais Front, as a focus for all those opposed to the Investiture. Because Cayo Evans 'was a good bloke', Griffiths was drawn back in as an active member, although constitutionally the army had no members, no rules, no officers and no subscriptions. The FWA was just a bunch of blokes with pretty wild ideas about how to achieve what many thousands of Welsh men and women might have dreamed of: independence. But Griffiths's plans for a revolution in the aftermath of the Investiture were doomed if they could not get Coslett off the front pages. Writing again to Cayo Evans, he warned, 'Believe me, pal, if we don't clear up our image of being a lot of bloody idiots and nuisances, then there will not be one ounce of support among the people for us in 1969.'[16]

Other documents recovered from Griffiths's home hinted at links between the FWA and MAC2, and outlined plans for an uprising to achieve Home Rule by 1975, when England would be issued with a 'get out of Wales' ultimatum. If England failed to, then a 'state of war' would be said to exist between the two countries. Bridges, roads, railways and communications would be destroyed and the reservoir system attacked with 'increased ferocity'.[17] Revolution was a pretty tall order for an army that had never had more than twenty-five members. As insane as it might sound, there was a plan to disrupt the Investiture, involving the kidnapping and coronation of a true descendant of the last native Prince of Wales. In the event, the FWA played no further part in opposing the Investiture, its war games ending in the pre-dawn swoop on 26 February 1969 led by Detective Chief Superintendent Jock Wilson. The nine arrested were:

> William Edward Julian Cayo Evans (31), horse-breeder, of Glandenys, Silian, Lampeter;
> Dafydd Glyn Rowlands (31), of Trosafon, Dafarn Newydd, Upper Corris, Merioneth;
> Dennis Coslett (29), rabbit-breeder, of Penycraig, Pontaber, Gwynfe, Llangadog;
> Anthony Harold Lewis (31), bus conductor, of Porthmawr Road, Cwmbran;
> David John Underhill (29), of Ystrad Fawr, Bridgend;
> David Bonar Thomas (48), of Brynawelon, Bryn, Llanelli;
> Keith Griffiths (22), of Ynysganol, Brynteg, Anglesey;
> Vivian George Davies (27), of Dove Road, Blaenymaes, Swansea;
> William Vernon Griffiths (35), of Cwrt Farm, Cwrtnewydd, Lampeter.

Remarkably, they were committed for trial within a fortnight of being arrested, when usually it takes several months before this stage is reached in most criminal proceedings. But there was uproar in court in Cardiff when the Stipendiary

Magistrate, Mr John Rutter, announced the venue for the trial – Glamorgan Assizes in Swansea, a largely monoglot English-speaking area. Some of the accused wanted to give evidence in Welsh, and believed they would have a better chance if tried by a Welsh-speaking jury. 'British justice', protested Cayo Evans, shouting, 'God save Wales' as he was led to the cells. Stepping forward in the dock, Coslett raised his arm and shouted in Welsh, 'What right has an Englishman to sit in a Welsh court?' Mr Gareth Williams, representing Bonar Thomas, said it was fit and proper for a man who was Welsh-speaking to be tried by his peers in either Carmarthen or Cardigan, where most of the offences were supposed to have taken place. All to no avail, Mr Rutter deciding no hardship would be suffered by appearing before Swansea Assizes.

Seven of the accused faced five counts under the 1936 Public Order Act, alleging they took part in the control or management, organisation and training of the Free Wales Army, whose members and adherents were organised, trained and equipped in such a manner as to arouse reasonable apprehension that they were to be employed for the use, or display of physical force in promoting a political objective. The offences were alleged to have been committed between 22 October 1965 and 31 December 1968 in the county of Carmarthen and elsewhere.

Evans, Coslett and William Vernon Griffiths together faced three charges under the 1965 amended Firearms Act of having unauthorised possession of a Sten machine-gun, a Mauser self-loading pistol and a .38 revolver. All three offences were alleged to have been committed at Lampeter on a day unknown in October 1967.

Coslett was charged under the 1883 Explosive Substances Act with having illegal possession of sticks of Unigel, detonators, a battery, electric wire and a timing device at Llangennech on 20 July 1968, with having unauthorised possession of a Mauser self-loading pistol, a revolver and a Sten machine-gun on various dates in 1966 and 1968, and with unlawful possession of an explosives timing device.

Evans was charged with having unauthorised possession of a Sten machine-gun between 1 January 1966 and 23 August 1966, and with possession of a Luger pistol at Lampeter on 14 July 1968.

David Bonar Thomas was charged with having unauthorised possession of a revolver at Lampeter on 14 July 1968, and Vivian George Davies with having unauthorised possession of a Mauser self-loading pistol at the same time and place. [18]

The admitted reluctance of the Director of Public Prosecutions to make martyrs of the FWA was no less valid three years later, when Cayo Evans and company were eventually rounded up. Nothing had changed. The police still did not know who was behind the sabotage campaign. By now they had the name of the organisation, but that was about all, despite the insertion of Jock Wilson's special squad into the investigation. The very least that Wilson could more or less guarantee was that the FWA would be locked up before the big day at Caernarfon Castle. Details of the precise circumstances prompting the government's decision to crack down on the FWA after ignoring its activities for five years were destroyed in June 1990, when, 'in accordance with good records management practice', file 18/16/103 'Activities of the Free Wales Army' was shredded by the Home Office.[19]

On the eve of the opening of the FWA trial at Swansea Assizes on 16 April 1969 a bomb exploded outside the lost property office at Cardiff's new police headquarters in Cathays Park. A wall and windows were damaged, but luckily the office was empty at the time. What was particularly bizarre about this incident was that while MAC2 had targeted the police headquarters that particular night, when the saboteurs arrived to plant their device they discovered one had already been placed in the central-heating duct! This, and the interception of a letter-bomb delivered to Detective Sergeant John Lavery at Cardiff police headquarters on the same day the detective gave evidence in the FWA trial, appeared to be attempts to disrupt the trial. Euphemistically described as 'The Pimpernel', Detective Lavery told the jury how he had infiltrated a mock FWA exercise with the password 'Llywelyn Rest in Peace', only to be told to make the tea. Were these two incidents, together with the unexplained shoebox bomb at the Pembrey RAF control tower, the work of some other agency, more deadly than MAC2? Unlike the bombs planted on water pipelines and at government buildings, all timed to explode when no one was expected to be in the vicinity, these three other devices were timed to kill or maim – and so was a fourth device, in a canvas bag pushed through a letterbox at Cardiff postal sorting office in Cowbridge Road East on the day the FWA leaders were convicted. No one was hurt, but the blast blew a three-foot-square metal casing thirty feet across a busy road.

Whatever preconceptions one had about the leaders of the FWA, their trial was widely regarded as putting Welsh patriotism in the dock. After Cayo Evans refused to plead and Coslett replied, 'I do not accept foreign law', the scene was set for a comic opera lasting fifty-one days.[20] Much of the prosecution case was pieced together from a thick file of newspaper cuttings, collected over the preceding six years by Detective Superintendent James Vivian Fisher of Carmarthenshire Constabulary. Convictions were obtained from a stream of journalists filing into the witness box to vouch for the accuracy of their reporting of the FWA's most outrageous statements, and not from astute police detective work. Of the seventy-two prosecution witnesses called, by far the majority were journalists giving evidence either willingly, or on subpoena, for appearances' sake, so that they would not be seen to be willingly compromising their sources. The *Western Mail*, *Llanelli Star*, *Herald of Wales*, BBC *24 Hours*, BBC *Good Morning Wales*, *Daily Mail*, *Daily Mirror* and the *David Frost Show* all trooped into the witness box to defend their stories. For its part, the prosecution produced only four ancient weapons recovered from the lake near

Tregaron, some incriminating documents about stopping the Investiture (which a large part of the Welsh population was opposed to) and Detective Lavery's evidence.[21]

Most observers agreed that the FWA trial, in which the barristers greatly outnumbered the accused, was an exercise in pure farce. One cannot help but wonder what the chief prosecutor Mr Tasker Watkins, QC – winner of the Victoria Cross for charging a German machine-gun post in the Second World War – really thought when he told the jury of the FWA's plan to invade England! Everyone agreed that the arch-clown Coslett talked of violence only to get his name in the newspapers. Beside him sat Griffiths, wearing a pair of dragon cuff-links throughout the trial, and described as a juggler throwing 'ideas in the air like little balls'.

No one could explain why it was left until February 1969 before the men in their ex-army surplus jackets dyed green were rounded up. Suggestions that the arrests were prompted by political pressure on account of the imminent Investiture were brushed aside. Superintendent Fisher cross-examined by Mr James Mulcahy, QC, for Cayo Evans:

> Fisher: I'm not a political policeman.
> Cayo Evans (from the dock): You are.
> Mulcahy: I am not suggesting you are in the category of political police-man. What I am suggesting is that something had to be done in view of these men's proclamations because of the forthcoming Investiture? [22]

Superintendent Fisher denied that the FWA were 'an easy target because of their public proclamations'. He had submitted his very first report on FWA activities to the Director of Public Prosecutions as long ago as April 1966. Between then and September 1968 there had been four or five such reports. The FWA's exhibitionism was a cover for something deeper, said the officer.

The following day Fisher was cross-examined by Mr John Gower for Bonar Thomas about the political dimension to the trial. Asked what he meant when he said he was not a political policeman, the superintendent replied:

> I read correspondence from the accused, one to another, in which it is alleged this trial is a political trial by political policemen to make sure they are in custody when Prince Charles visits Aberystwyth. I resent that suggestion. I am a policeman doing my duty.[23]

Detective Chief Superintendent Jock Wilson, the last of seventy-two prosecution witnesses, insisted he knew of no special reason for his appointment the previous August, other than that he had been seconded from the Met Special Branch at the request of the Welsh chief constables to take charge of the hunt for Welsh extremists. Asked by Mr Mulcahy for his definition of an extremist,

Wilson said, 'A person becomes an extremist by threats of violence, either directly or indirectly, to persuade the duly elected representatives to his point of view.' Wilson denied offering Cayo Evans a deal of immunity from prosecution if the weapons were surrendered.[24]

On day 29 of the trial, the *Western Mail* carried the headline, 'Nationalism is not crime, says Q. C.' Neither was membership of the Free Wales Army, Mr Aubrey Myerson for William Vernon Griffiths told the jury. Pivotal to the defence was the strong presumption that the State had put patriotism on trial.[25] The prosecution case was that legitimate protest had been taken too far. Winding up for the Crown, Mr Tasker Watkins said that while extremists and moderates alike could talk themselves hoarse in a democracy, the tipping-point came when they spoke of violence or threatened it. The 'great untruth', he said, was the suggestion the trial was politically motivated:

> We live in a very old, very experienced and very famous country, which has a history stretching back across many centuries of turmoil, change and progress. It has known its fair share of strife both within and outside these islands.
>
> Over these tumultuous times, a society in which you and I form part has come to be renowned for its tolerance, for its fondness of a peaceful existence and an orderly way of living. A society that does not keep peace within itself and does not preserve order is in an unhappy state. We allow extraordinary licence to people to express their views, however odd and unusual, in private and public […]
>
> Thus we are rightly described as a tolerant nation and a country of free speech. Violence and talk of violence is another matter … When someone resorts to unlawful methods of achieving his political object he puts himself in peril with the law … To attempt to prevent the investiture was a political object of the accused … Is there anything comic about the men who take it upon themselves to gather weapons … Is there anything comic about people who say they are prepared to use violence for political means?[26]

Of the six still in the dock – all charges against Rowlands, Thomas and Underhill had been earlier dismissed – Mr Tasker Watkins described Cayo Evans as the man who talked most frequently, the FWA's prime organiser, at 'the very heart of its affairs'; Dennis Coslett, one of twelve commanders, a lecturer on explosives, and 'very much a live wire'; Vernon Griffiths played a vital part in its control and management; Bonar Thomas very much had 'his finger on the trigger'; Tony Lewis provided the FWA with equipment.[27]

Winding up the defence on behalf of Cayo Evans, his counsel Mr James Mulcahy focused the jury's attention on the incongruities in the case. Was it not an extraordinary coincidence that the FWA weapons were not found until a few days after Detective Chief Superintendent Jock Wilson was sent to Wales? Why was none of the journalists who gave evidence interviewed by police before 1969? If the manner in which the accused men were organising was causing public concern, Mr Mulcahy wanted to know why it was left until February 1969 before arrests were made.

> What makes the case exceptional and extraordinary in another way is that most of the evidence does not come from secret investigations or commendable detective work, but from television, newspapers and magazines. It is not very often that a man charged with a criminal offence is in the position of committing it on television or to a whole team of journalists.[28]

Mr Mulcahy suggested the obvious explanation was that the authorities had decided 'something desperate should be done' about the FWA by the police because by the time they were arrested the Investiture was only four months away.

According to Mr John Mortimer, QC for Coslett, it was a political birthright, like the air we breathed, that people should be free to express their own views. Intemperate and high-flown words were part of the country's freedom and should not be disallowed. Just as cabinet ministers and statesmen were entitled to freedom of speech, so were men of little education. In fact, the FWA's cause was 'dear to the hearts of hundreds of Welshmen':

> They had done no acts of violence or sabotage. We are living in a time of Welsh history when acts of violence and sabotage have taken place. If one of these men was in a position of there being evidence against him of being connected with any such thing, to be sure the proper charges would have been levelled long before now.[29]

Mr John Gower, QC, representing David Bonar Thomas, was applauded from the public gallery after describing the trial as a historic one, the verdict likely to be remembered long into the annals of Welsh history. While no one knew why the Attorney General had sanctioned the trial months after the arms were found in the lake, it was clear that politics featured in the case. There were just too many coincidences surrounding the discovery of the weapons for this to have happened naturally, said Mr Gower.[30]

Summing up, at the end of a trial costing £130,000, Mr Justice Thompson said that nothing the jury had heard made it a political trial. The 1936 Public Order Act – this only the second time it had been used – was not against political objects but certain methods of obtaining them, said the judge. The trial, which he admitted had been a tax on judgement and common sense, was about whether the public had reasonable apprehension from the promotion of a political objective.[31]

On his directions, not guilty verdicts were returned on Cayo Evans on charges of unauthorised possession of a Sten gun, a Mauser self-loading pistol and a .38 revolver. Similar verdicts were returned with regard to a pistol and revolver in the case of Coslett.

Not guilty verdicts were also returned on firearms charges against William Vernon Griffiths, and formal not guilty verdicts returned on Keith Griffiths and Vivian George Davies on public order charges. Keith Griffiths had earlier changed his plea to guilty to organising FWA members or adherents. Davies had also changed his plea to guilty to a charge of unauthorised possession of a Mauser pistol. Underhill had been cleared of all charges in May.[32]

The two FWA leaders, Cayo Evans and Coslett, were each jailed for fifteen months, Coslett on eight Public Order Act firearms and explosives charges, and Cayo Evans on three charges under the Public Order Act alleging control and management, organising and training of FWA members, and a further two firearms charges. Keith Griffiths, who had earlier changed his plea to guilty to organising FWA members, was sent to prison for nine months. Tony Lewis for organising the FWA, Vivian George Davies for possessing a Mauser and William Vernon Griffiths for unauthorised possession of a Sten gun were jailed for eight, six and three months respectively, all sentences suspended for either three or two years. Dafydd Glyn Rowlands was cleared of organising the FWA, so was David Bonar Thomas and of a further charge of possessing a revolver.

After being sentenced, Coslett made an emotional speech in Welsh from the dock, in which he said he was trained to use violence by the British Army:

> That was to promote an English political object and this was regarded as honourable. English violence is honourable but Welsh violence is a terrible crime … I shall never forget Wales in my lonely cell and my last prayer shall be, May the God of all Freedom strengthen Wales to cast off her fetters. Tonight I shall sleep in my lonely cell and tomorrow I shall wear prison uniform, but for me it will be a far more honourable uniform than the costliest dress of the slave and the serf … I do not believe that it is possible to kill the soul that has been inspired by the spirit of freedom. The only arm I shall now use is the pen…I am ready for your sentence … Free Wales.[33]

The public gallery erupted with applause, the judge ordering it to be cleared, all except Coslett's wife who, in tears, was allowed to remain.

Evans and Coslett would have faced stiffer sentences, had it not been for their agreement to certain undertakings the judge hoped would help restore peace 'in this land of Wales which you and others have done something to disturb by your activities'. Sentencing the men, Mr Justice Thompson said that although misguided, he had also taken into account their love for Wales, and for this reason they would be dealt with more leniently:

> I hope and believe I understand patriotism … I hope, too, I understand the desire of men to improve the conditions of their fellows and their home-land. I also have a homeland, remember, whose poets have sung so eloquently. I know there is a Welsh way of life very dear to people in this land of Wales. The right to hold dear the matters I have mentioned has not been on trial in this case. None of you has been charged with loving Wales. Just as there is a Welsh way of life, so there is a civilised and orderly way of life which is international and which is cherished by the people of other lands. And crime has no place in it. Some of you caused among your fellow countrymen anxiety and alarm by your schemes, claims and boast-ings, and in the case of two of you, weapons. You have served Wales ill. It is said on your behalf there is no evidence connecting you with any of the bomb incidents. What is not known is what encouragement your public boastings, public displays and private propaganda may have given to those who were. What is also known is the approval some of you gave to evildoers, whoever they may be, and the encouragement for their future you offered.[34]

Evans and Coslett each gave undertakings: (1) not to take part in any military-style activity or handle weapons illegally; (2) not to associate with people engaged in military-like actions; (3) not to advocate the use of violence for a political cause; (4) not to form or attempt to form a military-like organisation; (5) not to use or advocate the use of violence and not to associate with anyone doing so; and (6) not to take part in any military-like organisation. Vernon Griffiths, Lewis and Davies gave similar but shorter undertakings. Only Keith Griffiths refused to make any declaration.[35]

Evans and Coslett were as good as their word, for the rest of their lives main-taining a respectable distance between themselves and other extremist organisations. Apart from the annual pilgrimage to Cilmeri to mark the death of Llywelyn, the last native Prince of Wales, the pair were never again actively involved, although for some they remain icons in the struggle for Wales.

A trial, which the prosecution and politicians had earnestly hoped would be over long before the Investiture of the Prince of Wales, ended with the FWA men being sentenced on the very day of the great event – and, significantly, within hours of two real saboteurs blowing themselves to pieces while on active duty.

# 9

# A MEETING WITH MAC

The very first clue to the identity of the activists crossed my desk at the *Western Mail* one evening in May 1968, when I received a telephone call from Ian Skidmore, a freelance journalist then based near Chester who occasionally did work for us. He was offering a story from a secret press conference given by Mudiad Amddiffyn Cymru, a clandestine organisation I had never heard of previously. Anything calling itself 'Movement for the Defence of Wales' sounded immediately suspect to someone whose newspaper life was spent warding off crank calls. Skidmore's description of how he and Harold Pendlebury, a reporter from the *Daily Mail*'s Manchester office, had been kidnapped by extremists and forced to listen to the saboteurs confessing was even more preposterous.

The story was that Skidmore and Pendlebury had met a go-between, Emyr Jones, a reporter on the *Wrexham Leader*, in the Grosvenor Hotel, Chester, on 1 May 1968. After moving on to the Talbot Hotel, where more alcohol was consumed and Jones made a telephone call, it was suggested by him they went to Skidmore's house at Picton Hall, Picton, about three miles away for a drink, by which time I was guessing that their fevered minds were capable of concocting anything to earn a couple of pounds from an unsuspecting *Western Mail*. It was not until they were en route to Skidmore's place that Jones said it was to be the location for the press conference with 'MAC'. By arrangement, the car drove past the house, returning a few minutes later after John Jenkins, waiting in a nearby telephone kiosk, had satisfied himself it was not being followed.

Two men stepped from the shadows on either side of the car immediately it stopped outside the entrance to Picton Hall, one of these men later being identified as Alders. The house was in darkness, the room where the interview was to take place illuminated by a single reading lamp. After searching the house and the three journalists, Alders groped his way in the darkness to a telephone, knocking over a low table in the process. Picking up the receiver, he dialled

Jenkins in the telephone kiosk and said, 'OK Mac, come in.' A few minutes later Jenkins arrived; on his instructions the lamp was switched off and Pendlebury given a small torch, so that he could just about see to take notes. Skidmore and the other journalist, Emyr Jones, just listened, as Jenkins introduced himself only as 'Director of Operations MAC', explaining that MAC had started in 1963 with the explosion at Tryweryn and had been resurrected a few years later. The organisation had originally been too much like the 'Boy Scouts', explained Jenkins, but now it had a Supreme Council of five and executive committee of three. Asked what its aim was, Jenkins replied:

> To reawaken the national consciousness of the Welsh people by propa-
> ganda and by action with explosives … We believe in every form of
> violence; we are peaceful men in the way an outraged father is a peaceful
> man, but there comes a time when you can't take it any further and you
> must dig your heels in. We believe extreme violence is a bad thing, but
> there are worse forms of inhumanity. Two wrongs don't make a right. One
> wrong may be the lesser of two evils. We are prepared to kill. We don't
> make the rules. We are dealing with a Government that apparently puts
> aside logic and reason. We aim to make them sit up and take action. The
> only way to make them see that we mean business is to carry out acts of
> extreme violence … I believe quite frankly that half of Wales had not
> heard of Tryweryn until they had read about it in the paper after the
> explosion there. It also offends the authority that there are people about
> who intend to do something about it.[1]

His role was 'Director of Operations', although he was not the head of the organisation. That was a 'much older man', known only as 'Mac', someone whose identity would be a complete surprise if ever it was revealed. Jenkins had told Alders the same thing, but claimed later that it was a smokescreen to confuse Special Branch:

> We have a battle plan. It is a declaration of war on anyone who attempts
> to compromise the Welsh people. We consider ourselves the soul of
> nationalism and the conscience of Wales. This is the first time we have
> come into the open. We feel that the people of Wales should know about
> our activities.[2]

Jenkins then proceeded to list for the journalists the five explosions for which MAC claimed responsibility, beginning with Clywedog, which he said took five weeks to plan. The explosion was detonated by passing a charge along a telephone line, just as police had suspected. After this came Llanrhaeadr-ym-Mochnant, the Temple of Peace, Snowdonia Country Club and the Tax Office in Cardiff. The last building was bombed because it symbolised a taxation system 'maintaining the trappings of an Imperialist Empire'. Another target had been aborted because the volume of water released by sabotaging a pipeline would have swept away a nearby village.

Pendlebury asked the questions, but Jenkins spoke more or less uninter-rupted for about four hours, his statements a mixture of conviction, tinged with sentiment, and denunciation of English rule in Wales. Sometimes what he said was plainly contradictory, one moment assuring the journalists that MAC2 wanted to harm no one, the next mentioning the existence of an 'assassination squad'. In reply to the question uppermost in everyone's mind – MAC2's attitude to the Investiture – Jenkins said bluntly, 'We plan that there won't be one':

> Strange as it may seem we have a lunatic fringe. There may come a time when some person fired only by patriotic ideals may perform a 'Lee Harvey Oswald'. Who knows! This Investiture ceremony is a bloody fiasco. There are members of my group who are prepared to do anything. This is the final insult. No one wants it. This is being forced on the Welsh people so it is right up our street … Everyone is powerless to stop it except us. People in favour of this are the usual 'honour-crazy councillors' and also people whose brains should have guided them better. No doubt that some lecturers in one Welsh university will make their future out of this. We have finalised our plans. They include explosives. If I were the Queen I would start thinking about being a mother … We have nothing against Charlie, but we hate and detest the Prince of Wales. To send him to Aberystwyth for a term is a mockery, a foolishness and a nonsense encouraged by certain university lecturers. He is not coming as a friend. He is coming as a political overlord into his inheritance by right of conquest.[3]

Noticeably, MAC2's concern for Wales was not confined to who ruled it. The insurgents claimed a cultural dimension to their activities. Unless the decline in the language was stopped, they feared there would be nothing left in ten years. The proportion of Welsh-speaking children in Cardiganshire, according to Jenkins, had fallen from 80 per cent to 50 per cent because of the lack of local employment and the influx of people from outside Wales, who were not prepared even to 'spend a second trying to pronounce a Welsh place-name'.

Towards the end of the interview, Jenkins touched on a grievance that a decade later would give rise to another outbreak of extremist activity: the influx of second-home owners from England, threatening Wales's indigenous culture and language. Their property would not be safe, he said, unless they accepted the Welsh way of life.

Apart from the beam from the torch Pendlebury had for taking notes, the room remained in complete darkness. Twice the interview was suspended for the reporter to use the toilet, each time Pendlebury being followed upstairs by one of Jenkins's accomplices. In the darkness it was impossible to see much of the MAC2 spokesman, except that he had a straight nose. Speaking vigorously and fluently with a soft Welsh accent, the man seemed to be about thirty; he smoked a number of cigarettes, blowing smoke rings when he wanted to emphasise a point. Because Jenkins spoke fluently and precisely the journalists later told police they thought their mystery man was a schoolteacher. Afterwards, schoolteachers with known nationalist sympathies found them-selves under increased surveillance.[4]

Little of this figured in the story Skidmore was offering the *Western Mail*. The focus was not upon the persons who organised this bizarre press conference or its purpose, but upon the alleged kidnapping of the three reporters. Skidmore made no mention of how it was arranged or explained anything about Mudiad Amddiffyn Cymru, an organisation few had heard of previously. As a result of my suspicions, I spiked what could have been one of the *Western Mail*'s greatest scoops. Not even the *Daily Mail* used it, as far as I have been able to tell, but a few paragraphs did make the *Daily Mirror* after the freelance Skidmore fired the story around Fleet Street.[5]

The reason for the press conference, Jenkins explained to me later, was to deliver a message to Special Branch and MI5 that MAC2 had the resources to threaten the life of the Prince of Wales unless the Investiture was cancelled. Since it would be another nineteen months before Jenkins and Alders were arrested, the message clearly never got through, even though reinforced by the explosion that blew out the windows of the main administration block at the Welsh Office in Cathays Park, Cardiff.[6] George Thomas, appointed Secretary of State for Wales by Harold Wilson the month before, immediately pointed a finger at Plaid Cymru, accusing it of having created a monster it could not control. Ted Rowlands, Labour Member of Parliament for Cardiff North, was prompted famously to remark, 'This is Cardiff, not Chicago.' For Thomas, the insurgency was nothing less than 'political terrorism', encouraged by Plaid Cymru after it had failed to stop Tryweryn. Facing a barrage of criticism from Labour members, Gwynfor Evans repudiated the allegations that his party had consorted with the extremists, adding, 'Plaid Cymru has condemned without reservation these outrages.'[7] The *Western Mail* censured both, Thomas for making political capital out of the insurgency, and the Plaid President Gwynfor Evans for claiming that the failure to catch the bombers was because it was all a plot by the government's own security services to discredit nationalists:

> Both Government Ministers and supporters and Nationalists would do well to call a halt to the mud slinging and concentrate their efforts on bringing every pressure to bear on the Home Office to institute the most thorough police investigation into the whole series of incidents. The

dangerous nature of these persistent attacks gives the situation an urgency, which dictates that the services of Scotland Yard should be called upon to aid local police forces.[8]

For George Thomas, events were hurtling out of control. On the same day that he confronted Plaid Cymru in the House of Commons came news of the failed attempt to blow up the pipeline at Lake Vyrnwy in north Montgomeryshire, and then the following month the saboteurs' most spectacular success, at Hapsford, where the railway line was flooded.

Thomas's impatience with lack of progress in the investigation could be measured by the increasing intensity of his condemnation of the insurgents. After each incident, his outrage ratcheted up a level, the more frenzied the nearer the saboteurs got to the Investiture. Thomas had invested a great deal of personal esteem in staging this historic event at Caernarfon Castle, for which this son of a Rhondda miner was widely regarded as the architect. Besotted with royalty, he never missed an opportunity to be seen at the side of even relatively minor royals. For him the most important person in the world after his widowed 'Mam', Emma Jane Thomas – to whom he referred endlessly – was the Queen Mother, otherwise 'Mam in a tiara'. What most delighted Thomas was that the friendships cultivated in high places meant he would officiate at the Investiture and, later, be chosen to read the lesson at the Prince's marriage to Princess Diana in Westminster Abbey. For the 'poor boy from Tonypandy', riding in the monarch's carriage, rubbing shoulders with royalty, was at the very top of his Richter scale of memories.

For all his folksy manner and melodious voice – characteristics he believed won him elections, affection and eventual appointment as Speaker of the House of Commons – Thomas was detested for his toadyism more than he was respected for his political achievements. For many, 'Mother's Pride' is remembered as the hammer of Welsh nationalism and the language. Bitterly critical of devolution, he nevertheless managed to combine attacks on devolution with a significant transfer of administrative power to the Welsh Office, which he regarded as merely an extension of the administrative reach of Westminster and Whitehall. Real power would always reside with his beloved House of Commons, his mother of parliaments. But for Thomas, bombs and Plaid Cymru meant the same thing, all nationalists tarred with the same brush. John Jenkins, whose mother's house was swallowed by the avalanche of slurry at Aberfan, thought Thomas a 'monster' for proposing that the charitable fund set up to aid victims of the disaster be raided to remove the tips. Although forced to back down by the ensuing public outcry, £150,000 was still taken from the fund towards the cost of moving the tips, creating resentment in the village not erased until the money was returned in the 1990s.

From the moment of the first bomb at Clywedog, the political knee-jerk reaction was always the same: expressions of outrage, followed by the determination of the political class to dissociate mainstream Welsh opinion from nationalist activists. They refused to countenance the possibility that there existed an undercurrent of admiration and covert support for the insurgents at 'war' with England.

# 10

## COUNTDOWN

George Thomas's first year as Secretary of State for Wales ended with the ninth act of sabotage for which MAC2 claimed responsibility, the target on this occasion a pipeline across the border at West Hagley, supplying water to Birmingham from its Elan Valley reservoirs. The explosion, on 2 December, occurred about a week after a twenty-four-hour police patrol was suspended. A five-foot gash was blown in one of four cast-iron pipes, the flood reducing Birmingham's water supply by half. This was followed by a three-month lull before MAC2 on 10 April 1969 targeted another tax office, this one in Hamilton House, a six-storey concrete block in Chester. Almost every window at the rear of the property was blown out and glass and income tax papers strewn across all floors by the blast, centred on a roof above an adjoining garage. Internal walls buckled, and buildings seventy-five yards from the seat of the explosion were also damaged.

But Chester Tax Office had not been chosen because it was 'an agent for the Imperial Empire'. The explosion was timed to coincide with a secret visit by the Earl Marshall, the Duke of Norfolk, to the headquarters of Western Command, Chester, for an Investiture conference. Hurriedly this was cancelled, and the Earl Marshall's helicopter diverted to Caernarfon Castle for an unannounced inspection of the venue. Not for the first time, Jock Wilson's special squad suspected the extremists had a police informant.[1]

Five days later the 'mystery' bomb exploded outside Cardiff Police headquarters, George Thomas told of this while listening to the Chancellor of the Exchequer's Budget Speech in the House of Commons. Incandescent with rage, he condemned 'these cowards who strike without knowing or caring (about) whom they are striking at':

> I understand that between 70 and 80 work in the building and the two rooms damaged in the explosion could well have been occupied at the time. I have repeatedly warned that serious injury or loss of life must

inevitably result if this course of rash and premeditated violence is followed. Today's deplorable incident came dangerously close to this. Those responsible are no friends of Wales. These acts are becoming more reckless, for clearly the risk was wantonly taken of killing people on duty in the office.[2]

Thomas returned immediately from London to inspect the damage and chair a press conference, alongside Detective Chief Superintendent Jock Wilson. All that emerged from this was that after the attacks on the tax offices in Chester and Cardiff security had been tightened at Inland Revenue offices throughout Britain. It was clear no one had a clue about the identity of the insurgents, Detective Chief Superintendent David Morris, Head of Cardiff CID, remarking that 'the saboteurs came from the north, the south, possibly the west or the east'.[3]

Inevitably, a bombing campaign that had most people waiting for the next one to explode spawned copycat incidents. Towards the end of April an explosive device was found in a briefcase in left-luggage locker C10 at Cardiff's Queen Street station. This was a hoax that went very badly wrong for the perpetrator Robert William Trigg (20), a student from Ely, Cardiff. If the chemical concoction had exploded it would have had the force of between six and twelve hand-grenades, according to an expert, the consequences for the crowded station 'quite disastrous, utterly appalling'. Discovered by a booking clerk who noticed a surcharge was payable on the locker, the bomb failed to explode because it had not been properly assembled.

Arrested three days later, Trigg pleaded guilty to possessing explosives and stealing smoke-grenades and was jailed for four years, for what he claimed was a hoax and not an attempt to overthrow the government.[4] Many thought the length of sentence only reflected the Establishment's frustration at the continued failure to apprehend the real bombers. Hoax or not, British Rail imposed an immediate security clampdown extending beyond the Investiture. Passengers at stations in Wales were required to produce proof of identity before leaving suitcases in left-luggage offices. Failure to do so meant suitcases being opened, searched and, if necessary, destroyed.[5]

The last explosion in Cardiff occurred six days after Trigg's hoax, on 29 April 1969, when the Central Electricity Generating Board's offices at Gabalfa were rocked. Only minutes before the device, hidden in a flowerbed, was detonated, a night watchman had passed the spot.

The Anti-Investiture Campaign Committee, now chaired by Owen Williams, after his acquittal on explosives charges, had stepped up a gear with a protest demonstration in Caernarfon on St David's Day. This attracted the attention of the BBC's flagship *24 Hours* news programme, and reporter Linda Blandford and a camera crew were dispatched to north Wales. The programme included a vox pop of local attitudes towards the Investiture and also an interview with

Cardiff Member of Parliament Mr Ted Rowlands (1966–70) said after the Welsh Office was bombed in May 1968, 'This is Cardiff not Chicago' (top). Bomb disposal experts and police inspect the extensive damage caused to the massive West Hagley water pipeline in December 1968 (bottom). Copyright: Press Association.

Owen Williams. The establishment class were aghast when reporter Blandford referred to the Prince of Wales as Charles Windsor. Welsh Secretary Thomas could not contain his anger and demanded to see a transcript of the programme. In the margin of this he scrawled 'untrue' alongside the comments of members of a local band who said they had rejected an invitation to perform at the Investiture because it was a 'calculated insult to their Welsh pride and heritage'.

Before sending the transcript off to Prime Minister Harold Wilson, Thomas heavily underscored other passages, which he believed were evidence of clear bias in Blandford's reporting. Her description of Caernarfon Castle as 'a shrine of Welsh nationalism' got a big black line, as did the response of men and women in the Welsh street who said no one wanted the Investiture or intended going near the castle, for fear of another bomb. Suggestions by Owen Williams that the Investiture was supported only by those hoping for recognition in the Investiture Honours also got a big black mark from Thomas. So did Blandford's claim that 350 special toilet units had been installed for the great day in a town where many of the old terraced houses 'still haven't got bathrooms, indoor toilets, electricity, hot water, or even a cold water tap outside'. According to her, the Anti-Investiture Campaign Committee had organised a commemorative mug-smashing campaign, with a book of Welsh poetry as a prize.

Introduced to viewers as chairman of the committee, Owen Williams admitted he was regarded as an extremist for bombing Tryweryn, but insisted the campaign to stop the Investiture was constitutional:

> Prince Charles is more related to the Germans and the Greeks, than he is to Welshmen. He will say that he comes from Tudor stock, well, that was five or six hundred years ago. That doesn't mean anything to Wales. I mean – you can trace back Welsh ancestry to Adam and Eve if you go that far back.

> I have nothing against Prince Charles as a person but people are using him and stepping on him to further their own ends and therefore they are bringing the Welsh nation down …[6]

Harold Wilson agreed that the description of Prince Charles as 'Charles Windsor' was 'extraordinary', and advised Thomas to pursue the complaint with Lord Hill, chairman of the BBC Governors, to whom he wrote:

> There is certainly *prima facie* evidence that the BBC directed its attention to well-known minority opponents of the Investiture. It would be possible for any slanted programme, which concentrated on minority groups to give a completely distorted and untrue picture of the feelings of a community on any subject. I have an overwhelming impression from the

evidence that has come to me that those responsible for the production of this programme had one intention only, to produce an anti-Investiture programme.[7]

The immediate concern for the government was the three months of the spring term the Prince of Wales was to spend at University College, Aberystwyth, considered by Thomas as a hotbed of nationalist intrigue. The visit had been planned some years previously, as it was generally agreed the Prince knew far too little about the history of his Principality, its culture and language. At least some spoken Welsh would be necessary for him to participate fully in the Investiture. His predecessor, Edward VIII, had been taught his part in the 1911 ceremony by the Liberal premier David Lloyd George.

The Prince's Welsh tutorial had started in 1967, when it was arranged for a free copy of the *Western Mail* to be delivered daily by special courier to his lodgings at Trinity College, Cambridge, and to Buckingham Palace during vacations. This, together with monthly reports compiled by the Welsh Office, helped keep the young prince informed of developments in Wales and potential problems. In addition, the great and the good from Wales were invited to a series of discreet luncheons with the Prince at Lancaster House. But George Thomas's biggest coup was in persuading the Archdruid of Wales to participate in the Investiture, which was considered a betrayal by those opposed to it. In return for his cooperation the Archdruid had anticipated that Charles would at least be seen to be taking a greater interest in Wales before his Investiture. The Queen, however, refused to allow this, insisting that the prince's Public engagements should be kept to the minimum until his education was completed. This impasse was partially overcome by the Gorsedd inviting the Prince to become a member at the 1968 Barry National Eisteddfod, another poke in the eye for nationalists.[8]

Prince Charles almost never got to Aberystwyth for his Welsh lessons under the tutorship of Edward Millward, then a prominent member of Plaid Cymru. Convinced by this time that Wales was far too dangerous for the young royal, Harold Wilson decided to advise the palace to cancel Aberystwyth, only to discover he had left it too late – the Prince was already there, and Home Secretary Callaghan and Welsh Secretary Thomas agreed it was unwise to disturb the arrangements.[9] Thomas added to the Establishment's unease when he reported having detected a nationalist bias creeping into the prince's speeches. This, he declared, 'boosted Plaid Cymru' while threatening the monarchy. In a handwritten note to Wilson he suggested the Prime Minister should have a discreet word with the Queen, because:

It has become quite evident to me that the Aberystwyth experience has influenced the Prince to a considerable extent … On two occasions he has made public speeches which have political implications. If the Prince is writing his own speeches he may well be tempted to go further. The enthusiasm of youth is a marvellous spur but it may lead to speeches that cause real difficulty.[10]

The explosion outside Cardiff Police headquarters caused hardly any damage at all, but the impact on Whitehall was considerable. On hearing about it, Sir James Waddell, Deputy Under-Secretary at the Home Office, asked for an urgent meeting that same evening with Callaghan and his Private Secretary Brian Cubban. There, they agreed that the hunt for the saboteurs was getting nowhere, even after sending in Williamson and Jock Wilson to run the investigation. Another top-level summit was called for 22 May, in Room 101 at the Home Office headquarters in Horseferry House. In the meantime, Williamson undertook yet another review of police operations, reporting to Callaghan that the situation was more alarming than he had thought. Welsh extremism, he told the Home Secretary, was not confined to the imminent Investiture: it would be an ongoing problem needing constant policing. His recommendation that Wales should have a 'central intelligence agency' was accepted by the seven Welsh chief constables when they met at the Home Office with their opposite numbers from Gloucestershire, Cheshire and West Mercia, as well as the heads of the security services.[11] For the time being this function was to be performed by Jock Wilson's Shrewsbury Unit. In the longer term, the plan was for an organisation in which English forces would share responsibility for policing nationalist activity.[12]

The meeting in Room 101, occurring as it did only five weeks before the Investiture, also dealt at length with security arrangements for the Prince. Access to documents detailing these have been refused to the author, on the grounds that this would compromise national security. After a request under the Freedom of Information Act, the Home Office decided it was not in the public interest to 'disclose police tactics for dealing with terrorist threats in the past, as disclosure would undermine current and future operations for dealing with similar threats'.[13]

Some insight into the scale of the security operation has been obtained, however, from a document declassified by the Home Office and deposited in the Public Record Office. Reliable radio communications were essential during the ceremony and throughout the three days of the Prince's Royal Progress through Wales, when he would be even more vulnerable to attack. W. O. Nichol, Director of Telecommunications at the GPO, briefed the high-ranking police, army officers and security chiefs assembled in Room 101 on the complex network of communications in place for the ceremony and beyond. Nothing was left to chance. Barbed-wire entanglements were erected around radio stations to prevent sabotage, and helicopters were flying round-the-clock patrols along every mile of the Prince's route. Telecommunication depots, stores, water pipelines and public buildings were under constant surveillance.

In the event that the main hilltop radio relay stations were knocked out, the Civil Defence was on standby to provide emergency fixed radio contact. Police motorcyclists had all been equipped with mobile radio sets linking directly to the regional crime squads and Special Branch. Caernarfon Castle had been sealed off for several weeks, closed circuit television and armed patrols preventing insurgents from approaching within several hundred yards. From Nichol's 'Signal Plan for the Investiture' it is possible to gauge the heightened sense of alarm, at a time when the police were no nearer apprehending the bombers than they had been when the sabotage started three years previously. Very specifically, Nichol had been told to provide telecommunications 'protection and counter-measures to deal with subversive activity, direct attack or interference with the communications of the law and order forces'. All this was to be in place well in advance of the Investiture, because incidents were expected in the weeks before the main event.[14]

Another tool in the fight against extremism was demonstrated to security chiefs attending the summit. The Home Office man Frank Williamson had been concerned at the delay by scenes-of-crime officers in detecting traces of explosive substances on suspects. If they were to catch the bombers, police needed to act more quickly than the existing procedure permitted, which then involved sending suspect pieces of evidence to the nearest forensic science laboratory for examination. At Williamson's request, the laboratory developed a mobile testing kit to detect small traces of explosive on the hands or property of persons suspected of handling explosives. Unfortunately, one of the chemicals used in the kit was concentrated sulphuric acid, corrosive and likely to cause severe burns if spilled.[15]

# 11

## THE ABERGELE MARTYRS

One immediate result of this final security summit before the Investiture was that a company of Royal Engineers was placed on standby by the Ministry of Defence to repair roads, bridges and railway lines in the event of sabotage. Prime Minister Harold Wilson also asked for troops to be deployed to guard key installations. Callaghan's Private Secretary at the Home Office (soon to become new Permanent Under-Secretary at the Home Office), Brian Cubbon, assured the Prime Minister that the necessary security precautions were in place, although it had not proved possible to guard every vulnerable point. Caernarfon Castle and the bridge over which guests would pass had been guarded since 1 June, while teams of detectives had checked all the premises along the processional route:

> The Security Service has identified important vulnerable points throughout Wales and in the border counties and the chief constables concerned have been advised of the need for suitable precautions. Precautions have been taken and, as the date of the Investiture approaches, they have been stepped up. All the most important points are being watched or frequently visited by the police.[1]

Wilson was especially concerned for the safety of the Royal Train and the two others carrying VIP guests, including himself and half his Cabinet, from London to Caernarfon. It was no secret that after leaving Windsor the Royal Train, with the Prince and members of the Royal Family, would, as customary, spend the night in a siding somewhere en route, before proceeding to north Wales, where it would be at greatest risk. Only days before the Investiture Wilson issued instructions for either a scheduled service or decoy train to traverse the track immediately ahead of the Royal Train, so that if the line was booby-trapped the decoy would take the full blast.[2] The same precaution would be taken when the Prince left Wales from Cardiff at the end of his Royal Progress on 5 July. No one appears to have expressed concern that a scheduled service was being suggested as a decoy.[3]

As it happened, apart from the 2,500 servicemen engaged on ceremonial duties, no additional troops would be deployed to guard the Prince.[4] The first that the Secretary of State for Defence, Denis Healey, knew about the Prime Minister's request for troops was five days before the Investiture, proving that the lack of cooperation was not confined to the Welsh police forces. The Defence Ministry took the view that a large-scale troop movement into Wales at that late stage risked creating the impression of a country on a war footing. In the circumstances, three Royal Artillery Sioux helicopters were dispatched to fly dawn-to-dusk missions across the whole of north Wales, the West Midlands and Cheshire, patrolling water pipelines, dams, roads and other public installations.[5]

While the government was fretting about security, MAC2 was preparing to plant four bombs to disrupt the Investiture. The first target was a memorial stone marking the spot on McKenzie Pier, Holyhead, where the young Prince of Wales had first set foot in Wales in 1958. It was also where he would board the Royal Yacht *Britannia* for a private dinner immediately following his Investiture on 1 July. With only days to go, Prime Minister Wilson's confidence in the security arrangements was badly shaken when No. 10 was told that an unexploded bomb had been found propped against the foot of the memorial stone on McKenzie Pier. Wilson, still unsure whether to allow the Investiture to proceed, demanded an immediate report from Home Secretary Callaghan, who in turn asked for this in a personal telephone call to the Chief Constable of Gwynedd.

It was shortly before 7 o'clock on the morning of 25 June when a blue canvas shopping bag, fifteen inches by nine inches with one side completely cut away, was found by James Crookston, a 50-year-old crane driver from Brighton, as he arrived for work with two mates at a jetty they were building at Holyhead harbour. The bag contained eleven sticks of dynamite, weeping and dangerously unstable. A fully charged battery and a badly corroded electric detonator, although still in working order, were wired to a Smith's alarm clock set to go off six hours later.[6] Assuming it was a perfectly harmless shopping bag mislaid by a holidaymaker, the crane driver peeped inside, before dropping it like a hot potato at the sight of the gelignite and the sound of ticking. Shouting a warning to his workmates, the three 'ran like hell' to the nearest police station. Meanwhile, back at the pier four Holyhead Council workmen, quite unaware of the commotion, continued hanging Investiture bunting around a ceremonial arch surmounted by a gilt crown, beneath which the Prince of Wales was due to pass before embarking on the *Britannia*. The bomb could have gone off at any time, blowing the commemorative plinth to pieces, according to Major Clifton Jefferies, head of Western Command's bomb disposal unit, who disarmed the device.[7]

If strong words could have blown away the threat to the Prince of Wales, then there were plenty. 'A vile act totally detestable to the people of Wales' was Welsh Secretary George Thomas's reaction to the McKenzie Pier bomb. For Cledwyn Hughes, Minister of Agriculture, in whose Anglesey constituency the bomb was planted, this was 'a wicked act which could have had the most appalling consequences'. For the Tories Welsh Affairs spokesman, David Gibson-Watt, the bombers were 'lunatics with no respect for what 99 per cent of Welsh people are thinking'. Even Gwynfor Evans, the Plaid Cymru leader, disowned the extremists as deserving 'the outright condemnation of all decent people'. What was certain, observed Welsh Liberal Party leader Emlyn Hooson, was that 'the whole atmosphere of Welsh life has been changed for the worse by talk of bomb outrages, terrorism and threats'.[8]

But the discovery of the McKenzie Pier bomb did produce a breakthrough in the investigation. Within twenty-four hours three young employees of Anglesey County Council planning department were arrested and questioned in connection with the incident, only because they were known to be outspoken critics of the Investiture. All three were named Jones – William Glyn Jones (22), of Trearddur Bay, Anglesey, Dewi Jones (22), from Porthmadoc, and John Allan Jones (20), from Tŷ Groes, Anglesey. While none was suspected of planting the device, Dewi and Glyn Jones were implicated in assembling it. Dewi Jones, killed later in a road accident, was certainly a member of MAC2, the others suspected of being part of the same cell through their association with him. The only contact that the cell leader Dewi Jones had was with an unidentified person, linked to what he only ever knew as 'The Organisation'. When arrested, Glyn Jones's left hand tested positive for traces of nitroglycerine. Fibres similar to those on the holdall were found on Dewi Jones's clothing. Glyn Jones and Dewi Jones would be jailed for eighteen months for offences concerned with explosives, Allan Jones for six months, suspended for two years, for offences connected with petrol-bomb experiments. A scrap of paper with the name, allegedly, of an IRA contact in Dublin was found in Allan Jones's car.[9]

Mr John Gower, QC, who defended one of the accused – and who had appeared for one of the defendants in the Free Wales Army trial – spoke of the three Joneses being caught up in a 'whirlwind of violence' at a time of terrible tension in Wales:

> Unfortunately, one's experience of public events in this country rams home the lesson that where there is division and unrest there are also subversive people willing to take advantage of it in order that the seeds of unrest may produce the whirlwind of violence.[10]

According to John Jenkins, the McKenzie Pier bomb was planted by one of the four 'units' sent to disrupt the Investiture. Another unit comprised Alwyn Jones

The 'Abergele Martyrs' George Taylor (left) and Alwyn Jones (right), who blew themselves to pieces while on their way, some say, to plant a bomb on the route of the train carrying the Prince of Wales to Caernarfon for his Investiture.

(22), of Glasrafon, Abergele, and his friend George Taylor (37), a father of three from Ffordd-y-Morfa, Maes Canol, Abergele. Eighteen months previously, Jones and Taylor had successfully blown up the Snowdonia Country Club near Caernarfon. Now, on the evening of 30 June, the eve of the Investiture, their target was a government building just a few hundred yards from the railway line along which the Royal Train was expected to pass, carrying Prince Charles and the Royal Family to Caernarfon for the Investiture. After finishing a game of darts at the Castle Hotel, Abergele, the pair collected a ladder and set off through the middle of the town, a paint pot dangling from the end. The pot contained a fifty-stick gelignite bomb, the largest ever assembled by the saboteurs, and clearly intended for a major target. Both men worked for Abergele Urban District Council, Jones a labourer, Taylor a painter, and they probably guessed that no one would see anything unusual in them carrying a ladder through the centre of town, even at that time of night on the eve of the Investiture

Stopping in a narrow passageway between Ministry of Health and Social Security offices off Market Street, they were thought to be assembling the bomb when it exploded prematurely, possibly because they tested it after the detonator was connected. The two men were blown to pieces, the body of Jones found forty yards away, and that of his accomplice, Taylor, stripped of all its clothing by the force of the blast. What remained of the pair was unrecognisable.

At the inquest, the West Denbighshire coroner Mr E. Talog Davies returning verdicts of accidental death, said:

> These men had no business to be handling explosives. Someone who knew more about explosives than they had given either one or both of them a substantial quantity, and you may well think that the greatest responsibility for their deaths lies with these people … I may say quite clearly they were not trying to injure anyone. It would have been extremely unlikely anyone would have been walking along that passageway at that time. A more futile exercise is hard to imagine. These two men without any reason we know of decided they wanted to cause an explosion at that point. They set up the explosive and one wire could have touched the other. I imagine something like that happened.[11]

Whether the pair intended to bomb the Social Security office at Abergele or the Royal Train, due to pass along the railway line a few hundred yards away, is disputed. John Jenkins, who supplied the Abergele bomb already assembled in a shoebox, says the target was the government offices. Other former members of MAC2 disagree because they see no reason in selecting the Social Security office, other than for its proximity to the main north Wales railway line.[12] When the bomb went off, the Royal Train was already on its way, but running late, after a fifty-minute delay at Crewe while police investigated a report of a bomb on the line. All they found was an alarm clock with sticks of plasticine attached.

Whatever Taylor and Jones had as their target, their deaths were a massive jolt that forced MAC2 to face the consequences of escalating their campaign of violent direct action. Neither man was on the police radar, even though they had bombed the Snowdonia Country Club. All that was known locally was that both were nationalists, particularly concerned about a threat to the town's Welsh character by a council plan to build a large new housing estate at Abergele.

The first that Sergeant John Jenkins of the Royal Army Dental Corps knew of Taylor and Jones's deaths was the following morning, when an army captain opened the flap of his tent on a disused army site near Caernarfon and said, 'We got two of the bastards.' Jenkins was a member of the army contingent on ceremonial duties for the Investiture, his job to look after anyone with the toothache. Desperate to know what had gone wrong, he hurried across to the sergeants' mess. They were watching football on television, joking and expressing delight that two Welsh extremists had died. 'I had a part to play and show that as a member of the Army I, too, was delighted with what had occurred. But inside it was killing me', said Jenkins.[13]

Years later, on his discharge from Albany Jail on the Isle of Wight after serving ten years as a category A prisoner, the very first thing Jenkins did was buy a rail ticket to Holyhead. The moment the prison gates closed, Special Branch officers were on his tail, on the assumption that the Holyhead rail ticket meant a ferry to Ireland, then in the throes of the Troubles. But Jenkins left the train at Abergele, where a friend was waiting, and together they went to the graves of Taylor and Jones to pay their respects. Taylor and Jones would be the only fatalities for whom MAC2 was directly responsible. Why that bomb went off prematurely has haunted Jenkins all his life:

> I had only ever met Taylor once. I still don't understand why the bomb I gave them exploded prematurely. All my bombs had a fail-safe device so they could be tested without going off. They were always delivered fully made-up in a shoebox. One theory is that they were killed by the Security Services.[14]

The deaths of the two saboteurs within yards of where the Royal Train was due to pass might have been expected to have had widespread repercussions. Owen Williams, then in Ireland after having been advised by police to leave Wales for the duration of the Investiture, discovered what had happened after asking why the Irish Tricolour was flying at half-mast above Sinn Fein party headquarters in Thomas Ash Hall, Cork. Picking up a local newspaper he read that it was as a mark of respect for 'two Welsh freedom fighters killed in Abergele while trying to stop the Investiture of the Prince of Wales'.

In Britain, where the police were no nearer catching the mastermind behind the bombing campaign, the Establishment had, however, successfully refocused public attention away from the activities of a small group of fanatics on to a ceremonial occasion only a few steps behind a coronation in its significance. The hunt for the bombers was slowly overtaken by time and a determination that since the pageant had to go ahead, it would be without a hitch. The embossed commemorative chairs for the four thousand guests had been delivered, so had the bulletproof vest for Prince Charles to wear beneath his regalia, capable of stopping an assassin's bullet at short range.[15]

For its part, the *Western Mail* did its level best to show the world that Wales was not awash with revolutionaries causing mayhem: that the majority of Welsh people waited in excited anticipation and adoration for Charles to be crowned Prince of Wales. Opposition was given as little space as possible. While it was impossible to rewrite the historical record of a Prince foisted upon a conquered nation, the *Western Mail* tried hard to ignore it.

What better man to reconcile the Prince's German descent with Celtic blood than that curious royal invention, the Wales Herald Extraordinary, created by the Queen in 1963 specifically to officiate at the Investiture when the Prince came of age? Squadron Leader David Checketts, equerry to Prince Charles, asked the *Western Mail* if it would publish an article written by the first Herald Extraordinary, Major Francis Jones, vindicating the anointment of the Prince of Wales by proving from the genealogical record that he had descended from all the main dynasties that formerly ruled Wales.

The angry response to the subsequent headline, 'How the Prince got his Welsh blood', filled the *Western Mail* postbag for days afterwards, hardly surprising in view of Major Jones's conclusion that,

> Genealogically, Prince Charles is as good a Welshman as any of us. He is a link between us and our storied past. When he comes to Wales, he comes to the Land of *his* fathers in a very special sense, among friends and kindred, his own people.[16]

Readers in the Welsh-speaking heartlands were nauseated by the newspaper's toadyism, their disgust rattling the editor into casting around for something to alleviate their sense of betrayal. The best the *Western Mail* could come up with was an article by the eminent Cambridge University archaeologist Dr Glyn Daniel, extolling Wales, the Celtic nation, but still managing to avoid any mention of the native princes. 'Not a race,' Dr Daniel wrote, 'but a Celtic nation defined by a matter of political geography after the pagan Saxons designated the area between the Irish Sea and Offa's Dyke as the land of the *wealas*, the foreigners, the people on the other side.' This did little to repair bridges with the newspaper's large Welsh readership.

Few of the hundreds of journalists descending on 'the Principality' bothered to investigate the strength of opposition to the Investiture or reasons for it. A process rooted in 800 years of cultural assimilation that had transformed Wales into an economic and social dependency was hardly the stuff of headlines. After a brief look at Caernarfon Castle, most correspondents headed back to Cardiff to get the official line from those of us at the *Western Mail* and BBC briefed to describe all opposition as belonging to the lunatic fringe. Being Welsh had long since been reduced to an exercise in diffidence. At a time of economic crisis the historical record could not be allowed to threaten the Holy Grail of inward investment.

The unrest in Wales was not seen through quite the same eyes in post-colonial Africa. One African newspaper spoke of Wales as being 'a small nation struggling for independence under the bureaucratic boots of Whitehall'. But most foreign observers failed to tear themselves away from the lyrical and romantic *How Green was My Valley* vision of a land filled with hymn-singing miners. *Time*, one of the most prestigious American publications to preview the Investiture, commented, 'Welshmen break into song as readily as lesser men tell jokes, and after an evening in any Welsh public-house it is perfectly possible to believe that all who sing off-key are packed off to England at the age of 15.'[17]

Nearer home, criticism of the restless natives was dismissive, at best condescending.

According to Paul Ferris, writing in the *Observer*, 'for every ardent patriot with Welsh on his lips and a mad dream of freedom in his brain, you can find ten Welshmen who are hardly more than Welsh-Englishmen'. The *Observer*'s conclusion was that there were simply not enough patriots around in Wales to make a revolution; that the opposition the Investiture had provoked was more a post-mortem by the Welsh on their fellow men, language and culture. Above all else, the Welsh suffered from their well-known inferiority complex. Other commentators thought that Welsh nationalism had had its heyday, the idea of separatism spurned by all but the extremists. Rather than revolt, the Welsh had cause to be grateful for the attention lavished on them by the Wilson government. Neither was such disparagement confined to English writers. Goronwy Rees, writing in the *Daily Mirror*, thought 'there are far more important, more interesting and more urgent matters in the world today than the condition of a small and poor country'. Ironically, the disdain of a fellow Welshman came from an academic and author who, thirty years later, was revealed to have been the fifth man in the Soviet espionage ring recruited by Guy Burgess in the 1930s.[18]

Despite the loud noises off-stage, Wales could not stop one of the great ceremonials in English history. It did not help that the opposition to it was divided. The protests organised by the Anti-Investiture Campaign Committee were identified with republicanism and the struggle for independence; that organised by Plaid Cymru and Cymdeithas yr Iaith Gymraeg regarded this as an opportunity to relaunch the language campaign. Special Branch officers mingled with the crowd of several hundred language activists who, after laying wreaths at the foot of the great slab of granite that serves as a memorial to Llywelyn's death at Cilmeri, listened to a tape-recorded message from Saunders Lewis before dispersing.

The Anti-Investiture Campaign Committee, supported by MAC2, had hatched an ambitious plot to kidnap R. O. F. Wynne of Ruthin, reputed to be a direct descendant of the last native Prince of Wales. Since Wynne had consented to this – and had twice stood bail for the committee's leader, Owen Williams – it was more of a conspiracy than a kidnapping. After blocking all the main roads, Caernarfon Castle was to be seized and Wynne crowned as Prince of Wales. But as the day approached the opposition melted away, leaving MAC2's chief bomb-maker, Sgt. John Jenkins, providing dental care for the troops on ceremonial duty – at other times wandering around Caernarfon and being abused by locals on account of his uniform.

# 12

## THE BIG DAY

The morning of the twenty-first Investiture of a Prince of Wales dawned dry and bright. Light drizzle was forecast for later, but at least the weather was not expected to disrupt the pageant. By 10 a.m., almost four hours before the ceremony was due to start, some of the VIP guests were already taking their seats inside the medieval walls, on crimson chairs bearing the motif of the Prince's three feathers embossed in gold and black. Any guest wanting a memento of the great occasion could buy a chair for £80.

The tradition of investing the male heir to the throne of England as Prince of Wales began in 1301. After completing the conquest of Wales in 1283 with the death of the last native Prince of Wales in the ambush at Cilmeri, Edward I began the construction of Caernarfon Castle as part of a chain of fortifications to encompass Gwynedd. The suppression of the Welsh coincided with the birth of his son in the castle's Eagle Tower in 1284, Edward reputedly presenting the child to the Welsh as 'the native-born prince who could speak no English'. Raised in the royal court, the language the prince eventually spoke was Norman French, his presentation as a native-born prince thought to be apocryphal, as it was not mentioned until three centuries later.

Although never completed, Caernarfon Castle withstood sieges and defied the rebellious army of Owain Glyndŵr. Like a gun emplacement at the entrance to the Menai Straits, its sheer granite walls rise from the water's edge as a reminder of 800 years of subjugation. Ironically, it was a Welshman, the former Liberal Prime Minister David Lloyd George, who revived the pageant in 1911 for Edward VIII after it had been dormant for several centuries.

Set at the very heart of this great fortress and enacted before the most powerful people in the land, the Investiture symbolised for many the reaffirmation of ownership, in the unfurling of the Prince's banner above the Eagle Tower as his procession entered the concourse, to a fanfare of trumpets. To the dismay of nationalists, the Prince's procession was led by Archdruid Gwyndaf and the President of the National Eisteddfod Court, Cynan, guardians of the last bastion of Wales's cultural independence.

Wearing the uniform of Colonel-in-Chief of the Royal Regiment of Wales, the twenty-year-old prince was followed by the Queen Mother in pale apple-green, Princess Margaret in pink and Princess Anne in a shade of turquoise, and a sea of red, gold and blue. On reaching the dais the Prince knelt on a scarlet cushion before the Queen as the Letters Patent were read, first in English by the Home Secretary, James Callaghan. According to the *Western Mail*, the Prince gave 'a full warm smile' as the Queen girded him with a sword and invested him

Queen Elizabeth II invests her son as Prince of Wales at Caernarfon Castle on 1 July 1969. Copyright: *Western Mail*, Cardiff.

The ceremonial procession through Caernarfon following the Investiture of the Prince of Wales. Copyright: *Western Mail*, Cardiff.

with the insignia of his Principality and Earldom of Chester: coronet, mantle, gold ring and gold rod. When the crown was placed on his head Charles raised both hands, adjusting it to sit more comfortably. The only noticeable hitch was that Welsh Secretary George Thomas took too long reading the Welsh text of the Letters Patent, the Queen placing the ermine mantle around the Prince's shoulders a shade too soon.

The ceremony was a fairly brief affair, although long enough for a 16-year-old Army Cadet of the Royal Welch Fusiliers who fainted behind the dais, where he lay covered with blankets until it was all over. By the time the newly invested Prince of Wales came to address his subjects from a castle balcony, drizzle was falling and storm clouds gathering across the Menai Straits. But with a smile and evident pride in his new Principality, he dedicated himself to the service of Wales, 'whatever the demands may be': 'It is indeed my firm intention to associate myself in word and deed with as much of the life of the Principality as possible. And what a Principality. To do so I seek your co-operation and understanding.'[1]

Few of the 4,000 guests noticed that the celebratory twenty-one-gun salute at the conclusion of the ceremony actually added up to twenty-two, the last

Caernarfon Castle, where the first Prince of Wales was invested by his father Edward I after Welsh resistance was finally crushed and the Welsh subjugated at the end of the thirteenth century.

report a derisory augmentation detonated by MAC2 in Love Lane, at the bottom of the Chief Constable's garden. Several days later bomb disposal experts found the crater and parts of the timing device, embedded in a tree. The *Western Mail* reported that not even 'an angry puff of Welsh extremism' could disrupt the standing ovation the shy young prince received from his guests. Cheers followed him all the way as his carriage headed out of the castle, past the ironmonger's yard where MAC2's fourth bomb was hidden, though it failed to explode until five days later. At the Ferodo Works, Charles transferred to a car for the journey to McKenzie Pier, Holyhead, and a banquet aboard the Royal Yacht *Britannia*. As he did so, the band of the Royal Regiment of Wales played *Charlie is My Darling*.

Across Wales a chain of twenty beacons was lit at the end of a triumphant day. The one disappointment was the small turnout. Instead of the 250,000 expected in Caernarfon, officials estimated 70,000, blaming this on the televising of the proceedings. By the evening, however, the street celebrations around the castle were augmented by 2,700 troops, released from their ceremonial duties. It was their first night out for several days, having been confined to barracks for fear of being infiltrated by subversives, the most important of whom, John Jenkins, was already in their midst.

Back at the *Western Mail* I was satisfied our coverage had gone like clock-work. On set-piece occasions most of the words are written in advance, leaving the reporter to top and tail with an adjective or two where appropriate. By 9 o'clock that evening the editor, in Caernarfon with his £80 chair as a guest at the Investiture, felt it was safe enough to reward the reporting team with a crate of beer for a job well done. Based at a hotel within the shadow of the castle walls, the six reporters soon polished off their bonus and were well into a lot more when all hell broke loose. Mansel Jones, normally our district reporter at Aberystwyth but drafted in for the occasion, was screaming down the tele-phone at me, 'The castle is on fire. We can see the flames from here. There was an explosion.'

It's another bomb, I thought. After the explosion at Abergele the night before, the Investiture had so far passed without incident. Most of the Language Society activists were thinking of new campaigns, after their chairman Dafydd Iwan had exhorted them to turn the failed protest against the Investiture into a campaign 'to give the Welsh language its rightful place in Wales'. Apart from a youth who tossed a banana skin under the hooves of the Household Cavalry as it rode past, another pair of youngsters who made a V-sign at the Royal Carriage and someone who held up an anti-Investiture placard – each fined £5 – nothing had happened to disrupt the ceremony. The bomb in the ironmonger's yard that should have frightened the horses had not exploded. Nevertheless, no one expected the extremists to let the occasion pass without staging something spectacular. Now they had. They had bombed the castle!

For me and the night editor, John Cosslett, this was a critical moment in our careers. In front of us on the news desk was the front page-proof, waiting for our final approval before it became a metal plate bolted to a press spewing out 25,000 papers an hour, its twin sitting alongside producing an equal number. Besides a very large picture of the moment the Prince was invested by the Queen with his regalia, the page carried only two other stories: 'Joke in pub before killer blast', an account of the Abergele bombing the night before, and 'Three go to jail in FWA case', the report of the end of the Free Wales Army trial. It was what newspapermen call a strong page dominated by a single story. No one anticipated breaking news big enough to replace the set-piece account of the Investiture. Cosslett and I both knew that if extremists had indeed detonated a bomb inside the castle, even after the Prince had long gone, this meant an immediate front-page change, making the explosion the lead and demoting the Investiture from its top spot. It is at moments such as this that newspapermen earn their corn. Get it right and you are acclaimed for having a nose for news; get it wrong and no one will trust your judgement again. Weighing heavily upon us was that we were both mindful that the *Western Mail* considered itself a newspaper of record. What might historians make of a newspaper that replaced its account of the Investiture with a story of a very large firework exploding somewhere in the vicinity of the castle?

Thank heavens there were not too many occasions in my newspaper career when I was required to take a decision that was utterly irremediable, and for this to be taken within minutes and acted upon immediately. The Aberfan disaster in 1966 was one such occasion. The entire issue of the *Western Mail*, twenty-eight broadsheet pages, was devoted to the varied aspects of a single massive story. The picture of the school buried by thousands of tons of black slurry covered most of the front page, below it the headline that 144 had perished, 116 of these children. Just as we were about to start the presses that night I received a call from our London desk to the effect that the *Daily Mail* was claiming that twenty children had survived the horror. There had been no suggestion of this from the *Western Mail* team camped out in the Aberfan Hotel, our operational base for the duration. If it were true, then for the *Western Mail* to publish a story that there were no further survivors was unforgivable, not forgetting the terrible anguish this would cause parents clinging desperately to the slightest chance a loved one might still be found alive in the wreckage of the school. Denis Gane, leading our team in Aberfan, confirmed nothing was known of more survivors since the little girl had been carried to safety in the arms of a policeman, one of the most graphic disaster pictures ever published. Time was pressing, and Cosslett could not hold back the first edition much longer as I waited for Gane to get back to me. Within minutes he was on the line from the Aberfan Hotel. John O'Sullivan, one of the *Daily Mail* reporters covering the disaster, knew nothing about the story. The theory was the story had been developed on the news desk to give the *Daily Mail* the jump on its Fleet Street rivals. On that occasion Cosslett and I took the correct decision to stick with our original report. There were no other survivors.

The implication that the security surrounding Caernarfon Castle had been breached by extremists produced a similar explosion of adrenalin. The *Western Mail*'s front page was a celebration of the monarchy and its adoring Welsh subjects. The same theme continued across several inside pages. With some relief, it dawned on me the castle could not be on fire – it was built of stone, I shouted down the telephone to Mansel Jones, with instructions to check it out immediately. Minutes later, he was back with an update after a rapid sortie of the scene. It appeared that a Military Police Bedford van had exploded on the quay, close to the outer wall of the castle. Someone was trapped inside, but whether this was the work of a MAC2 bomber or not, there was no immediate way of knowing. Cosslett and I stared at each other, our news instinct telling us to lead with the explosion as a new front-page splash, relegating the account of the Investiture from the top spot. Given the extremist track-record, there was no reason to suppose it was not another bombing. But deciding to demote an event that was the equivalent of a Welsh Coronation was a huge call. Lingering in the back of my mind was the memory of being one of only three members of the *Western Mail* staff chosen to represent the newspaper at a gala banquet in London marking its hundredth anniversary, hosted by its Canadian owner, Lord Thomson, in the Ritz Hotel for a thousand guests, from royalty to ambassadors to prime ministers. And me – selected by the editor because I was acknowledged to be a safe and trusted pair of hands. At a stroke, while the editor was collecting his Investiture commemorative chair at Caernarfon, Cosslett and I could seriously dent the *Western Mail*'s reputation. We were both of a mind to update the front page with the account of the explosion on the quayside beneath the castle walls as the new lead. But before I had time to worry too much, Cosslett succeeded in reaching the editor, Giddings, on the telephone at his Caernarfon hotel. The instruction was to change nothing, even if the latest incident was the work of Welsh extremists. Eight paragraphs were cobbled together in a hurry under the headline 'Soldier killed in van blast'. It was the correct decision. As the night wore on, it emerged that Ronald Anthony Berry (21), from Northwood, Kirby, Liverpool, a corporal with a signals unit stationed at Llanddwrog Camp, Caernarfon, had been arrested for being drunk and disorderly and locked by his Military Police escort in the van on Slate Quay while they returned to the town centre. Petrol from an open jerrycan leaked through the floor of the van and was ignited, possibly by a discarded cigarette, apparently no one aware the young soldier was trapped inside when the vehicle exploded in flames. Not a terrorist attack, just an accident, but it testified to the prevailing edginess, when even a car backfiring could be another extremist bomb.[2]

The following day, when the Prince began his Royal Progress, no one would have guessed public opinion had been so divided over the Investiture. The Royal Yacht followed him down and around the west and south Wales coastlines, immediately on hand to provide a safe haven each night in a potentially dangerous country; not that there was any need for concern. Where once insurgents were suspected of lurking in every nook and cranny, there was bunting and pavements lined with flag-waving schoolchildren. Adoration replaced hostility. At every scheduled stop, establishment figures waited in line with a warm Welsh welcome, chests filled with pride, fluttering, perhaps, in anticipation of receiving a special Investiture honour. For three days exultation became a national pastime. For opponents, the sight was distressing. Not only had they failed to stop the Investiture, but the Prince of Wales, through royal patronage and presence, had shown that Welsh loyalty was easily bought.

The fourth of the bombs intended to disrupt the Investiture was a sorry metaphor for failure: it exploded late and hit the wrong target. On the day that the Prince of Wales's Royal Progress ended at Cardiff, ten-year-old Ian Cox, on holiday in Caernarfon from Chalfont St Giles, Buckinghamshire, climbed over a wall into an ironmonger's yard to retrieve his football. It was not the first time Ian and his five-year-old brother had kicked the ball into the yard for Ian to chase after. But this time his foot was badly injured by a bomb extremists had planted against some oil tanks to disrupt the Investiture five days previously. As in the case of the Abergele bomb that killed two saboteurs, the timing mechanism had misfired. Immediately afterwards, Gwynedd Police, on the instructions of its Chief Constable, issued a press statement to the effect there were no suspicious circumstances; that it was unconnected to extremist activity. That it was a bomb and not an accident came to light only after questions were asked in the House of Commons by the Merioneth MP, William Edwards, about conflicting statements emanating from Gwynedd Police. But when Frank Williamson, the Home Secretary's man on the spot in Wales, investigated, what he found was a damning indictment of the incompetence and obstructionism that had so frustrated the efforts of Commander Jock Wilson and his special squad to crack the conspiracy.

It was not until 12 July, seven days after the young boy was injured, that Williamson confronted Gwynedd's Chief Constable, the recalcitrant Colonel William Williams. The Home Office man was told in the clearest posssible terms that the policy of Gwynedd Police was to issue as few press statements as possible, a policy Williamson believed only aggravated the situation. Even then, after twenty acts of sabotage and a manifest threat to the life of the Prince of Wales – recognised by everyone, from the Prime Minister down – the autocratic Colonel Williams still resented the presence of Commander Jock Wilson's special squad. Now that the Investiture was over, he wanted it disbanded, in direct contradiction to Williamson's recommendation that the Shrewsbury Unit continue to operate, because there was no reason to assume that 'the activities of extremists will decline'.[3]

By now Williamson was openly contemptuous of the Gwynedd police operation and its stubborn chief constable. If the Home Office man had not intervened, then the three Jones boys accused in connection with the McKenzie Pier bomb would have been released on bail for the duration of the Investiture. Worse still, he suspected that vital prosecution evidence in that case had been leaked by a Gwynedd police officer.

The erroneous press statement issued by Gwynedd after the boy was injured in the ironmonger's yard was approved by the Chief Constable to 'allay public concern'. Gwynedd Police saw no significance in the 'few bits and pieces', comprising the remains of a tin, a sock bearing a boy's name, pieces of twisted metal, one PP6 battery, electric flex and detonator wire, recovered from around the seat of the explosion. It was not until Williamson telephoned the forensic science laboratory himself that he learned that parts of a clock also recovered from the scene had tested positive for explosives.

And there was worse. Despite all the undertakings given by the Chief Constable prior to the Investiture, no designated Special Branch officer was ever appointed by the force to liaise with Commander Wilson's special terrorism squad. The Home Secretary, James Callaghan, had asked for a detailed report of everything that had occurred at the time of the Investiture, but was told by Williamson he could not have it because the police incident-room at the Caernarfon headquarters had failed to compile a proper log of the incidents.[4]

Even seven days after the explosion in the ironmonger's yard it was evident to Williamson on investigating the blast that there was sufficient evidence to identify it as the work of extremists. The explosive charge had been placed at the foot of a paraffin storage tank, the base and side of which had been dented by the force of the blast. Fortunately, the sealed tank was empty, but the bomber would not have known this. Only three yards away, there was another tank containing paraffin – this just forty yards from the processional route. It was immediately clear to Williamson that the intention was to disrupt the Investiture by causing an explosion and fire. Although couched in diplomatic language, Williamson's report drew for the Home Secretary a picture of police incompetence:

> The result of my examination of all the facts in these cases has been to confirm in my mind the absolute need for the Shrewsbury office to continue.

> I have made due allowance in my comments for the impact made on the Gwynedd Constabulary by the Investiture. It should be realized, however, that part of the preparations for this occasion should have been the establishment of an efficient Special Branch unit. My impression that this arrangement has not been made is confirmed by the letter from the Chief Constable, Gwynedd, dated 8th July 1969 (copy attached). The contents of this letter appear to be a confession of failure to implement agreements made by the Chief Constable at various meetings that Shrewsbury could only operate with the support of a strong Special Branch unit. It is necessary once again to emphasize the need for Special Branch units in all forces affected by the activities of Welsh extremists.[5]

Williamson's recommendation for continuing vigilance inaugurated the era of the secret policeman.[6] Activists of all persuasions would, henceforth, be under constant surveillance. On the explicit directions of Home Secretary James Callaghan, nothing should be done to 'weaken the police security forces now available to counter Welsh extremism'. The team at Shrewsbury would remain for as long as was needed; warrants authorising the bugging of telephone lines would be issued when required; and Gwynedd Constabulary reconstructed to combat mid-twentieth-century subversives, its nineteenth-century chief constable retired gracefully.[7]

Whether it was because of the difficulties encountered in Wales or for the 'personal reasons' he cited, Commander Jock Wilson requested a transfer back to the Met. So did his number two, which meant a new team would lead the

Shrewsbury Unit for the next two years, during which 'the future pattern of Welsh extremism' was to be established. Detective Chief Superintendent C. Dixon and Detective Sergeant Ray Kendall, both from the Met's Special Branch, took over the special unit. Kendall, with more than twenty years' experience of counter-subversion, would eventually become head of Interpol. Still a tightly knit team of only seven, the other officers were recruited from Dyfed-Powys (two), South Wales, Gwent and Gwynedd, with two administrative staff from West Mercia. The realisation that the age of the 'secret policeman' had dawned for Wales sat uncomfortably with a nation that prided itself on freedom of speech and action, and for whom Special Branch was synonymous with 'political police'.

The concern of nationalists was not helped by the knowledge that the original name for the Special Branch was the 'Irish Special Branch', formed to suppress Irish nationalism. Many of its members had experience of fighting nationalism in Africa, Cyprus and Aden, fuelling Plaid Cymru's conviction that it was the government's intention to suppress the growth of Welsh nationalism, by whatever means necessary. Gwynfor Evans, Plaid's solitary Member of Parliament, raised this concern when, on the day of the Investiture, he condemned the Free Wales Army trial as 'political' and intended to discredit all nationalists:

> It was a dangerous precedent against which Welshmen and others who cherish the right of freedom of speech must be on their guard. Plaid Cymru rejects the idea of the FWA and will not admit its members into the party. Yet it is alarming when ideas whatever their character are put on trial in a court of law and this is what happened in this case. Finally, I must say that the police-state manner of the arrest of the nine men, following a swoop on their homes by a large fleet of police cars in the early hours of the morning was repugnant, and that keeping the men in solitary confinement while in prison was utterly abhorrent.[8]

Gwynfor Evans and other nationalist leaders would have had much more to complain about had they known at the time that one of the main reasons for the proposal to establish a 'Welsh intelligence agency' was Plaid's decision to contest every constituency in Wales at the 1970 General Election.[9] The Home Office feared 'there may be repercussions', in which event the Shrewsbury Unit would be useful as an intelligence-gathering centre.[10] Ferguson Smith, Commander of the Metropolitan Police Special Branch, agreed, as did Dennis Trevelyan, a former Principal Private Secretary to the Leader of the House of Commons. In Trevelyan's view, the Welsh police forces had 'completely failed to establish an intelligence organisation of their own', were uncooperative and did not know enough about Special Branch work. The activities of MAC2 had put Welsh nationalism bang in the middle of MI5's radar, to the extent that the

Home Office even contemplated asking ratepayers in Birmingham, Manchester and Liverpool who received water from Wales to contribute towards the cost of the increased intelligence presence in Wales.[11] While MAC2 was driven underground, only to resurface in another form a decade later, nationalists would, henceforth, be synonymous with extremism, and phone tapping commonplace. Was this the end for the Welsh freedom fighters? Might those fighting for constitutional change in future be treated in much the same way as militant Islamic fundamentalists?[12]

# 13

## ARREST AND CONVICTION

The deaths of three men – two saboteurs and a soldier – and the maiming of a ten-year-old boy when he climbed into the ironmonger's yard were blamed by John Jenkins on those who imposed the Investiture on Wales. A draft 'statement' found in his home, and allegedly written by him on the back of Army-issue notepaper, was, according to police, intended to be issued to the media by Jenkins as a eulogy to the dead men, whom he described as 'heroes tired of licking boots with a smile':

> For our men who died, we weep. For their wives and children we feel great sorrow. But we hope that in time they will realise the nobility of their husbands and fathers who could not live with their consciences and died trying to be free. It is strange that no character assassination has taken place regarding our dead, but again, on deep reflection, perhaps it is not. Sober, respectable married men who liked their pints and their darts, one of them married to a charming West Indian girl, so it would be rather futile to fit them into the category of yobbos.

On the injury to the small boy, the statement added: 'Words would be wasted on those who set up a fund for a child whose parents came perhaps unknowingly to exult in the domination of our nation by theirs.'[1] Not only was the statement never issued, Jenkins adamantly denies having written it. If the original that helped convict Jenkins exists, then it is probably contained in a file of exhibits prepared for his trial, but still closed to the public after the Lord Chancellor extended the thirty-year closure rule.

The hunt for MAC2 did not end with the Investiture, although Jenkins felt reasonably secure hiding out in the bosom of the Army at Saighton Camp. Indeed, he was planning further explosions, the first of these at the South Stack Radio Relay Station on Holyhead Mountain, Anglesey. The station relayed messages between Ireland and Britain, and Jenkins reckoned on disrupting communications by knocking it out. For this, he approached Wynne Jones, a Holyhead ferry man. Jones had previously been assigned to plant the McKenzie Pier bomb, the various parts of which were delivered in a carrier bag to his home by Jenkins and Alders. When Jones's wife asked what might happen to her husband if he was caught, Jenkins replied, 'I'm the one they are trying to catch, but they will never catch me because I am too clever for them.' The carrier bag contained eight sticks of gelignite wrapped in greaseproof paper. In another package was an alarm clock. No one explained how to assemble the bomb, but Wynne Jones figured it out for himself.[2]

Every day, on his way to join the ferry at Holyhead Harbour, Jones passed the commemorative stone MAC2 wanted destroyed. It was a busy place, and an explosion would almost certainly have injured someone, so he abandoned the mission, deciding instead to hide the explosives in a disused farm on Holyhead Mountain. Later he told police he was more surprised than anyone when a bomb was found in a carrier bag at the foot of the McKenzie Pier memorial.

Some weeks later on 14 August 1969 part of that explosives cache was used to blow out the windows of the Relay Station on South Stack. The remainder was eventually detonated in Holyhead Park.[3] The very last bomb built by Jenkins was given to Alders to plant outside a building in Chester. By now a very worried man, Alders fixed the device so that it would not explode.[4]

Jenkins first suspected that the police were on to him in October 1969 when he was approached by a police officer as he repaired a set of false teeth in the dental centre. The officer wanted him to act as an agent provocateur. Having discovered Jenkins was born in the Valleys, the proposition was that he returned to south Wales to renew his contacts at the Halfway public house in Bargoed, then a haunt for republican nationalist supporters. Suspecting a trap, Jenkins agreed to do it, on condition he was given a letter explaining that he was working undercover.[5] That was the last he heard of it. But it was a warning that the gelignite, stacked in a locker at the dental centre, needed a new hiding-place. Alders had married a few weeks earlier, Jenkins his best man, so they stashed the explosives beneath some linoleum in a cupboard in the newly-weds' house.

A month later the police were back, catching up with Jenkins on a Saturday night as he left the TA Centre, dressed in his distinctive red bandsman's uniform. This time the story was that money was missing from the band's funds and he was to accompany them to Wrexham police station. 'When I asked how long it would take, they said "just ten minutes" … but it was ten years before I returned', was how Jenkins described his last moments of freedom. Held on remand with Alders at Risley in adjoining cells, Alders one night shouted through the bars that the police had offered him a deal. Jenkins told the younger man to take it. After all, Alders had been married only a few months.

The deal was a lighter sentence in exchange for a confession that helped convict Jenkins.[6]

Moved to Shrewsbury Prison to await trial at Flintshire Assizes, Jenkins agreed to be interviewed by representatives of the security services. It might help his case, his solicitor explained, as he was ushered into a room to face ten men in dark suits asking about MAC2:

> They couldn't understand this was an indigenous fightback. Because they knew from my army record that I had served in Cyprus and Germany, they tried to prove I had accomplices there. They refused to believe we were acting on our own. Yes, we did have dealings with 'Red' Rudi Dutschke, the East German Marxist. It was he who contacted us, not the other way around. The authorities couldn't understand why Dutschke suddenly left a conference in London to travel to Swansea. Dutschke wanted to organise us but we said no. As for the IRA, one or two came over for a chat but there was no alliance, no specific arrangements. The Breton National Army offered us an alliance, training facilities, safe houses. But there was nothing in it for us at that stage. Harri Webb was our go-between with the Bretons. Dai Pritchard had the IRA contacts. It was he who got me involved with MAC2. He had been a member of MAC1 but apart from providing a safe house and a meal for members, Pritchard wasn't active in MAC2. At the time I was arrested we were planning to take our campaign to London. Big Ben, the symbol at the centre of Empire, was the target. The News at Ten was always accompanied by the strokes of Big Ben. Initial planning proved it was feasible. Whatever we did had to be seen as being relevant to the then current situation in the country. Our aim in planting bombs was always the nuisance value and damage they would cause without hurting anyone.[7]

Jenkins faced nineteen assorted charges linked to the extremist bombing campaign, fifteen of these jointly with Alders. The charges related to conspiracy to cause explosions between January 1966 and November 1969, procuring and counselling people unknown to cause explosions, possessing and supplying explosives, breaking and entering, and theft. The explosives found in Alders's house were traced back to Saighton Camp, where Jenkins's car and a pair of gloves found in a coat pocket tested positive for nitroglycerine. Jenkins said nothing during his police interrogation, denying all nineteen charges against him. Alders admitted to eight joint charges, his not guilty plea to seven others accepted by the prosecution in exchange for his confession.[8]

Seven days into a trial that was expected to last several weeks, even months, Jenkins, to the surprise of his defence team, suddenly changed his plea to guilty on the same eight charges Alders had already admitted. As the evidence was produced, he had become increasingly concerned that if the case continued the identities of other members of MAC2 would be revealed. Much later he confided:

> We had 20 members or so divided into self-contained cells. There was no contact between the cells other than the contact each cell leader had with me. Even though they recognised my face, the cell leaders never knew who I was. If they had been offered a million pounds to inform on me they couldn't because they had no idea who I was. The communication was very much one-way, from me to them, a system that would later be copied by the Provisional IRA. I carried the bombs in the back of my car. No one knew I would be arriving with a bomb in a shoebox. But I knew certain people went to certain places on certain nights of the week. I would arrive there with the bomb and detailed instructions about the target. They were left to do the job.[9]

On 20 April 1970 Sgt. John Bernard Jenkins (36), of Range Road, Wrexham, was jailed for ten years and his accomplice Frederick Ernest Alders (21), an aerial rigger of Pearson Street, Rhos, Wrexham, for six years. They have never met or spoken to each other since that day. Alders had given evidence against Jenkins to 'cleanse his whole being', according to his barrister Mr Alun Talfan Davies, QC. Once the younger man had come under the influence of Jenkins, a man of 'status, experience and authority', and helped to plant the first bomb, on the pipeline at Llanrhaeadr-ym-Mochnant, there was no turning back. The judge in the trial was Mr Justice Thompson, who had also presided in the Free Wales Army trial. Jailing the real bombers, he expressed the hope the sentences would discourage others from taking extremist measures in pursuit of an independent Wales.

'"Wales disowns you", terrorists are told' was how the *Western Mail* splashed the verdict across its front page. From my recollection this was the first time the saboteurs were actually described as terrorists. In fairness, it was the *Western Mail* that used the word, not Mr Justice Thompson, although the judge did condemn the two men for a terror campaign that might well have landed them in prison for life, adding:

> The motives prompting you were not personal gain but a misguided motive that you were patriotically promoting the interests of Wales. But you were not. Wales will not approve or applaud what you have done. On the contrary she will condemn the terror you contrived to spread by your wicked deeds. Wales will disclaim and disown such methods of promoting her interests and those who use such methods. She will expect you to be punished both for your own misdeeds and to discourage others who might be disposed to imitate you.[10]

In purporting to speak for Wales, the judge was only echoing the published sentiments of politicians and the Establishment. No one asked the Welsh public what it thought about the campaign of sabotage and the reasons for it. The only test of public opinion, by the *Western Mail* almost three years previously, after the Temple of Peace bombing, indicated substantial support for the struggle for independence to which the bombers were committed.

The unexpected decision by Jenkins to change his plea to guilty on the eight charges, and the jury's acceptance of his not guilty pleas on others, have left a lot of questions unanswered, not least the extent of the extremist organisation. Because of the geographical spread of the various incidents, it is manifestly clear the pair were not alone. Indeed, they were only ever convicted, by their own admission, on three counts of actually causing explosions: at Llanrhaeadr-ym-Mochnant, at Lake Vyrnwy and at Hapsford, Cheshire. Additionally, they pleaded guilty to procuring and counselling unknown people to blow up the Tax Office at Llanishen, Cardiff, and with supplying explosives for the McKenzie Pier time-bomb at Holyhead. The other charges related to the break-in at Hafod colliery explosives store, with the all-embracing one of conspiracy to cause explosions between January 1966 and November 1969. This last charge conveniently terminated the police hunt for others involved in the insurgency.

So who did cause the explosion at Clywedog Dam in 1966? Not Jenkins or Alders, since neither was involved with MAC2 at that time. Two men, Marcus Gale (27), a waste-paper sorter, of Abbey Road, Llangollen, and Harry Hones (25), an ex-miner, of Heol Avon, Cefn Mawr, near Wrexham, fell under suspicion, but police were later satisfied that neither had anything to do with the affair. Both were placed on probation after admitting possessing explosives.[11]

Clywedog is not the only unsolved act of sabotage. No one has to this day been charged with sabotaging the Tax Office at Llanishen, Cardiff, the Temple of Peace (Cardiff), the Welsh Office (Cardiff), Police Headquarters (Cardiff), Central Electricity Generating Board Offices (Cardiff), the pipeline at West Hagley (Cheshire), or with planting the bomb on McKenzie Pier (Holyhead) and the bombs in the ironmonger's yard (Caernarfon) and Love Lane (Caernarfon).

The sudden end to the Jenkins/Alders trial caught most of the media unprepared. Behind the scenes of every large showcase trial, press and television prepare their background stories in anticipation of a conviction. None of these can be published until the trial ends, unless the editor wants to go to jail for contempt. From the moment a jury returns a guilty verdict the convicted person is fair game for the sometimes exaggerated accounts newspapers are waiting to roll out about his or her life and times. On such occasions half a fact carries the force of a sworn affidavit, and rumours are assumed corroborated, because convicts are generally deemed to have no rights or reputation to impugn.

According to the *Western Mail*'s background story, Jenkins 'peeped through a crack in the curtains whenever someone knocked on the door'. The man described by the prosecution at his trial as a 'clever, ruthless fanatical' head of a terrorist organisation had good reason to check who was calling. That Alders, his co-defendant, confessed to being frightened of him might surprise anyone who meets the much older Jenkins. When I did, almost the very first thing he said was, 'Don't describe me as sinister just because I wear black'. By then he was a slightly crumpled seventy-four-year-old, not wearing black, nor threatening, but still a little intimidating. Above all else, he was understandably reticent, because this was the man who elected to go to jail rather than risk revealing the identities of his accomplices in a conspiracy that struck at the very foundations of the governance of Wales.[12]

# 14

# FREEDOM FIGHTERS OR TERRORISTS?

Images of the violence committed by the Baader–Meinhof Gang might well spring to mind for those contemplating the dreadful consequences if MAC2's plans had just once misfired. Much was made afterwards of the assertion by Jenkins and others that they never intended harming anyone; that the explosions were designed to awaken Welsh national consciousness and deliver a message to government that Wales would no longer tolerate its colonial status, as represented by the Investiture of the Prince of Wales. For this reason, the explosive devices were timed to detonate when the saboteurs were reasonably sure the target areas would be deserted. Apart from George Taylor and Alwyn Jones, who blew themselves to pieces, the others were lucky. None of the insurgents were experts in handling explosives, and at the outset they relied on advice from the man in south Wales. When that source of sophisticated Venner time-switches dried up, they improvised with alarm clocks, purchased for a few shillings from Woolworths. One wrong connection, and the bombs planted at the Temple of Peace and the tax offices in Cardiff and Chester could have caused carnage, catapulting MAC2 into the world of Baader–Meinhof. That the left-wing student leader Rudi Dutschke saw MAC2 activists as fellow souls and a potential recruiting-ground for his revolutionary ambitions shows they were paddling in dangerous waters.

But there the comparison ends. None of these men were students in revolt against social and political norms. Apart from Emyr Llewelyn Jones, for whom direct action ended with Tryweryn, not one had seen the inside of a university. Having completed formal education at fifteen, they went to work, on the farm, down the mine, into a factory, or joined the armed services because that was what was expected of youngsters from working-class homes in the 1950s and 1960s. Unlike the urban guerrillas of the Baader–Meinhof gang, submerged in left-wing politics, MAC2 had no discernible political creed. During his imprisonment Jenkins wrote to friends about wanting a Welsh-speaking socialist republic. But the Welsh-speaking bit came later. Initially, MAC2's insurgency was more spiritual than anything else, an accumulation of petty grievances derived from oppression that became magnified and embedded in the psyches of the insurgents. For some, like Jenkins, identity loss resulting from cultural deprivation had degraded his sense of self-esteem. A curious mixture of poorly educated and low-paid, Welsh- and English-speaking, these activists were essentially fundamentalists resisting further assimilation through violent direct action. Sometimes, unable to articulate their enmity and frustration beyond the bar-room door, they turned to violence because they saw no other way to pursue their legitimate grievances. For them, symbolism, like Saunders Lewis's burning of the RAF bombing school on the Llŷn, was capitulation. Suffering the same inferiority that afflicts the Welsh nation, these men drew upon what remained of their national pride to resist the corrosive forces of assimilation. The inevitable focus for their hostility was England.

As a nation, Wales is often represented socially, culturally and economically, as a sum that never adds up. On the one side, those whose conviction is naturally rooted in its cultural heritage, confident Welsh-speakers like Owen Williams, concerned about its demise; on the other, lost souls, like John Jenkins and his Valleys' monoglots, searching for a way home. Paradoxically, Jenkins talked a lot about saving the language and Williams about republicanism. The only manifesto that both agreed to was that independence was a prerequisite for cultural survival, to be achieved, if necessary, through violent direct action. There was nothing remarkable about this from the perspective of those former colonies – Cyprus, Malta, Aden, Kenya – whose freedom fighters legitimised violence in their progression from extremist terrorist to ambassador to the Court of St James. For these former colonists, what was at stake was far too precious to be left to English vested interests. Seen in this context, the 'war' waged by MAC2 was a colonial struggle, and for all its eccentricities and blurred message it was the only authentic Welsh uprising since Owain Glyndŵr.

Among MAC2's enemies were those Welsh who had jettisoned their cultural heritage and assigned independence to history in return for socio-economic dependence. If nothing else, by attempting to turn back the pages MAC2, and for that matter the FWA, caused a convulsion, which reverberated throughout Wales and especially down the corridors of power. By confronting government with the constitutional implications of cancelling the Investiture, MAC2 helped restore Welsh self-determination to the political agenda.

But because the saboteurs did not have the same widespread support as the holiday-cottage arsonists a decade later, the authorities were partially successful in quarantining the 1960s insurgents as mad dogs. Ironically, while the secrecy Jenkins insisted upon frustrated detection, it also thwarted attempts to establish a political base, unlike the IRA, which had Sinn Fein as its

Freedom fighter or extremist? John Jenkins returns to Cardiff after serving his ten-year sentence. Copyright: *Western Mail*, Cardiff.

mouthpiece. Not until the final twelve months of the insurgency was MAC2 even rumoured to exist. Instead, the focus was almost entirely upon Cymdeithas yr Iaith Gymraeg as the means for shoring up the culture. Apart from one or two whose republicanism bridged the language divide, MAC2 never had a clearly defined constituency. While this by default was perceived to lie in the Welsh-speaking heartlands, the insurgents probably had more in common with the republican tradition of the south Wales valleys.

If the insurgency succeeded at all, it was by providing the background crackle for the devolution of administrative power to Wales. The year following the sabotaging of the transformer at Tryweryn, a Secretary of State for Wales was appointed with a seat in the Cabinet, followed by the creation of a Welsh Office, to which increasing administrative powers accrued throughout the next thirty years. Three months after Clywedog in 1966, Gwynfor Evans won Carmarthen, and for many of those subsequently drawn to Plaid Cymru, especially from the Anglicised south of Wales, the reinforcing of national identity corresponded with their support for an independent

After befriending the anarchist Dafydd Ladd when he was on the run, Jenkins was jailed a second time. Copyright: Andrew Wiar.

Wales. Evans's epic victory was followed in 1967 by the first Welsh Language Act, and then, at the height of the violence immediately preceding the Investiture, Prime Minister Harold Wilson appointed the Kilbrandon Commission on the Constitution. If renewed self-respect and raised aspirations helped, then the insurgents can claim at least some credit for these concessions.

The years spent in Albany as a category A prisoner gave Jenkins plenty of time to reflect. Why he was rated such a high security risk he never did discover, but it meant no parole, no home leave or any sort of rehabilitation. Visitors were closely scrutinised, on one occasion the Home Office refusing permission for Jenkins to receive a visit from Eileen Beasley, wife of the language activist Trefor Beasley, and a teacher with whom Jenkins wanted to discuss his sons' education at Rhydfelen, then the only Welsh-medium school in south Wales. The authorities, however, eventually relented and permitted Mrs Beasley to take Jenkins's eldest son Vaughan to visit him in Albany.[1]

A naturally solitary individual, Jenkins survived prison by isolating himself with his books and his Open University course, which he would eventually complete at University College, Cardiff, on his release. Correspondence was restricted to writing one letter a week, with permission to buy another from the prison authorities, if a prisoner had the cash. All his correspondence was vetted by the Home Office. Jenkins, who never had a radio for his first two years in Albany until sent one by Dai Pritchard's widow, envied the Provisional IRA detainees for the support they received. [2] From them, he learned to wave 'a big stick' if warders treated him badly:

> There was an established way for treating people in Albany. On one occasion a new screw from Swansea began to throw his weight around, bursting into my cell shouting and bawling. Next day I complained to the governor about his behaviour. 'I'm only thinking of his family', I said. 'If my friends heard about this who knows what might happen to the officer's family?' The following day the screw apologised and was especially careful how he treated me in future. In prison you carry a big stick but don't use it. [3]

As far as the regulations would allow, Jenkins was a prolific correspondent, his letters explaining and justifying his actions, and never once expressing regret. Some were published in *Planet*, the Welsh current affairs magazine, whose executive editor, Sara Erskine, wife of the editor, Ned Thomas, was a regular correspondent. Excerpts also appeared in the Welsh-language weekly *Y Faner*, but never in the *Western Mail* or *Daily Post*. Although contemptuous of the *Western Mail*'s repudiation of anything it suspected in the aftermath of the 1960s' bombing campaign of having nationalist associations, Jenkins, nevertheless, considered it his vital link with Wales. The *Western Mail* – 'the mule', he called it – was a dreadful paper, he told Sara Erskine, nothing but a rag, but it had a monopoly and was essential. 'Could you ask Harri Webb to arrange for copies to be sent to me?' he added. [4]

Jenkins had guessed more or less correctly: hell froze over for nationalism at the *Western Mail* after the turmoil of the bombing campaign. The editor, Giddings, had only two more years in the chair and for most of that period the door was bolted. His hostility was palpable, like tiptoeing through a minefield for those of us responsible every night for delivering the news agenda. Giddings never banged the table or shouted his orders at his evening news conference. He simply sniffed the air for the smell of someone offering rotten eggs.

Cyril Hodges, the poet, was Jenkins's most regular correspondent. They had not known each other previously and would never meet, Hodges dying before Jenkins was released. Hodges provided a conduit for Jenkins's explanations and reflections, which earned the prisoner of Albany a savage rebuke in Plaid

Cymru's *Welsh Nation* for using his incarceration to moralise.[5] Jenkins remained ambivalent towards Plaid, his main criticism that the party contained too many eminent academics and 'culture vultures'. By now a staunch socialist, he believed that only a party that was predominantly socialist had any chance of winning the votes of the *gwerin* (the common people), without whom the battle for independence would be lost. 'History might be bunk but cultural nationalism is cock unless accompanied by political power', he wrote to Sara Erskine.[6]

The description of Jenkins during his trial as a 'ruthless fanatic' did not seem to worry him unduly. The Director of Operations of MAC2 sought to make a virtue out of fanaticism, explaining in a letter to Hodges that he needed the strength of ten men because the other nine 'couldn't be bothered':

> You should not really denigrate fanaticism as such; perhaps, if you regard the matter as one of semantics and think of it as an obsession with an ideal, or a deeply dedicated sense of purpose, or even an unswerving objectivity, it will not cause such fear. I will say three things about fanaticism: firstly that it is true that a fanatic has the strength and drive of ten men … Secondly, it is not always true that a fanatic doesn't count the cost of taking action … Lastly, if Wales is to survive and her culture and heritage flourish, it will be done only by the ferocious and unswerving devotion to Wales above all else … including family, prospects, careers, health freedom and life itself. I know that Wales can inspire this sort of fanaticism … the essential catalyst to move the majority of people.[7]

Besides a fairly constant stream of correspondence, Jenkins received some practical support. Cynon Dafis, a founder member of Cymdeithas, gave his sons Vaughan (11) and Rhodri (6) a holiday, and Audrey White and Gwyn Williams administered a fund set up to help his family. His wife Thelma had promised to wait for her 'kind husband and father', whose only fault, she told reporters after his trial, was that he 'cared too much for Wales'.[8] In the event, they were divorced within a year and Jenkins was awarded custody of the children, rare for inmates of Britain's most secure prison. His status was reduced to category B one year before his release, after a campaign run by the Welsh Political Prisoners Defence Committee and representations to the Home Office by the Plaid Cymru MP, Dafydd Elis-Thomas.[9]

There is no doubt from his prison letters that Jenkins continued to reach out to supporters, who regarded him as the standard-bearer for Welsh republicanism. When a general election looked likely, the Welsh Republican Party asked Jenkins whether it could nominate him as its candidate for Caerphilly in 1974. If the party formed by disaffected nationalists had contested Caerphilly it would most certainly have split the nationalist vote in a constituency Plaid thought it could win. Realising this, Jenkins declined the invitation to stand, although by then there was no longer any law debarring a convicted felon from contesting a parliamentary election. Seven years later, the Provisional IRA prisoner Bobby Sands contested and won a parliamentary seat while in the Maze prison in Northern Ireland.[10]

Before his release from Albany in 1976 Jenkins struck up a friendship with another inmate, one destined to land him in more trouble. Dafydd Ladd was jailed in 1973 for five years for causing an explosion at the Army Officer's Club in Aldershot. An anarchist, Ladd had a pretty impressive track-record. Born in Germany, the charismatic son of a former British Army sergeant, he was well educated, fluent in both German and French. In the early 1970s Ladd joined a revolutionary organisation called Freedom Fighters for All, dedicated to the violent overthrow of society, this culminating in an explosion at the Army Officers' Club in Aldershot for which he was jailed for five years in 1973. On his release, Ladd helped form another anarchist group, Black Aid, in support of the jailed Baader–Meinhof gang in West Germany. At that time, Scotland Yard's Anti-Terrorist Squad was investigating armed raids on supermarkets, the purpose appearing to be to fund the purchase by anarchists of weapons and bomb-making materials. During searches, a stockpile of false passports was found and also two holdalls full of guns. Ladd was arrested with four other men and a woman, their subsequent trial known as the 'Persons Unknown' case, because other gang members remained at large. Not expecting a fair trial, Ladd jumped his £17,000 bail and went underground, assuming the identity of 'Jim Llewellyn', a name he picked off the gravestone of a dead child. Not even his girlfriend had an idea of his true identity.[11] In the meantime, an Old Bailey jury acquitted four of Ladd's co-defendants, jailing a fifth for nine years. The trial is probably best remembered for allegations of police jury-vetting. While on the run, Ladd was quoted in the *Leveller* magazine as saying, 'I find any violence against the ruling elite justified.' Three years later, in May 1982, Ladd surrendered himself to the Old Bailey and was formally cleared of all charges. Waiting outside, however, were detectives from south Wales to arrest him for questioning about his involvement with the Workers' Army of the Welsh Republic. Ladd was one of those implicated in 1980–2 in attempted explosions outside the British Steel Corporation premises in Celtic Road, Cardiff, and an Army recruitment centre in Pontypridd, and attacks on Conservative Party offices in Cardiff and Shotton.[12]

A loner, Ladd shunned social contact. Few were aware of his anarchist past, Jenkins regarding him as 'a rootless individual looking for roots'. For aiding and abetting Ladd to avoid arrest by providing him with the address of a 'safe house', Jenkins was sent to Dartmoor for two years. At the time of his arrest he was at a critical stage in a university course and felt he could ill afford to waste time in custody. To obtain bail, he says, he was advised to make a statement admitting only to having given Ladd an address to go to. That would result in a fine, rather than a custodial sentence. Eighteen months later, when the case finally came to trial, instead he was sentenced to two years in Dartmoor as a category B prisoner for giving assistance to a man he says he never even met, while on the run.[13]

There was no one waiting for John Jenkins when he walked out of Albany on the Isle of Wight, apart from the pair of Special Branch men wondering why he had bought a rail ticket for Holyhead. After paying his respects at the graves of the Abergele Martyrs he might have carried on to the farm at Llanllyfin where Owen Williams had given him a plot of land. The site of an agricultural worker's cottage, all that remained were the stone walls, but the foundations had been restored by supporters, using the proceeds of a fund raised for renovations and furnishings. For this, the pacifist organisers of the fund were criticised by the *Western Mail* for parading as a hero a man once regarded as a danger to Welsh society. Whatever the reason, the cottage was never renovated, but Jenkins still owns the site, even though Owen Williams offered to buy it back for £10,000.

After paying his respects to his fallen comrades, Jenkins headed back to Cardiff to complete his university course in social work. Rejected by University College, Swansea, on account of his extremist activities, he had applied successfully to Cardiff, whose Principal, Professor Bill Bevan, did not have the same reluctance about enrolling Jenkins as an adult student. By then Jenkins was living with his partner Lowri Morgan – daughter of the Welsh insurance millionaire Trefor Morgan – in Pontcanna, Cardiff, and as an active member of the Students' Union was elected as its representative on the University Court of Governors. The Chancellor, none other than the Prince of Wales, would customarily have personally welcomed new Governors to their first meeting of the Court, but on this occasion was taken ill. In his absence, the formalities were undertaken by Lord Elwyn Jones, who as Attorney General in the Wilson government had initiated proceedings against Jenkins and Alders. Instead of a handshake, Jenkins was not surprised to receive only polite applause.[14]

Piece by piece Jenkins was getting his life back together. His relationship with Lowri Morgan was to last many years, surviving even his second term of imprisonment. A new Drum and Fife Band was formed in Cardiff, with himself as conductor. Known as the Republican Band, it performed at the annual commemoration for the Abergele Martyrs and also during the commemorations at Cilmeri, where John Jenkins and Owen Williams as leaders of Cofiwn – a group formed to draw attention to Welsh history – were instrumental in erecting the commemorative stone to Llywelyn, last native prince of Wales. The police, understandably, believed the only tune the Republican Band played and its Cofiwn supporters marched to was a revolutionary one, a cover for something more sinister, as it had been at Wrexham. Jenkins was still seen as the spider at the centre of the extremist web.

On his release from Dartmoor in 1985, Jenkins returned to live with Lowri Morgan at Pontcanna. When they eventually split up he decided to leave

Wales, having lost count of the number of times he had been arbitrarily arrested. He refused to possess a computer, for fear that incriminating evidence might be planted on it. Deciding after one police swoop that it was only a matter of time before they pinned something on him, Jenkins moved to London to work for Brent Mind from 1988 until he retired and returned to Wrexham in 1996. As a counsellor with the National Association for Mental Health (Mind), working with people suffering mental distress, John Jenkins excelled. His greatest strength had always been that people felt able to trust him.[15]

# 15

## MAC3: THE COTTAGE ARSON CAMPAIGN

From inside the high-security wing at Albany Prison John Jenkins made the extraordinary prediction that MAC2 had not been defeated: it had simply gone underground, to be reorganised in the future. An investigation that was estimated to have cost £7 million in the 1960s had ended with two dead, two in jail and two activist cells dismantled. Jenkins has always believed his cover would never have been broken had it not been for 'a woman from the north, a Welsh-speaking friend of an associate', who recalled that night his red bandsman's tunic was illuminated by the beam of a car's headlights. Despite his imprisonment, four, maybe five, MAC2 cells had survived to fight another day. 'My greatest achievement', he wrote to a correspondent, 'was not so much the cost to the state … but that the complete system of safe houses, dumps, dead letter boxes, active supporters and sleeping sympathisers have to this day completely escaped detection.' What happened next was to wait for Glyndŵr to reawaken. But for Jenkins there would be no further part to play. He was, he wrote, putting himself 'out to graze'.

Many nationalists believe that the catalyst for the next stage in the struggle was the crushing defeat for self-determination in the 1979 devolution referendum, a defeat that reputedly drove Gwynfor Evans, president of Plaid Cymru, to the point of suicide; if not that, to endorsing the cottage arson campaign that followed. In the event, he did neither.

Welsh activism in the 1970s was largely about saving the language. Increasingly, the subject of independence was ushered into the sidelines by those for whom the 'I' word was an anathema. Such a person was Dafydd Elis-Thomas, who shared a flat with Evans in London and would eventually succeed him as party president. No sooner was he elected to the House of Commons, than Elis-Thomas condemned the arsonists, even though of the 12,000 houses in his constituency, 2,500 were second homes.[1] The focus for concern for Evans and many others had become the heartlands, *Y Fro Gymraeg*, centred on the most vulnerable parts of north and west Wales, where the influx of more prosperous incomers, mostly from England, was overwhelming indigenous communities. Emyr Llewelyn Jones, one of the three convicted for sabotaging Tryweryn, helped found ADFER to combat this cultural erosion by advocating policies for providing a stock of affordable housing for locals, unable to compete with prices offered by the retirees arriving in droves from the English Midlands.

These were the golden years of Cymdeithas yr Iaith Gymraeg, its members lionised after having been dragged kicking and screaming from court for daubing English-language road signs that left motorists peering through the whitewash for directions. For this, some language activists were elevated to the pantheon of Welsh cultural heroes, eventually providing the seedcorn for the Welsh Language Board and the Welsh-language television channel, Sianel Pedwar Cymru (S4C). At the same time, MAC2 was painstakingly airbrushed out of history, leaving Cymdeithas and Plaid to profit from the rising tide of national sentiment prodded into life by those who tried to prevent the Investiture. Even though no one spoke for MAC2, unlike the language campaigners, who had the implicit support of Plaid Cymru, its activities contributed to the background hiss of independence that eventually persuaded Prime Minister Harold Wilson to respond to the democratic deficit. The Kilbrandon Commission Wilson had set up at the height of the troubles in Wales recommended legislative and executive assemblies for Scotland and Wales, the Labour Party committing itself to devolution at the 1974 General Election. After Wilson's sudden resignation two years later, the new Labour Prime Minister, James Callaghan, was hanging on to office by his fingertips and needed the parliamentary support of the Scottish National Party (eleven seats) and Plaid Cymru (three). In a cynical electoral ploy to retain power, Labour introduced separate devolution bills for Welsh and Scottish assemblies, but critically amended them to appease their own bitter opponents of devolution by allowing a clause pledging the government to repeal the Acts unless 40 per cent of the electorate voted 'yes' in post-legislative referendums. Most observers thought that the referendum commitment meant the Welsh bill in particular stood little chance of succeeding, especially when no attempt was made by the government to rein in fierce opponents like Neil Kinnock (Bedwellty). For a self-serving politician like Kinnock, devolution was a concession to Welsh nationalism that threatened his chances of securing the leadership of the Labour Party, which he did four years later during Labour's wilderness years. Kinnock and five other renegade south Wales Labour MPs – Leo Abse (Pontypool), Donald Anderson (Swansea East), Ioan Rees (Aberdare), Fred Evans (Caerphilly) and Ifor Davies (Gower) – resorted to playing the language card and the slippery-slope argument to destroy Wales's devolutionary aspirations by ruthlessly projecting the language as being as great an obstacle as the Protestant/Catholic divide was proving in Northern Ireland.

As proof that the Anglicised majority were doomed to become second-class citizens, Kinnock and company had only to point to the language campaigners, whose activities were incomprehensible to the vast majority. High-profile prosecutions of Cymdeithas activists, like the popular Welsh folk-singer Dafydd Iwan and Ffred Ffransis, Gwynfor Evans's son-in-law, fuelled suspicions that devolution meant a Welsh-speaking Wales, especially after the concessions of the 1967 Language Act failed to satisfy language activists. Perversely, monoglot English-speakers welcomed plans for a separate Welsh-language television channel, but for entirely selfish reasons: it removed the irritation of having to switch channels to avoid the latest instalment of the Welsh soap *Pobol y Cwm*! The *Western Mail*, run predominantly by English speakers, also wanted the airwaves cleansed – ignoring the possibility that Sianel Pedwar Cymru (S4C) might become a language ghetto watched by a handful, surviving on subsidies and run by an elite cadre of Welsh-speakers.

At the *Western Mail* the 1979 referendum was a defining moment. Unlike many issues on which newspapers offer advice to readers through their editorial comment column, there was no wriggle-room this time. The 'on the one hand and on the other hand' prescription would not work. By now I was deputy editor to a new editor, Duncan Gardiner. Gardiner, a Yorkshireman, had worked in Wales previously, but he wanted someone beside him who understood the competing interests that influenced the *Western Mail*. As well as me, the candidates for the deputy's job were a Norfolk man, Rex Reynolds, parachuted in from Fleet Street as chief assistant editor to teach the locals a thing or two about running modern newspapers, and assistant editor Geraint Talfan Davies, generally considered far too Welsh-Welsh for some. The office bets were, however, on Talfan Davies, a Welsh-speaker believed by most to have the perfect pedigree to edit the *Western Mail*: his father, formerly programme controller at BBC Wales, and his uncle, Sir Alun Talfan Davies, an eminent judge who as a QC prosecuted Owen Williams unsuccessfully and later defended Ernest Alders in the bombing trial. That Geraint was being groomed for the job seemed obvious from his various training stints around the Thomson group, including a spell at the *Times*. Besides twenty years' experience at the journalistic coalface, also in my favour was the *Western Mail*'s inherent distrust of Welsh-speakers, from whom it had always felt estranged, having been founded to represent the interests of south Wales coal- and shipowners. In the circumstances, the new editor decided that the thoroughly Anglicised boy from the long line of terraced houses in Newport was a safer pair of hands on the brake if the *Western Mail* headed in the direction of some Welsh cul-de-sac. While Gardiner, our English editor, encouraged debate, unlike his predecessor, the 1979 devolution referendum was a minefield through which he needed a reliable guide.

The first question was whether the *Western Mail*, or rather its owners, wanted devolution at all if, as Kinnock predicted, it meant a step on the slippery slope to separatism. The pressure on the editor was vociferous and devious. Feeling especially vulnerable, Gardiner resisted admirably, but knew the newspaper could not procrastinate forever. A decision had to be taken on whether a referendum was needed to ratify devolution.

The debate inside the office was robustly split between the Welsh-speakers, firmly in the 'yes' camp, and the English-speakers, with their traditional suspicions and prejudices. Having made it from district reporter to the number two spot on one of the most prestigious newspapers in the country, there was no way I intended sacrificing my career on the altar of devolution. I might not make editor of the *Western Mail* when Gardiner went down – as all editors do eventually – but neither would I stand a chance at any other Thomson title if it were thought I was a closet nationalist.

As an Englishman, Gardiner remained somewhat detached from the debate, faintly amused that such a boring subject could generate such intensity among his executive team. The truth is he was more interested in watching a good game of rugby. A resident of Wales for many years, he had as much right to influence the debate as any native-born, but preferred instead to be persuaded as to what line the newspaper should take. Around him were three principal protagonists: Geraint Talfan Davies and his co-conspirator on devolution, John Osmond, the *Western Mail*'s knowledgeable Welsh Affairs Correspondent, and me. Davies and Osmond wanted the lot: a full-blown legislative parliament with law-making and tax-raising powers. Significantly, they were dead set against holding a referendum and rightly so, because of the way the referendum would be skewed towards a 'no' vote. That, plus the size of the immigrant (English) population, meant that put to the vote devolution was doomed. From my Newport perspective all I could see was Kinnock's slippery slope. Mindful that I had been appointed to apply the brake, I argued that the *Western Mail* should support the holding of a referendum. After interminable discussions between the four of us, Duncan Gardiner remained undecided, but resolved finally to settle the matter on the basis of written submissions from the opposing camps.

Newspapermen do not read, they scan. Before computers with automatic spelling and grammar checks, newspapers had 'readers' to speed-read every word every night before a single line was published, all errors sent back for correction. The *Western Mail* had about twenty of these men sitting in pairs beneath reading lamps in an otherwise darkened room, one reading the proof aloud, the other correcting, their monotonous hubbub sounding like the drone of an aircraft passing slowly overhead. A journalist had not the same skills or the time to read every dot and comma. His experienced eye picked out the salient points and ignored the packaging. What this usually meant was a retention span of between 300 and 500 words, beyond which nothing much else registered.

Shortly after Duncan Gardiner had asked Geraint Talfan Davies and me to produce written submissions, Geraint went sick. Back at the office, with the clock ticking towards the crucial meeting, I struggled in between other duties to piece together the case for the *Western Mail* advocating little more than a talking-shop assembly, crucially endorsed by a referendum. I was about halfway through, having already typed four foolscap sheets, when the editor's secretary, Madelaine Morris, who had that morning delivered some cuttings from the library to Geraint's sickbed, whispered to me that he was sitting up in bed scribbling furiously. His submission for the editor was already in double figures! Like a flash, I knew that no matter how well reasoned Geraint's argument the editor would scan it, the law of diminishing marginal returns kicking in after a few hundred words. My one-page argument was all that was needed to persuade our English editor to advocate an executive assembly backed by a referendum.

To this day I regret having put personal ambition before the longer-term interests of Wales, because the *Western Mail*'s advocacy was certainly a factor in the government's decision to allow the devolution bill for Wales to be amended to include the referendum commitment. After all, besides being Prime Minister, Callaghan was a Cardiff MP, the *Western Mail* delivered daily to his desk in Downing Street. From this, he would have seen that Kinnock and company were not voices in the wilderness pressing for a referendum: they had the support of a newspaper usually regarded as Labour's enemy. The result was, as Davies and Osmond predicted – and I had facilitated – a rout for the devolutionists, unable to muster the 40 per cent of the electorate needed to pass even this emaciated piece of legislation. Opponents of devolution had relentlessly exploited the spectre of a Welsh-speaking minority lording it over the cowed majority of monoglot English-speakers in a banana republic. The result: four to one against devolution.

This result gave me no pleasure. I was as stunned as anyone by the overwhelming rejection. Devolution was dead, and I had helped hammer in the final nail. All that lay ahead was further integration into England until the moment the light was finally switched off for Welsh national aspirations. Not long afterwards, Labour were defeated in the General Election of 1979 and headed off into the wilderness, led first by Michael Foot and afterwards by Kinnock. The Conservatives, under Margaret Thatcher, performed the last rites by repealing the 1968 Wales Act. For some, the frustrations of the devolution debacle found an outlet in the intensified campaign for a Welsh-language television channel. For others, language and culture became quite literally, burning issues, with the start of an arson campaign in December 1979 directed at holiday homes.

The torching of holiday cottages was designed to draw attention to rising house-prices and the erosion of cultural life caused by inward migration, problems that the democratic processes had failed to address, in much the same way that they had not prevented the drowning of Capel Celyn. In resorting to direct action the arsonists were no different from the insurgents of MAC2. Because the first cottage fires occurred a few months after Welsh aspirations were dashed by the devolution referendum, it is not inconceivable some of the arsonists were frustrated insurgents from the previous decade. In fact, they followed in the footsteps of MAC2, which had planned to move on to second homes after water pipelines.

Responsibility for most of the 200 acts of arson between 1979 and 1992 – culminating in the fire-bombing of estate agents in several English cities and London – was claimed by Meibion Glyndŵr (the Sons of Glyndŵr), a mystery organisation first rumoured to exist as early as 1966, after the bombing of Clywedog. Nothing was heard of it again until 1979, when it re-emerged as branding for the cottage arson campaign. Was Meibion Glyndŵr no other than MAC3, involving the same people? Was there an umbilical cord linking thirty years of insurgency, beginning with Tryweryn? 'MAC2 still existed and could have been reorganised', according to Jenkins, who had predicted as much in Albany Prison.[2] The possibility that some of the same people were involved was taken seriously by Ray White, the former Chief Constable of Dyfed-Powys, on whose patch forty-three incidents occurred.[3] If MAC2 was not directly involved, police were convinced that members still at large after the 1960s bombing campaign were providing the arsonists with advice.

It probably escaped the attention of most that the English translation for Tyddyn Gwêr at Nefyn on the Llŷn Peninsula – the very first holiday home torched – is Wax Cottage, particularly appropriate since wax was part of the preferred timing-device for many of the arson attacks. The would-be arsonist dipped a test-tube in melted wax so that it formed a hollow tube when it cooled. Sulphuric acid was then poured into the wax tube, the end of which was sealed before being slid into a condom, the acid perfectly safe so long as it was contained by the wax. This the arsonist carried in his pocket to the target. When the tube was snapped in half, the sulphuric acid burned through the rubber, igniting the inflammable material in which it had been placed. In the meantime, the arsonist made good his escape. Although there was not a year between 1979 and 1992 without some kind of arson attack, Meibion Gyndŵr activity was most intense at the beginning of the 1980s and again in 1988, when the arsonists switched their attention to estate agents in England suspected of selling second homes in Wales. The phases of the campaign, and arsonists involved, are evident from the different types of incendiary devices employed. In the later stages the fire-bombs comprised a clock and battery timer connected to a chemical explosive and accelerant. Although more sophisticated, the devices were unstable. Whether on account of this, or because a new group had become involved, the incendiary device changed again when estate agents and building societies just over the border in England became the target. A device recovered by police when it failed to explode at the Worcester Building Society offices consisted of two brown envelopes, one A4 size and about an inch thick, the second smaller. One envelope contained the firing device and some inflammable powder, the other an accelerant chemical. Another Meibion Glyndŵr timer, similar to that used by the Vietcong during the Vietnam War, consisted of a clothes-peg, the jaws held apart by a piece of solder, with drawing pins attached to the inside edges of the jaws. The pressure of the spring-loaded peg made the electrical contact triggering the firebomb. When the arsonists graduated to letter-bombing their police pursuers and politicians, the video-cassette posted to a target was timed to explode when the lid was opened by the recipient.

Rather than the two or three 'hobby' arsonists police believed were initially responsible, it would seem from the geographical reach of a campaign lasting twelve years and employing different incendiary devices that Meibion Glyndŵr was well organised and tightly controlled. As was the case with MAC2, the arsonists had no intention of harming anyone, the majority of incidents occurring in midwinter, or at other times when the target properties were known to be empty. Unlike the sabotage campaign of the 1960s, no one was ever injured by the arsonists, apart from a fireman when a staircase collapsed in the offices of a firm of London estate agents.

That there were at least two cells engaged in burning down holiday homes was evident from the outset on the night of 13 December 1979. The fire at Tyddyn Gwêr was one of four that night, two within ten miles of each other on the Llŷn Peninsula at Nefyn and Llanbedrog, the other two within one hundred yards of each other in the village of Llanrhian, near Fishguard. Not only were the locations on the Llŷn Peninsula and Pembrokeshire almost 150 miles apart, the fire-bombs were detonated almost simultaneously, ruling out the possibility of a single arsonist being responsible. Ten years later more than one group would have been needed to plant fire-bombs on the same night at estate agents in six English cities along a 250-mile front from Merseyside to Bristol, even though the chosen targets were located close to motorways.

The Welsh police seemed no better prepared to deal with extremism, although each force had been required following the Investiture to recruit additional Special Branch officers, augmented by others stationed at all the Welsh ports. Before the arson campaign ended, the 1980s equivalent of Commander Jock Wilson's Shrewsbury Unit would be established in north Wales, a twelve-strong specialist team responsible for gathering and distributing intelligence and investigating the mounting number of unsolved arson attacks.

Suspicion fell immediately on two organisations: Cymdeithas yr Iaith Gymraeg and Adfer. Both were campaigning to halt the sale of second homes at grossly inflated prices. When Cymdeithas began disrupting the auction of such properties in Caernarfon in July 1972, Wales had an estimated 20,000 second homes and a council-house waiting-list of 50,000. The Welsh-speaking areas were worst hit by the influx, 16 per cent of all properties in the districts of

Meirionnydd and Dwyfor being owned by affluent incomers, outnumbering locals in some villages. After Gwynedd, where one in ten properties was a holiday home, came Powys and Dyfed, with 6.5 per cent of the housing stock owned by incomers.

There were two reasons for the influx. The increase in incomes and property prices in south-east England meant that pretty little Welsh cottages were easily affordable trophies for even the moderately well-off. The other was 'white flight'. The day predicted in Enoch Powell's 'rivers of blood' speech a decade earlier, when England's inner towns and cities would become 'wholly foreign, alien territory', had dawned for many. With plenty left over after selling a semi-detached in London or the Midlands, plus the prospect of a more relaxed, environmentally friendly lifestyle, rural Wales was an irresistible attraction for these 'white settlers'. Holiday homes soon became permanent residences, the incomers moving on to run cafés, guesthouses, supermarkets, garages and newsagents, in the process squeezing out locals from once wholly Welsh-speaking communities. Many made no effort to integrate, preferring instead to Anglicise everything and everybody in their path. Where properties were intended for summer use only, in winter the incomers left behind ghost villages.

Before this, rural Wales was already suffering from the depopulation caused by the introduction of modern farming techniques, which drove thousands off the land in the twentieth century. By 1991 fewer than 20 per cent of those who remained spoke Welsh. Perhaps no different to the economic crisis in many other parts of depressed rural Britain, in Wales the dilution and destruction of a distinctive culture added an extra layer of injustice to the economic imbalance between the indigenous Welsh and prosperous settlers from England. The increasing domination of one linguistic group by another, and the failure of the democratic process to alleviate the economic and cultural inequalities, served only to reinforce the sense of oppression. In the absence of a democratic solution, following the referendum defeat, the tensions manifested themselves in an arson campaign whose activists were regarded as modern Robin Hoods – 'social bandits' defending the oppressed against those whose interests were protected by the law.

In the eyes of Meibion Glyndŵr, the invasion of rural Wales by predominantly English incomers and the extinction of the Welsh way of life was state-sponsored ethnic cleansing, not very different from Henry VIII's plantation boroughs for suppressing the Welsh after the Acts of Union. According to Dafydd Wigley, Plaid Cymru MP, later its president, unless 'we protect[ed] our own people' against the influx from England, the local tension created by the incomers would give rise to a 'very awkward situation'. His solution was to force immigrants to pay more for their houses, at the same time preventing them from buying council houses. Not only was this impossible to implement, especially since the UK had become a signatory to the European Charter of Human

Rights, but by the time it was proposed inward migration had already peaked (1988).

With no sign of a democratic solution, the arsonists acting in the name of Owain Glyndŵr tapped into Welsh mythology and its heroic sagas to protect the weak and poor from exploitation. Folk heroes exist not so much for what they achieve, but for identifying with common grievances. The crisis in rural Wales was another injustice to add to those of the preceding millennium, none of which had been forgotten by a nation that survived in the mind, if not in body.[4]

Saunders Lewis was considered a modern Robin Hood when he burned down the RAF bombing school in 1936, and again in 1962 with his call to arms to save the language. The campaign to prevent the drowning of Capel Celyn and, sixteen years later, the fire-bombing of second homes won widespread public support by defending Wales's cultural identity. Those responsible were exonerated in the eyes of their compatriots, if not by the law-makers. Even the Anglo-Welsh poet and pacifist R. S. Thomas justified the fire-bombing of English holiday cottages, observing, 'What is one death against the death of the whole Welsh nation?' Without popular support the cottage arson campaign would not have lasted ten minutes, let alone twelve years.

Unlike the arsonists, the pipeline bombers of the 1960s were not embraced by Mother Wales. Secretly admired by some, the vast majority of nationalists refused to lift their heads above the parapet when the bombs were exploding. Striking at water pipelines, government offices and the Investiture of the Prince of Wales was revolutionary – and the overwhelmingly Anglocentric dependency that Wales had become feared revolution more than it did English domination. The drowning of a Welsh-speaking community to construct a reservoir for Liverpool was in a different league from the explosive activities of MAC2. The sabotaging of Tryweryn could be excused because it was in response to a cultural crime against the nation; what MAC2 did was widely regarded as simply criminal.

On the night of the first arson attack, 13 December 1979, the owners of three of the four targets were from Twickenham, Croydon and Huddersfield. The one from Twickenham happened to be a Welsh-speaking Welshman, brought up at Betws-y-coed, who spent five months of the year at his Welsh cottage. The Welsh Language Society and Adfer immediately denied their members were in any way involved. Rhodri Williams, deputy chairman of Cymdeithas yr Iaith Gymraeg – and eventually one of the first chairmen of the Welsh Language Board – insisted that the group's campaign against second homes was dormant; that instead it was concentrating on obtaining a Welsh-language television channel. By the end of the year another four properties had been torched, three successfully at Blaenau Ffestiniog, and a failed attempt at Pwllheli. Local Plaid Cymru MP Dafydd Elis-Thomas described the actions as 'senseless'.[5]

Twelve years later, 197 separate incidents of arson or attempted arson would be officially attributed to Meibion Glyndŵr by the police: 134 in North Wales,

43 in Dyfed-Powys and 20 in England.[6] In addition, there were some copycat incidents, staged by people trying to swindle insurance companies. Neither does the official police list include every suspected Meibion Glyndŵr attack. Television coverage on 3 February 1981 of a burned-out boat being dragged from a barn at Gwnhinhar, Boduan, near Pwllheli, where it had been stored with twenty others, made no mention of another incendiary device placed aboard a second boat, *The Prince of Wales*, which failed to explode.

The arson attacks covered such an extended period that those involved at the outset were unlikely to be the same people active at the end. The only person ever convicted was Sion Aubrey Roberts, jailed for twelve years for possessing explosive materials and sending incendiary devices to Welsh Office Minister Sir Wyn Roberts, Conservative agent Elwyn Jones and the detective leading the hunt for Meibion Glyndŵr. Roberts was just nine years of age when the campaign started.

Fires were rarely extensive. Properties were almost always not occupied, some in the process of renovation in remote areas infrequently visited by their owners. All of this happened before the police central computer database existed to provide immediate access to information about suspects. Crucially, it was also before DNA testing.

For the first seven or eight years the police made little or no headway, apart from concluding from the geographical spread that as many as three groups of arsonists could be involved. For the Home Office and security services faced with the IRA, what was happening in Wales was low-grade extremism, probably best remembered for the music-hall joke, 'A cottage in Wales? Come home to a real Welsh fire.' Newspaper headlines were dominated by the Falklands War (1982), miners' strike (1984–5), more pit closures and the laying-off of thousands of steelworkers. The 1980s were also the high-water mark for Thatcher's privatisation programme and the demolition of trade union power.

The first communication with the arsonists was just after Christmas 1979, in a letter received by Geraint Talfan Davies, who by then had left the *Western Mail* to take over as head of news at HTV in Cardiff. Posted in Shropshire on 20 December, after the first attacks on second homes, and written in Welsh capitals with a ballpoint pen, it explained:

> The houses were burnt with great sadness. We are not ferocious men. It was an act of despair. The rural areas are being destroyed all over these islands. Wales is our concern. These homes are out of reach of local people because of the economic situation. We call upon individuals of goodwill to take steps before these sorry acts take place.[7]

Copies of the same letter were sent to four Welsh county councils, the BBC, four newspapers, including the *Western Mail*, and to three MPs, Dafydd Wigley and

Dafydd Elis-Thomas (Plaid Cymru), and Geraint Howells (Liberal, Ceredigion). Responsibility for the arson attacks was not immediately claimed in the name of any organisation.

The acid-filled condom was identified as the incendiary device when an attempt to burn down an eighth cottage on the Llŷn Peninsula failed. Breaking in through a window of the empty property at Tan y Ffalt, Mynydd Nefyn, the arsonists piled furniture and carpets together, but when it was snapped in half the wax tube failed to ignite the bonfire. At about the same time the *Western Mail* received a letter from the arsonists, this one in English, saying much the same thing about the destruction of local rural communities by market forces, and ending with a plea to 'all men and women of goodwill to act now … to reverse this trend before these deplorable acts escalate'.[8]

The first clue to the identity of the arsonists was contained in a letter to the BBC in Bangor and postmarked Bala, the day before the fourteenth holiday-home blaze destroyed a two-storey house, Bryn Meilwch, Gwynfe, near Llangadog in west Wales. Written in English, it was signed 'Cadfridog Gwynedd (Gwynedd General)' on behalf of 'Cadwyr Cymru (the Keepers of Wales)'. To prove they were responsible, the letter-writers said they had left a plastic bowl on the step of a house at Rhosygwaliau near Bala in an earlier fire-raising attempt. 'The police are hiding the facts', the letter continued. 'An organisation has claimed responsibility for the holiday cottage fires. What the IRA has achieved so shall we.' By now the special police incident-room in Caernarfon had received two other anonymous letters, posted at Bala and Oswestry, claiming that the 'Keepers of Wales' were responsible. One letter, quoted by the BBC, stated the activists were a coalition of groups operating as independent cells – much like MAC2's structure and command – and that they were supported by the IRA and the Basque separatist organisation ETA. John Jenkins, MAC2's Director of Operations, while denying any personal involvement, told the BBC he would not be surprised to discover that members of MAC2 were involved in the arson campaign:

> We are about to see a campaign, which is based on a last-ditch stand by people who are determined to resist, in any way possible, the infiltration, and basically cultural genocide of all they believe in. Obviously they are not going to achieve their objectives. You can't achieve objectives as vast as what they obviously have by burning holiday homes down. But they will obviously try to take it further … they have come to the end of their tether. They feel all constitutional means have been exhausted. This is not a democratic society in which the wishes of a fairly significant minority can be tolerated or encouraged. Therefore, they feel inclined to take the matter further as indeed any man of spirit would do in similar circumstances.

Asked by the interviewer how the arsonists might pursue their campaign and how this action could be justified after the 1979 referendum defeat, Jenkins replied:

> Who knows until the circumstances arise. It is time there was a bit more commitment and self-sacrifice involved in the word patriotism … The people of Wales have been brainwashed for close on 800 years. You can hardly expect someone who hasn't had full control of his environment or control of any decisions concerning his environment, suddenly to get up and take a great step forward as this [the referendum] would have been.[9]

As the number of arson attacks multiplied, so did the number of holiday homes, according to returns from local authorities to the Welsh Office in February 1980. Merioneth was the most seriously affected county, while in Ceredigion and Carmarthen there had been a sharp increase in the number of immigrants moving permanently to Wales from England.[10]

By late March 1980 the number of properties torched had risen to thirty, the apparent centre of activity the Llŷn Peninsula, where the arsonists seemed to be swimming in a friendly sea. If the damage to property was not great, the damage to Wales's chances of attracting new jobs to replace the thousands being lost in the coal and steel industries was considered huge. The economic and cultural crisis in rural Wales did not wash with the Valleys miners and Port Talbot and Shotton steelworkers facing redundancy.

The political pressure on police intensified after the discovery of explosive devices at the Welsh Conservative Party's headquarters at Whitchurch, Cardiff, and the East Flint Conservative Association's office in King George Street, Shotton. Two days later, forty people were arrested in a series of dawn raids across Wales on Palm Sunday, 30 March 1980. Telephone calls warning of the devices in Cardiff and Shotton were received by police before the fire-bombs were timed to explode. As it happened, the one in Cardiff never did, the other only partially and causing slight damage. Both devices were fairly crude, comprising a plastic container filled with what appeared to be petrol, with a battery, detonator and timing device attached. The immediate assumption was that the arsonists had stepped up their campaign by attacking political targets. For the first time, English police forces were alerted to the possibility of extremist activity spreading across the border. But a letter to the *South Wales Echo* in Cardiff hinted that the cottage arsonists were not responsible for the two latest incidents – that the Conservative offices had been attacked by another group, in protest at the steel and coal closures in Wales. The letter signed, 'Free Wales – Cymru am Byth', added, 'As with second homes, Wales is under attack. We call on Welsh people to resist the British Government and its lackeys who care nothing for us. The Tories will not close South Wales down without a fight.'[11]

The police responded with 'Operation Fire' (Operation Tân), a massive round-up of known nationalists on Palm Sunday 1980. Roadblocks were set up across north Wales, and dozens of nationalists arrested and questioned throughout that weekend, even though there was no evidence to implicate any in the fire-bombing campaign. The attack on Conservative Party offices might have raised the bar, but some senior police officers thought the Palm Sunday round-up premature and forced upon them by political pressure. Roy Davies, a former Detective Chief Inspector and head of Llanelli CID at the time, believes the intelligence they received was badly flawed:

> On the basis of the intelligence collected, warrants were drawn up to arrest people and search their homes for items such as magazines or maps that showed the locations of holiday homes, or sodium chlorate or those kind of things. So a few teams went around arresting people. I have to say from the absolute beginning there was no evidence against any person I questioned – they were absolutely innocent and not guilty. And as the questioning went on I could see that these were not involved with the campaign at all. The intelligence wasn't correct, that's obvious. There was possibly suspicion or the magistrates wouldn't have issued warrants to arrest anybody unless there was some information, so the arrests by the police were lawful.

> There was absolutely no co-operation by the public when crimes such as the burning of holiday homes was committed, because there was sympathy as people saw their Welsh communities dying even though they didn't support the campaign.[12]

Not even during the pipeline bombings and campaign to stop the Investiture of the Prince of Wales had there been such a blatant abuse of judicial powers. Applications for arrest warrants were not always made to magistrates within whose jurisdiction offences had allegedly taken place, and magistrates rubber-stamped warrants without scrutinising the information in support of applications. Statements taken afterwards from many of those arrested appeared in *Fire/Tân*, a report by the Welsh Campaign for Civil and Political Liberties. Commissioned by assorted individuals and organisations, including the Cardiff Direct Action group, International Marxist group, Cymdeithas yr Iaith Gymraeg, Plaid Cymru, Welsh Socialist Republic Movement, Labour Party, National Council for Civil Liberties (Cardiff), trade unionists and academics, the report revealed a disturbing picture. Police questioning, searches and seizure of property were indiscriminate and threatening, more reminiscent of a police state, according to the statements of those arrested:

> Plaid Cymru papers were taken, addresses of local members and supporters; anti-nuclear energy statements and facts plus badges; details

of Cofiwn AGM, and papers which contained John Jenkins's address, membership forms; papers on the fourth TV channel campaign …

They searched everything in the house, also in the village hall, the village library, every room in the hall, and came back in the day to search the safe of the Community Council …

A large number of items were removed: all my business papers, many photographs, candles, petrol oil (for the chainsaw), roll of masking tape, books, jungle knife, all my Cofiwn literature … shoes, boots, trousers etc. and passport … I was given no receipt for my property which apart from what was on me at the time is still being held by them …

When I returned from work there were three policemen in plain clothes in the garage … They looked at my son's vehicle … one of the back tyres was taken away …[13]

Most people were picked up between 4.30 a.m. and 6.00 a.m. by scores of police officers on the grounds of being suspected of arson or criminal damage, or 'in connection with the fires at holiday homes'. Some said later:

A sergeant told me that I was being arrested concerning the causing of damage costing £750,000 to holiday homes …

I was told I was a terrorist and had caused £250,000-worth of damage to property …

Eventually at the point of arrest after a three-hour house search I was told it was to do with holiday homes …

The first words that were spoken as I opened the door at 5.30 a.m. were, 'You're under arrest. We want to search the house.' I can't remember whether there was any reference to a particular offence …

I was told I would not be allowed to go home until my alibi was checked …[14]

A young mother faced the embarrassment of breastfeeding her infant in a busy police station until released after a flurry of telephone calls from solicitors. Even she was detained for two hours, much shorter than some, held for three days before being released without charge. Another suspect locked in a cell overheard one officer say to another, 'These men are hardened terrorists and should be treated as such.'

Bickney cottage, Llanrhian, December 1979, one of the first holiday homes torched at the start of the Meibion Glyndŵr (Sons of Glyndŵr) arson campaign, which continued for the next ten years affecting more than two hundred properties. Copyright: *Western Mail*, Cardiff.

Two of the Palm Sunday suspects were required to provide tape-recordings of their voices. Another was asked to write out a threatening message with regard to a particular arson attack so that his handwriting could be checked against something the police already possessed. Some of the tactics used by police investigators terrified suspects held for no reason other than being known nationalists. One of those acquitted in the Free Wales Army trial in 1969, after which his marriage broke up, complained of being subjected to psychological torture during his thirty-seven hours in custody:

> The police knew of my loss, trying to work on my mind, that the same type of thing would happen again. Threatening to arrest my wife and put the small children into care of the local authority. I was threatened about halfway through Monday when the two detectives left my cell to do this – I didn't know where the family was until about 6 o'clock at night and the police said they couldn't find them. By the way, the family hadn't been out of the house at all.[15]

In another instance a suspect's spectacles were removed, the police refusing to return them throughout the interrogation. Another complained of being questioned simultaneously by four officers firing questions at him non-stop, a technique he recognised from his service in the Army. One middle-aged suspect, held for more than three days, was confronted by a senior officer holding up the *Western Mail* containing a report about the arson campaign and shouting, 'You're a terrorist', then striking him across the face with the folded newspaper: 'I was struck by him afterwards (not very badly) twice on my body. We shouted at each other for a few minutes with myself replying to his comments by calling him a "Nazi" and a "thug".'[16] Neither was the questioning confined to those arrested. Family members, friends and relatives were interrogated. According to one, his wife was asked about his mental state, whether he had suffered a nervous breakdown, was impulsive or craved fame:

> She was asked if she really knew me and throughout her questioning felt that the police questions were designed to undermine her confidence in me as a reliable husband. She was also questioned about our sex life. She was told that all terrorists are sexually perverted, and that because I was a terrorist I must be perverted too. She was asked what method of contraception we used and if there were any vibrators around the house or any pornographic literature.[17]

The Palm Sunday round-up of nationalists unearthed not one scrap of evidence about the arsonists. For many, it only confirmed what they suspected: that since the 1960s' extremism it had become an offence to be a Welshman; that campaigning for a free and just Wales by patriots was now considered terrorism.

The Prevention of Terrorism Act (1976) had started life as a temporary measure in 1974, the bloodiest year in the Northern Ireland Troubles after the proposed all-Ireland Council (Sunningdale) foundered. When Harold Wilson won the ensuing General Election for Labour, the UK was gripped by its worst period of post-war violence. The M62 coach bomb killed eleven, another thirty-three died in bombings in Dublin and Monaghan, and thirty-three were killed by the Birmingham pub bombs. Before the end of the year 294 civilians and soldiers were dead, direct rule had been restored and the Labour government had rushed through the Prevention of Terrorism Act. A Welshman, Merlyn Rees, was in the hot seat as Northern Ireland Secretary.

The Palm Sunday swoop in 1980 was the first occasion in Wales that the new powers had been used to detain people for up to seven days without charge if it was suspected they belonged to, or supported, a proscribed organisation. The methods employed in the 1960s by Commander Jock Wilson and his special squad were just the start of a crackdown that pushed patriotism into the path of those combating terrorism.

Subversives were described by Lord Denning, Master of the Rolls and the most celebrated English judge of the twentieth century, as people contemplating 'the overthrow of government by unlawful means'. But it was Merlyn Rees who, as Home Secretary in 1978, widened the definition to cover just about any activity a government thought undesirable. In a House of Commons speech defending the role of the Special Branch, Rees said subversive activities were those that 'threaten the safety and well-being of the state, and are intended to undermine or overthrow parliamentary democracy by political, industrial or violent means'. The boundaries between terrorists and freedom fighters, political and industrial agitation, were being blurred, starting to sound like the same thing. In much the same way as the British government sought to criminalise the IRA 'freedom fighters' by refusing them political prisoner status, the subsequent raft of anti-terrorist legislation has major implications for future political protest in Wales. One thing is certain: those involved with Tryweryn, the pipeline explosions, the Investiture protest, cottage arson, even language campaigners, could not expect the same consideration and leniency in the current terrorist-charged environment.

The Palm Sunday round-up did have some success, leading eventually to the arrest of Dafydd Ladd, alias Jim Llewellyn, the self-confessed anarchist John Jenkins had befriended. Of the thirty-seven incidents occurring in Wales in 1980, five were not claimed by Meibion Glyndŵr but believed to be the work of the clandestine anarchist/socialist organisation calling itself the Workers' Army of the Welsh Republic. More interested in overthrowing the state than in the cost of Welsh rural housing, it had piggybacked on the upswell in home-grown insurgency. But its targets were quite different: three Conservative clubs in Cardiff, another at Shotton, Clwyd, and, most seriously, an explosive device slipped through the window of a bedroom at Welsh Secretary Nicholas Edwards's Crickhowell home, just feet away from where his eldest son Rupert (16) was asleep. The following year an Army recruitment centre in Pontypridd, British Steel offices and a Welsh Office building, both in Cardiff, were all hit. The campaign also extended across the border, with Severn Trent Water Authority offices in Birmingham and National Coal Board Offices in London and Stratford-upon-Avon all targeted.

Judging from the claims made following these bombings, they were protesting at the closures in the coal and steel industries. A letter posted to the *Western Mail* at the time when devices were found at the Conservative clubs in Cardiff and Shotton, and signed 'Celtic International Brigade', warned, 'The lackeys of the English state … together with their families will be treated as legitimate targets for punishment.' The name used by the bombers in this letter was regarded by the police as a derivative of the Workers' Army of the Welsh Republic. A day after a device had been found at the Army Recruiting Office, Pontypridd – not far from where the Prince and Princess of Wales were soon to visit – a letter to the BBC warned that in the struggle for a free socialist Wales 'all aspects of English cultural, economic and political rule' would be attacked. The following New Year's Eve a bomb rocked celebrations and shattered windows at the Birmingham headquarters of the Severn Trent Water Authority. Twenty-four hours later the NCB London office and another office in Stratford were both hit. For the first time gelignite was used. The bombing of the Water Authority offices in Birmingham was linked to protests over the disparity in water tariffs between England and Wales.

After his arrest Ladd took police to a site at Castell Coch, near Cardiff, where four detonators were buried. In the Cardiff conspiracy trial that followed, Ladd admitted two charges of possessing explosives and was jailed for nine years at Cardiff Crown Court. Five others alleged by police to be connected in some way with the Workers' Army of the Welsh Republic were cleared of all charges – charges they claimed were based on fabricated evidence and confessions. Before their trial, the case was at the centre of a legal storm over the length of time the accused men had been held in custody, ranging from nine months to as long as seventeen months in the case of Ladd himself. Lawyers and the media also protested to the Home Office about a news blackout imposed by magistrates at the committal stage of proceedings, even though reporting restrictions had initially been lifted.[18]

The cottage arson attacks would continue undetected for another ten years after this.

# 16

## THE LONG ROAD BACK

The Cardiff conspiracy trial was of little interest to me. By the time the Palm Sunday raids took place I had already left the *Western Mail* for Brussels to become Chief of the European Bureau for Thomson Newspapers, the paper's parent company. The move was fortuitous. Within months of my packing my bags the editor, Duncan Gardiner, was replaced. In newspapers, deputies rarely step directly into the editor's chair. They have to prove themselves via stints on less prestigious publications before claiming the prize. From my new location in Brussels I would be responsible for supplying the group's seventeen daily newspapers with news from the European Union and western European countries. The total daily readership was in excess of 3,000,000, from Belfast to Cardiff, Edinburgh to Aberdeen, Newcastle to Blackburn, Middlesborough and the Home Counties. For five years I followed the European story wherever that took me. The cost for Thomson Newspapers was prodigious. I was their first and last foreign correspondent.

As it happened, terrorism figured large on the news agenda from the moment I signed on as one of 4,000 correspondents accredited to the European Commission. Only a few months previously the first directly elected elections were held for the European Parliament, soon to become a political stage for the main players in the Northern Ireland drama. For the very first time, Sinn Fein confronted its *bête noire*, the Revd Ian Paisley, across the floor of a democratically elected parliament. Because the *Belfast Telegraph* was in my stable of newspapers, Paisley regarded me as a conduit for delivering his fiery messages to his followers back home. After fierce exchanges with republicans, Big Ian and his entourage invariably stormed the press-room, booming, 'Where's the man from the *Telegraph*?' About the only sanctuary was the bar, or so I thought, until one evening, during a break in the parliament session, Paisley, on the prowl for publicity, spotted me imbibing with a group of pretty German interpreters celebrating *Fasching*. This is the day German women take over decision-making, marking it on this occasion by chopping off the expen-

172

sive silk ties of every member of the European Parliament propping up the bar. By way of compensation, we all received a glass of pink champagne. A devout teetotaller but unafraid of entering alien territory, Big Ian pushed his way through the throng, slapped an outsize hand on my shoulder and bellowed above the hubbub, 'John, that's the Devil's buttermilk.' I cringed, feeling like a berated member of his congregation, which he seemed to assume I was, simply because he had studied at a theological college in Barry. He might have left me alone with the pretty German interpreters if he had known I was a Catholic!

The *Belfast Telegraph* saw the European Union as an escape from counting bodies every day. It was a source of news to relieve the siege mentality of its readers with stories about straight bananas or 'Picnic sites in bandit country', after the Parliament approved special grants to build leisure facilities in Crossmaglen in South Armagh, the most IRA-infested area in the whole of the province.

In a different dimension was the death of Bobby Sands on 5 May 1981 after sixty-six days on hunger strike in the Maze Prison in support of republican prisoners' demand for political status. Sands was the third post-war IRA prisoner to starve himself to death. The first was Mickey Gaughan, a fellow inmate of John Jenkins in Albany on the Isle of Wight until moved to Parkhurst for force-feeding in April 1974. At the time of Gaughan's hunger strike, Britain force-fed protesters, a brutal process whereby the jaws were painfully forced open with clamps and a pipe rammed down the throat into the stomach. Sometimes it went down the windpipe by mistake. By the time he died, Gaughan's throat had been ripped to shreds by the procedure, which not long afterwards ceased. A supporter of the struggle for Welsh independence, Gaughan each year joined Jenkins at a special communion service for Dewi Sant in the prison's Anglican chapel, while on Saint Patrick's Day Jenkins reciprocated at the Catholic service.

News of the death of the twenty-seven-year-old Sands provoked a parliamentary outcry among liberally minded members, needing little invitation to censure the British government for human rights abuses in Northern Ireland. In their vanguard were those from the Republic, the most vociferous being Neil Blaney of Independent Fianna Fáil and a champion of the IRA hunger-strikers, ten of whom were to die. While revulsion over the death of Sands prompted a surge in support for the IRA, it was the use of plastic bullets for crowd control that indirectly crystallised for me the depth of the psychological divide between the warring parties. The relatives of one of seventeen killed by plastic bullets appealed to the European Court for Human Rights, based in the Parliament complex at Strasbourg. After months of deliberation, the Court ruled that plastic bullets should be banned. At that time, the UK was not a signatory to all clauses in the Charter for Human Rights, but invariably it amended legislation in line with rulings by the Court. Since Northern Ireland was the only part of the UK where plastic bullets were used, the decision was of great interest to the *Belfast Telegraph*. Telephoning its news desk, I explained the implications to the news editor who, after pausing a moment, said, 'Yes, John. We agree they should ban plastic bullets. We think they should use real ones.'

Besides a platform for all-Ireland politics, the European Union also provided a snapshot of how a small, independent nation, the Republic of Ireland, was seizing the opportunites created by membership.When Ireland first joined, a not-insignificant proportion of its budget came in grants from Brussels. Within a generation the republic's economic growth was outstripping that of the EU's founding countries. Ireland was a young, unfettered nation on a roll, and I was deeply envious of my Irish colleagues, who had clear sight of the national implications of EU decisions. The benefits of membership to Wales, however, were buried inside the overarching interests of the UK. What was good for England was good enough for Wales. The very occasional Welsh presence in Brussels was usually a worthless exercise in flag-waving.

Very soon, the biggest story around was the Falklands War. Like the Kennedy assassination and the first landing on the moon, most people remember where they were when the Task Force sailed in April 1982. At the end of a European Parliament session in Strasbourg I had made a detour via Munich to spend the weekend with friends. Heading back to Brussels, I had parked the car just off the autobahn on the outskirts of Munich to fiddle with the car radio when I picked up the first newsflash. Deciding to return to base as quickly as possible for the inevitable diplomatic repercussions, I was about to set off when I saw a road sign pointing to 'Dachau'. Britain had embarked on a war thousands of miles distant in the South Atlantic, and I was a few kilometres from one of the most notorious concentration camps of the Second World War. The coincidence was too great not to break the journey and visit a place I was unlikely ever to see again. At the entrance to the camp stood an elderly German in a peaked cap, directing traffic. I grimaced as he waved the queue of cars through with a cheerful, 'Parking on the right, gas ovens on the left.'

A month later HMS *Conqueror* had sunk the Argentine cruiser *General Belgrano* with the loss of more than 300 lives, rendering Britain virtually isolated among its European Union partners. If Margaret Thatcher wanted EU support for economic sanctions against the Argentines, then she had chosen a bad time to block farm subsidies in the battle over the British budget rebate. The Irish Defence Minister said what most member states thought in describing Britain as the 'aggressor' for sinking the *Belgrano*. The prevailing view in Brussels was that Thatcher needed a war to win the next election. Tam Dalyell, Labour MP for Linlithgow, thought so too, and embarked upon a crusade to prove that she deliberately ignored a peace plan drawn up by the Peruvian President hours before the cruiser was sunk. Vigorously denied by the former Prime Minister as 'malicious and misleading nonsense', Dalyell's allegations are not that easily repudiated, if a conversation I had two years later in Lima can be believed.

The opportunity had arisen, as it sometimes does for newspapermen, for a free trip to Peru. This coincided with a sabbatical I had negotiated with Thomson Newspapers in return for agreeing to remain in Brussels for a further three years. If there is one thing everyone should do before they die then it is to visit Machu Picchu, the ruins of the almost inaccessible jungle city where the Incas hid their women and wealth from the conquistadors. But first I had to get there, not as easy as it sounds since my flight was with pre-glasnost Aeroflot, which probably explains why it was free. At that time, the only west European connection the Soviet flag-carrier had was through Luxembourg. But it did fly routes no other airline bothered with, such as Luxembourg–Havana–Lima. Aeroflot's giant Ilyushin airliners were reputedly held together with sticking plaster and flown by retired Soviet MiG fighter-pilots. Sure enough, when I boarded at Luxembourg the seats were torn, dirty and held together by strips of sticky brown paper, and the take-off was fast and vertical. Only chronic indigestion induced by in-flight meals served strictly according to Moscow time wrenched my thoughts away from the Ilyushin's shuddering frame during the twelve hours to our refuelling stop in Cuba. The breakfast I had eaten at midnight almost resurfaced as the aircraft dropped precipitously on Havana in the middle of a power blackout, the runway lights no more illuminating than flickering candles.

Herded into one dimly lit room, the door guarded by a pair of Cubans armed with Soviet AK-47 assault rifles, passengers crowded around a solitary drinks dispenser, which finally gave up dispensing after being growled at in Russian and thumped once too often. If there is such a person as an archetypal arms-dealer, then I was surrounded by them, square men, all shoulders and thick necks. For most of the flight they sat sullen and tight-lipped, occasionally jerking into life to order another vodka, and always with tonic, I noted. This confirmed what Boris the man from *Isvestia* told me once at a NATO press conference in Brussels, that what Russians liked most about working in the West was that they could get tonic with their vodka. Once the Ilyushin was refuelled we were led across the blacked-out runway for the flight down to Lima, arriving safely except for my suitcase, which sailed around the carousel, ripped and spilling clothes en route, but remarkably with nothing having been stolen.

Lima sits on a narrow coastal strip, the giant breakers of the Pacific Ocean at its feet, desert and the high Andes at its back. Tropical and humid, the city's climate is influenced all year by the upwelling of the cold, nutrient-rich water of the Humboldt Current flowing northwards along the Peruvian coast. The collision with the warmer surface waters spews out dense fog-banks, wrapping Lima's coastal suburbs in a shroud of dank humidity. The dampness climbs the walls of coastal apartment blocks like gangrene, rotting the very fabric of the buildings. But a half-hour's drive into the city's desert backyard are some of the driest places in the world, where nothing decays, the roadside marked by cairns built from rusting tins discarded years previously. In the 1980s Lima was too dangerous a place for a European to linger. Stray a few hundred yards from the hotel and there was every chance of being mugged. The Peruvian economy was in a mess, the gap between the rich and poor huge and growing wider by the day, the wealthy living in fortresses behind walls lined with razor-wire, and patrolled day and night by what were euphemistically called 'watchmen'. Each had a weapon or two hidden up his jumper. Even the Peruvian equivalent of Mr Whippy, tempting the children out of their affluent redoubts with his musical chimes, carried an automatic beside the tub of vanilla ice-cream. Far from these prosperous pockets on the outskirts of the city were the *pueblos jovenes*, overcrowded shanty towns for hundreds of thousands of Peruvian peasants who had fled the countryside to escape the grinding poverty and the violence. Much of this was attributed to the Shining Path (*Sendero Luminoso*), the Communist Party of Peru, a Maoist guerrilla organisation seeking to overthrow a corrupt government. One of the most brutal groups of revolutionaries the modern world has known, Shining Path was designated a 'foreign terrorist organization' by the United States and European Union twenty years before 9/11. When not executing recalcitrant peasants, kidnapping journalists was the favourite and most lucrative pastime for these revolutionaries. I had no immediate plans for an interview, but I did want to get to Machu Picchu.

After three days in lawless Lima I flew to Cusco, the ancient Inca capital, and from there travelled by tourist train, snaking up narrow mountain passes to the Incas' ruined city, strung along a mountain ridge 10,000 feet above the jungle-covered slopes of the Urubama Valley. The Peruvian cure for the altitude sickness which kicks in at this height is a wad of coca leaves chewed constantly. Not strictly a narcotic, although the source of cocaine, it first numbs the mouth like a dental anaesthetic and then the whole body, if enough of the juice is swallowed. The nausea eased as the tourist train headed back to Cusco, but the weather deteriorated until a fierce thunderstorm broke. Not to worry, I would soon be flying down to Lima, I thought, as I collected my suitcase from my dirty little hotel. Very quickly I discovered I was going nowhere. The airport had taken a battering and all flights were cancelled, no one knew until when. I was stranded, my only companions a Japanese family on holiday from Panama. Desperate to get back to Lima to catch their flight, they hired a minibus after discovering Cusco had another airport, a short distance outside the city. The tiny landing-strip, only large enough for small aircraft, was expecting one the next morning, bringing in a group of government officials for a meeting with striking Peruvian goldminers.

My second night in that scruffy hotel was mostly spent swatting bedbugs and swigging tea infused from coca leaves. Next morning I hitched a ride with the Japanese to Cusco's second airport, which I discovered had only a dirt runway. The check-in desk in the corrugated shed serving as the terminal building was cracked, as was the cistern of the toilet behind a curtain in a corner. Several hours later the plane landed, the placard-waving deputation of goldminers shuffled forward menacingly to surround Peru's Minister for Mines – and the pilot, after one look at the churned-up runway and the thunder clouds circling overhead, retired to Cusco until the weather improved. Our last hope of escape was by train and a ten-hour journey across the *altiplano*, the high Andean plain running through the interiors of Peru, Chile and Bolivia. A train was scheduled to depart shortly for the southern capital, Puno, and from there to Arequipa and an airport with planes that flew. But it was the first train out in two weeks, after the one that went before had been ambushed by Shining Path guerillas.

Cusco railway station was a tidal pool of humanity, spilling across the platform and bobbing with red and blue woollen bobble-hats, with ear-flaps instead of bobbles. The entire population, it seemed, was intent on catching what might be the last train for two more weeks. Most had been camped on the platform for several days, by which time it had been transformed into an Andean market, women with baskets of bread weaving between improvised fruit and vegetable stalls, others squatting and swatting flies swarming over slabs of raw meat dripping blood. There were even takeaways, chunks of unidentifiable meat sizzling on braziers of red-hot coals spluttering amongst the throng. Health and safety had not penetrated this far. Occasionally from among the mêlée of brightly coloured ponchos and straw hats came the flash of the green battledress of the army guards detailed to accompany the train through Shining Path territory. In the stampede for the train, I could think of nothing but holding on to my wallet with one hand while using the suitcase in the other to carve a path through the struggling mass. Tickets and reservations were forgotten in the fight for a foothold. As the train steamed out on to the *altiplano* I spotted my Japanese travelling companions stranded on the platform, waving their tickets in the face of a railway conductor.

Once aboard, so tight was the crush of bodies, bundles and slabs of raw meat, that no one could move. Then, like a tightly packed football terrace before kick-off, the crowd swayed just long enough to reveal a solitary empty reserved seat. Mine. One of four, the others were already occupied by three travellers of European descent – among them the pilot of the private aircraft who had abandoned the Minister of Mines in Cusco. The second was a young Irish Catholic priest in jeans and sweater returning to his parish somewhere on the *altiplano* after a holiday in Lima teaching slum children how to read, his only luggage a plastic carrier bag. The third was an American, claiming to be an agent for the US Drug Enforcement Agency looking for drug-smugglers.

Crossing the *altiplano* by train at night, in the middle of a Peruvian winter, through territory controlled by Shining Path guerrillas, was not the usual stuff of 'wish you were here' postcards from foreign parts. Not only were all seats double-booked, so was the aisle it seemed, not a spare inch visible beneath the sprawling bodies in ponchos. Outside the temperature had plunged well below freezing, but not for this reason was every window in the compartment tightly bolted. Each time the train slowed or screeched to a halt, as it often did, a deathly hush descended, passengers in unison peering into the inky blackness beyond the condensation dripping off the windows. As it happened, it was a lack of oxygen, not the Shining Path, that threatened my life. When the train reached 12,000 feet it felt as though its human cargo collectively drew a deep breath, draining the compartment of the very last gasp. Choking, I ploughed through the bodies spreadeagled in the aisle to the far end of the carriage to throw open the window, under the nose of a Peruvian armed guard. Gulping down a lung full of icy Andean air it was not hard to imagine the last days in the Black Hole of Calcutta.

Apart from this, the only other incident of note occurred just after dawn. The dry, flat *altiplano*, studded with frosted clumps of dwarf shrubs and grasses, like small oases in an otherwise barren desert, was appearing through the half-light when the train stopped once more. The young priest pulled on his sweater, picked up his carrier bag and, after bidding us farewell, jumped on to the track and headed off into his parish. Nowhere could I see a platform, a station, any sign of habitation, just a snow-covered ridge of volcanic peaks rising in the distance from the flat plain, the first rays of the morning sun turning their slopes blood-orange. For all I knew, he was not a priest but a smuggler, with a carrier bag stuffed with drugs.

Back in Lima after a flight from Arequipa, Peru's capital city took on an entirely new perspective, safe and civilised. I even had a welcome call from a member of the British Embassy staff and a gentlemanly reprimand for having failed to tell them I was on their patch. Because of the country's political and economic instability, visitors, especially journalists, were advised by the Foreign Office to check in before disappearing into the hinterland. Anyhow, all was forgiven and the nice man invited me around for embassy drinks that evening. Having scoffed one or two dozen bottles of champagne at the taxpayer's expense in my time, I was familiar with embassy drinks parties. Embassy staff, especially those in distant postings like Peru, love to gossip, hungry for titbits about colleagues ploughing the Foreign and Commonwealth Office furrow elsewhere in the world. Not even the Official Secrets Act stops them swapping the most confidential information so long as it is non-attributable. I must have been good company, because before we dispersed I was invited to join my new pals for brunch the following day, a Saturday, at their favourite watering-hole in the Peruvian desert. The drive took about an hour, nothing more interesting than sand and those rusting tin cans until we reached a green oasis surrounded by date palms, with a bar run by an eighty-year-old Lancastrian. Stripped to the waist and wearing boxer shorts, his skin like lightly tanned leather, he shuffled around serving Bloody Marys, taking care not to trip over an assorted group of tiny tots scampering around his feet. His name escapes me, sufficient to say he had arrived in Peru not long after the Second World War to help run a textile factory and never left. Nor had his broad Lancashire accent. The children, of whom I counted five, were supposedly the issue of his most recent marriage.

By the time brunch had become supper, one of my hosts from the Embassy, by then well into his cups, opened up a new front in the conversation: the Falklands War and the Peruvian initiative. According to what he whispered in my ear, Fernando Belaunde Terry, the Peruvian President, had with the support of the five Andean Pact countries – Peru, Venezuela, Ecuador, Bolivia, Colombia – put together a peace plan which should have prevented the sinking of the Argentine cruiser *General Belgrano*, and the Falklands War. Whether or not the peace plan was communicated to London in time or at all was central to Tam Dalyell's charge that the *General Belgrano* was sunk for political reasons, not military ones; that the cruiser was sailing away from the total exclusion zone when torpedoed. If my source was correct, the Peruvian President had been unable to communicate the peace plan to the British Embassy in Lima on 1 May for transmission to London because no one could be found: it was a Saturday, and they were out to brunch! The following day, Sunday 2 May, Margaret Thatcher was having lunch with her War Cabinet and Chiefs of Staff at Chequers when Admiral Sir John Fieldhouse, Commander of the Fleet, reported that the *Belgrano* and her two destroyers patrolling at the edge of the 200-mile exclusion zone posed a threat to the advancing Task Force. On the basis of this, Thatcher issued the order to attack the Argentine cruiser, HMS *Conqueror* sinking *Belgrano* at 8 p.m. that Sunday evening.

The significance of all this did not really dawn on me until the following day. But I needed to check it was not just Bloody Mary talk. By the time I did, the story had changed: the peace plan had, after all, been transmitted to London in time. Either way, this account contradicts what Margaret Thatcher says about the incident in her autobiography: that those who took the decision at Chequers that Sunday morning knew nothing about the peace plan.[1]

Throughout my time as a foreign correspondent it never ceased to surprise me how much the Foreign Office knew about my movements. By the time I returned from Peru it was evident from certain remarks dropped into conversations that there was concern that I had poked my nose into the Falklands. The United Kingdom Permanent Representation in Brussels – the UK embassy to the European Union – had a person whose job was to hang out with the media, professionally and socially. While it was always helpful to get the British angle on a story, I had no desire to see him later over my pint. Amiable enough, he knew too much, and not for the first time was I reminded of that.

The previous year, along with a group of mainly foreign pressmen covering a session of the European Parliament, I had been invited to dinner at an exclusive Strasbourg restaurant by Mr Bora Atun, representative of the government of a rogue state, the Turkish Republic of Northern Cyprus. The Turkish Cypriots in the northern half of Cyprus had declared themselves independent in 1983 after repulsing, with the aid of Turkish troops, a Greek Cypriot coup backed by Athens. After being pulled off each other's backs, Greek and Turkish Cypriots were separated by a buffer zone patrolled by United Nations troops. Since only Turkey recognised the new rebel state, Mr Atun's job was to lobby on its behalf for European Union recognition. The dinner in a private room at the restaurant was part of that process.

As the meal progressed, it became apparent my host knew far too much about me – personal stuff known only to colleagues back in Wales. Intrigued to find out how, I agreed to meet him for lunch on our return to Brussels. After toying with my curiosity over a plate of pasta and a bottle of wine, Mr Atun finally revealed that his source was none other than his wife, Cheryl Willis, a former advertising representative at the *Western Mail*. When the island was partitioned and an economic blockade imposed, the bottom fell out of the tourist market and the only way to get to Turkish Cyprus for anyone wanting a holiday in a danger zone was via Istanbul and then on to a military airfield on the island. Visitors were waved through with a smile, without even a passport stamp, because that automatically made them *persona non grata* in the Greek south. Greek Cypriots became apoplectic at the sight of anything suggesting de facto recognition of their rogue neighbour. Cheryl Willis was one of the first tourists to risk their wrath by taking a holiday, at the very time the master of a cargo ship unloading at Limassol in the Greek south was thrown in jail when his manifest revealed he had previously called at Famagusta in the Turkish north. It was on the beach at Famagusta that Ms Willis had met Bora Atun, then mayor of the walled city, from whose battlements he led the Turkish Cypriot resistance until help arrived from the mainland, in the form of 20,000 Turkish troops.

Our lunch ended with an invitation to join a party of European journalists on an exploratory, all-expenses-paid week in Northern Cyprus. It was one of those 'come and see for yourself' invitations during which every journalist expects to be subjected to intense propaganda. A few days into it, a splendid dinner was held for the visiting press and representatives of the Turkish Cypriot government at the Dome Hotel in the picturesque fishing village of Kyrenia, unquestionably the jewel in the new republic's tourist crown. For rooms with a view the Dome was unbeatable, perched upon a rocky outcrop, at its feet the blue Mediterranean and in the distance just eighty miles away the beaches of war-torn Beirut. The Dome was also a watering hole for the 'Old Brits', expatriate refugees from Malta who spent their afternoons playing bridge and drinking tea amongst its faded splendour. After relocating to Greek Cyprus when the Maltese threw them out, they had chosen to move again and take their chances with the Turks before the island erupted in civil war.

Not surprisingly, movement between the north and south of the island was keenly debated over dinner, as earlier that day a group of us had been turned back at the Ledra Palace checkpoint in Nicosia by an outraged Greek Cypriot police inspector, demanding to know why a party of European Union pressmen were breaking sanctions. Since partition the two sides were separated by the Green Line, an assemblage of walls and barbed-wire entanglements running across the island through the centre of Nicosia and patrolled by United Nations troops. Whereas the Turks permitted free movement through the main checkpoint at Ledra Palace, no one had crossed in the other direction for ten years. For the Greeks to allow this was tantamount to recognising the rogue state. That was about to change.

For the life of me I could not see what prevented anyone with a little initiative crossing the Green Line. Not only were large stretches unmarked, the obvious place to cross for someone with a British passport was through the British sovereign military base at Dhekelia, straddling the buffer zone and where John Jenkins's son was born while he was serving in Cyprus. Much later, and full of Dutch courage, I agreed to have a crack at being the first to cross the border in both directions since partition. At the time it sounded like a good idea if I pulled it off. If not, it almost certainly meant a spell in a Greek Cypriot cell!

Early the next morning a car drew up at the Dome Hotel, with two Turkish Cypriots on their way to work at the Dhekelia military base. Clutching my passport and press card I jumped into the back, and we headed for a back door into the base guarded by a young soldier with a rifle on his shoulder and sleep in his eyes. My companions waved their work permits and as I pretended to do the same the soldier lifted the barrier. Within a few minutes I was being dropped off outside the NAAFI. Now for the difficult part: getting back across the border at the Ledra Palace checkpoint in Nicosia. The first stage was to take a taxi from outside the NAAFI, the driver dropping me at the edge of the buffer-zone. Between there and the Ledra Palace lay a half-mile-deep belt of war-torn Nicosia, the ruins as deserted as the day the civil war ended and the opposing armies pulled back. Nothing moved, not a soul, not even a bird, my footsteps echoing around the bombed and burned-out buildings as I pressed on towards the checkpoint. Just occasionally a Greek Cypriot soldier with binoculars stuck his helmet out of the upper floor of some bombed-out building to take a closer look at whatever was happening on the far side of the wall.

Twice in my life I have tasted real fear: the first time, when I smelled petrol after crashing my car into what must have been the only ravine in tiny Luxembourg, and now, as I approached the Ledra Palace. My heart sank, my tongue a lump of leather. Ahead, on the other side of the checkpoint, I could see colleagues, cameras poised waiting to record the historic moment. But blocking my path, arms akimbo, was the very same police inspector who the previous day had given us such a hard time. And now I was on his side, the penalty for which, he reminded me in perfect English, was to be thrown into jail 'until the second coming of Christ'. No way would I cross on his watch, as if his very life depended on it. The argument raged back and forth, my colleagues yelling their support in several languages while taking photographs from the sanctuary of northern Cyprus. Eventually the police inspector called for assistance from his Ministry of Information, this arriving in the shape of a heavily pregnant press spokeswoman. A former BBC correspondent, she had no sympathy for my predicament, and but for the presence of a couple of armed Greek Cypriot soldiers loitering at the edge of the argument, I was tempted to jump the barrier into the arms of my colleagues. 'Jump, jump', one shouted in French, and another the same in Dutch. Then I played what I thought was probably my last card by reminding the mum-to-be that the arrest of a British journalist was certain to trigger an international incident. By now it was midday and the Cypriot sun beat down. Suddenly, Mrs BBC wilted in the heat, shuffled uncomfortably as if her baby was due any moment – and instructed a very unhappy police inspector to lift the barrier. Instead of cheers my colleagues seemed positively disappointed at missing an even better story. The Turkish Cypriot media, however, celebrated a propaganda coup by flying in a camera crew from mainland Turkey to interview the first person to cross the border both ways since partition.

Back in Brussels the spook from the Foreign Office cornered me in the middle of a press conference to offer a 'few words of advice'. I needed to be more careful where I stuck my size ten boots. An already difficult situation had not been helped by my Ledra Palace stunt. In fact, the British Ambassador had been obliged to apologise for my activities. By the time I left Brussels in 1985 the Foreign Office and its agents probably had a pretty fat file, which I imagine will follow me to the grave.

My career as a foreign correspondent ended abruptly and painfully. During the early summer of 1985 my eldest son Mark visited me in Brussels at the end of a long trip around Europe by train. The lad was exhausted and slept most of the time, quite understandable after heaven knows how many nights bunking down on railway platforms. I thought nothing more about it until, returning some weeks later from covering a story in Germany, I received a call from my wife back in Wales. Mark, then 24, was desperately ill with leukaemia. Potentially terminal illnesses like this usually affect other families. I just wrote about it. For the very first time in our lives, we were at the centre of a real-life drama, a fight to save our son. I knew I had to get back to Wales and into a job where I could help. My contract stated that if I were to return to the UK it would be to a position commensurate with my experience. That meant editor somewhere, but not necessarily in Wales. For six months I waited for this to be resolved, agonising over whether I should pack it all in to be at my son's bedside. Thomson Newspapers were sympathetic, allowing me as much leave as I felt necessary. But that really did not wash with colleagues on other newspapers, who said they would have expected, and received, immediate compassionate leave. The position I was eventually offered was in London, as city editor for the group.

Still a long way from home, it was to prove fortuitous when Mark ran out of options for treating his leukaemia. After contracting septicaemia from one of the many blood transfusions, he almost died in intensive care. Although his doctors got the leukaemia back into remission after powerful doses of chemotherapy, treating the disease was becoming increasingly difficult. His best hope was a bone-marrow transplant, but for that he needed a sibling with an identical match. Ironically, his sister and brother had matching bone-marrows and could have saved each other, but not Mark. His only other chance was an autologous transplant, which meant killing off the leukaemia with heavy doses of chemotherapy, after which a litre of bone marrow, a blood-like substance, is extracted. The bone marrow is then returned to the body after it has been treated, although with the risk of reinoculating the patient with his or her own leukaemia. The best place for what was still an experimental procedure was University College Hospital, in London, where I was working.

As Mark underwent what can only be described as a vicious course of treatment, I was hammering on the door of the Anthony Nolan Trust, at the time the only organisation in Britain with a list of potential unrelated bone-marrow donors. Finding one was a long shot. Even if you struck lucky there were all kinds of complications, such as host versus donor disease, invariably fatal. Hiring a car, I drove around south-east England knocking on doors with the addresses of donors long since gone, and finally giving up the search as hopeless. Back at University College Hospital, the punishing side-effects of the chemotherapy meant it was impossible for Mark to continue the treatment.

Those were desperate days for the entire family. We did not know where to turn. Without a proper register of potential donors people such as my son never stood any chance of a transplant. It could not be clearer that the National Health Service needed a register of potential donors, fully screened so that they could be matched with leukaemia sufferers at the touch of a button. But there was no money, no NHS resources for this. Finishing work one evening I joined some colleagues in the Cartoonist public-house, around the corner from our office in Fleet Street. Suddenly, someone I had never met tapped me on the shoulder and asked whether I was the man he had been searching for all over London: the man looking for a donor for his son. Malcolm Thomas, from Bridgend, who like me was then working in London, was desperate to find a donor for his twelve-year-old daughter Alex. That evening we decided the only hope for Alex and Mark – and for others in a similar situation – was to recruit in the shortest possible time 150,000 new donors. I don't know why we chose that figure, other than that it sounded large enough to improve the odds.

Our first move was to persuade the Anthony Nolan Trust to provide the facilities. Tennis courts behind the Trust's laboratories in Kensington were commandeered as a site for mobile laboratories for testing blood samples from the tens of thousands of potential donors from all over Britain. From each sample, tissue-typers could identify a person's bone-marrow type. I recruited forty of these experts from all corners of the world, some travelling from as far as India and Australia. They came from abroad, because to use those in Britain would have denuded the National Health Service of vital expertise. Malcolm persuaded British Airways to donate flights; I convinced the owner of a hotel chain to provide accommodation for the tissue-typers while they were in Britain. Woolworth's, where Mark was a trainee manager, collected the money to help fund this military-style exercise. Doctor members of the Round Table took the blood samples at temporary clinics set up all over the country for overnight dispatch to London by Red Star in special containers, all for free.

By the end of six weeks we had hit our magical target, as a result of which many would find transplants. But not Mark, whose tissue type was so rare there was not a single match, nor young Alex, for whom there were four hundred potential matches, but who tragically died before they could all be fully tested. That convinced the pair of us that if there was to be a national register, potential donors needed to be thoroughly tested when first recruited, because leukaemia patients had no time to wait. The result was that we founded the British Bone Marrow Donor Appeal in 1987, the year before I eventually returned to the *Western Mail* as editor. After raising more than £6 million towards the cost of testing potential donors, twenty years later Wales would have a register of 50,000 and England and Northern Ireland one of 250,000. Better still, the government in 2001 agreed to fund the register, after a meeting in Downing Street between Prime Minister Tony Blair, the parents of another desperately sick child and myself. Not many charities can declare themselves redundant, job done. Miraculously, Mark, who never found a donor, survived to start a new life, teaching through the medium of Welsh. And I have a native Welsh-speaker for a grandson. Those punishing courses of chemotherapy had knocked Mark's leukaemia out for the count.

# 17

## HIRAETH!

I returned to Wales as Editor of the *Western Mail* in January 1988, having jumped through all the hoops from lowly district reporter to the top job, probably the very last time anyone would achieve this from a standing start. No doubt some brows wrinkled with incredulity that someone from a long line of terraced houses, in Newport of all places, had landed one of Welsh journalism's plum jobs. Fortunately, the man then running Thomson Newspapers was a Scot who had risen through the ranks himself. Besides increasing circulation, cutting costs and re-establishing the *Western Mail*'s pre-eminence as truly the national newspaper of Wales, chief executive Bill Heeps handed me the additional task of founding another newspaper, *Wales on Sunday*, at the same time as I was editing the *Western Mail*. Thomson wanted a lot for his money!

With all my time and energy accounted for, the discovery that the cottage arson campaign was still going strong was a minor distraction, until Meibion Glyndŵr stepped up its campaign by targeting four estate agents across the border in England. The first attacks outside Wales were in Chester on the night of 27 February 1988. Little damage was caused by the incendiary devices, which were either left outside or pushed through the letter-boxes of the agencies. In the window of one were advertisements for cottages for sale in Wales. Two others in Liverpool city centre, one in Shrewsbury and another at Llangefni were attacked two months later on 6 May, in each case the explosive device being popped through the letter-box and a warning call made to the Samaritans at Rhyl. After this, Merseyside, Cheshire and West Mercia joined Gwynedd and Dyfed-Powys in forming a special squad based in Bangor to coordinate the hunt for the arsonists.

The arsonists laid low throughout the summer months until holidaymakers and second-home owners had departed. Then on 3 October Meibion Glyndŵr struck again in spectacular fashion along a 250-mile front, fire-bombing seven estate agents in England. Starting at Wellington in Shropshire, two agencies were hit at 8.50 p.m. and 9 p.m., after which they moved on to West Kirby (11 p.m.), then Chipping Campden in the Cotswolds (11.07 p.m.), on to Neston in the Wirral (11.45 p.m.), back to Worcester (2 a.m.), before finishing the night's blitz in Clifton, Bristol (9.46 a.m.). In view of the times when the incidents were reported, the logistics of the operation suggest more than one group was involved. The immediate result was that Avon and Somerset, and also Gloucestershire, were drawn into an investigation involving seven constabularies. Police throughout the country were also alerted to an escalation in the arson threat, condemned by the *Western Mail* as being:

> Not so much anti-English as anti-Welsh … Though it poses a serious threat to innocent individuals … It is liable to hit Wales hard … Far from helping the movement to give new vitality to Wales's culture, language or tradition the latest series of incidents in a disreputable campaign only threatens to sabotage that great movement … [it is] mean-minded, manically inhospitable, violent and reckless of life and limb.

The following month, on 26 November 1988, the arsonists were even more ambitious. The fire-bombing spread to London, where six estate agents in the fashionable West End were targeted. One of these, Strutt and Parker's four-storey Mayfair office block, was gutted, the staircase collapsing and injuring a fireman. From amongst the wreckage police recovered a brochure advertising Welsh properties for sale.[1] For the very first time, Scotland Yard's Anti-Terrorist Squad, already on high alert for an IRA Christmas bombing campaign, became involved, while before long, MI5 would, at various times, assign thirty-eight agents to Wales to assist police in the investigation.

When the BBC *Crimewatch* programme featured the investigation the only clues it offered viewers were a few spots of blood and strands of hair, and a solitary footprint recovered from the scene of one fire. Anonymous letters sent to the media and signed 'Rhys Gethin', the legendary lieutenant of Owain Glyndŵr, confirmed that English incomers and their businesses were very much in the firing line.[2] 'There is no welcome for the English in Wales' was the gist of an anonymous call to the *Western Mail*'s Welsh Affairs Correspondent Clive Betts after the London fires. But despite this dangerous escalation, the groundswell of public support held fast, an opinion poll for HTV showing 57 per cent of those questioned backed the aims of Meibion Glyndŵr. What previously had only nuisance value was taken more seriously when property was attacked in densely populated parts of London. Until then it had been regarded as low-grade terrorism with 'woolly and vague' motives.[3]

Speculation about the identity of the arsonists was intense. Quite a number of people within Plaid Cymru, among them Dafydd Iwan and party leader Dafydd Wigley, believed it was all the work of the government's 'dirty tricks' department. Police frustration boiled over in February 1990 after receiving a tip-off about an incendiary device hidden in the wall of a house at Penygroes.

As a result, the Welsh pop singer Bryn Fôn was arrested, partly on account of suspicions arising from a line in his song 'Sons of the Flame'. After more than ten years the police had resorted to sifting through the lyrics of a pop song for clues. Eventually released into the arms of supporters besieging Dolgellau police station, Bryn Fôn demanded an inquiry, this eventually recommending the disciplining of two officers for acting precipitously.[4]

That year, 1990, was the year of the letter-bombs, the first arriving on 20 July at Land and Sea, a centre serving the well-heeled and largely English yachting fraternity at Abersoch on the Llŷn Peninsula. Instead of a condom stuffed with a wax tube filled with sulphuric acid and thrown through a broken window of an empty house, the letter-bomb was a video-cassette posted to the target and triggered to explode when the lid was lifted.

Suspicion fell on Sion Aubrey Roberts (21), a known nationalist living on the top floor of a block of flats in Llangefni, Ynys Môn. Roberts was an associate of Dewi Prysor Williams and David Gareth Davies. All three had formed the Meibion Glyndŵr 'Colour Party' at the annual ceremony in Abergele commemorating the deaths of the MAC2 saboteurs George Taylor and Alwyn Jones. With Roberts their prime suspect, two MI5 agents broke into his flat and planted a bugging device in November 1991. When a second pair of agents returned thirteen days later to retrieve it they stumbled across bomb-making equipment, alarm clocks modified to incorporate batteries and wires, and a packet containing explosive substances. Whatever incriminating evidence, if any, was gathered by the bugging devices was never revealed, not even in court, when the agents, referred to only as A, B, C and D, gave evidence from behind a screen.[5]

The police arrested Roberts, of Plas Tudur, Llangefni, Williams (25), an electrician, of Dolgain Farm, Trawsfynydd, and Davies (32), unemployed, of Y Wern, Gwalchmai, after letter-bombs were intercepted at Bangor post office by a postal worker, who spotted a suspicious package with a stencilled address. Inside each was a video-cassette box. The moment the box was opened an electrical current fired a modified flash-bulb, igniting an incendiary mixture. The intended victims were the head of North Wales CID, Detective Chief Superintendent Gwyn Williams; the senior detective leading the search for Meibion Glyndŵr, Detective Chief Inspector Maldwyn Roberts; Welsh Office Minister Sir Wyn Roberts; and Conservative Party agent Elwyn Jones. All three accused denied charges of conspiracy to cause explosions; Roberts and Davies denied a charge of sending explosive materials and Roberts denied a further charge of possessing explosive material. Lasting forty-one days, it was the longest bilingual trial ever held and cost about £3 million. Halfway through, a juror found a message on his windscreen: 'Wales is not for sale'. Roberts, a callow youth of low intellect, generally regarded as only a footsoldier acting on instructions, was jailed for twelve years. More a dupe than a terrorist, many thought that Roberts, who was nine years old when the arson campaign started in 1979, had been made a judicial scapegoat. Dewi Prysor Williams and David Gareth Davies were acquitted of all charges.[6]

Much was made of the fact that after the conviction of Roberts the cottage arson campaign stopped, which is not exactly the case. Three further incidents occurred while the trio were being held in custody for fifteen months, the length of their detention before the trial generally regarded as a denial of their human rights.[7] The hunt for the arsonists continues. As recently as 2004, the Deputy Chief Constable of North Wales Police, Clive Wolfendale, said that material gathered during the investigation would be subjected to DNA testing to discover whether it could yield new clues.[8]

A measure of police frustration over the failure to break through the wall of silence was the £50,000 reward offered by the North Wales Constabulary for information. I added another £30,000 from the *Western Mail*, but still no one came forward. Asked to launch a campaign for a review of Roberts's sentence, I declined, partly because I thought it unrealistic and also because I was by then too busy saving my own neck. The inevitable had happened. After five years as editor, during which the circulation had reached an unprecedented 80,000 a day, and I had also launched *Wales on Sunday*, like so many editors before me my time was up. Editing a newspaper is a bit like being adrift in an open boat in

In 1993, 21-year-old Sion Aubrey Roberts of Llangefni, Ynys Môn, was jailed for twelve years for sending letter bombs. Only nine years of age when the cottage arson campaign started, Roberts is thought by some to have been made a scapegoat for the failure of police to identify the mastermind behind the arson attacks. To this day, no other person has been convicted in connection with the cottage arson campaign. Copyright: *Western Mail*, Cardiff.

dangerous seas: invariably you get torpedoed, no matter how fast you duck and dive. In addition to the usual fortunes of war I was aware that in refocusing the *Western Mail* on Welsh national issues, after a decade of relative indifference, I had upset those who regarded the 1979 devolution result as the last throw of the Welsh dice. By resurrecting the debate about the democratic deficit and the need for a Welsh Assembly I was rocking the boat again. That was fine so long as the managing director backed me, but once Robert Tilsley was dispatched I was exposed to those who cared only for the balance sheet and not a jot for Wales. Late one afternoon I was called upstairs and told by the new managing director, imported from England, that London had decided it was time for a change of direction: I had taken the paper as far as I could and now they wanted someone else. I would, of course, be compensated. I did not put up a fight, because by then not only was I exhausted from editing one newspaper and creating a second from scratch, but what no one else knew was that I had cancer, which at the time seemed much more serious than it proved.

Redundant newspaper editors of a certain age are unemployable by being over-qualified. Instead of shuffling off into some consultancy, as most do, I embraced retirement as an opportunity to shed my impartiality. No longer expected to be a political eunuch, I could even join a political party, if one would have me. Plaid might have, in view of the sentiments expressed in a letter from Gwynfor Evans. Of the many I received, most sounded like commiserations on the part of contemporaries who had suffered the same fate. Gwynfor's, because it resonated with what I had tried to achieve throughout my editorship, would be the only one I kept:

> I have meant to write to you since I first heard of your intention to leave the editor's chair in order to thank you for your splendid leadership. Your strong support for the Welsh language and for a parliament has made the *Western Mail* a truly national daily. This has put Wales and those who struggle for a national future deeply in your debt. I look on your coming retirement as a grievous national loss. I hope you will find other ways of strengthening Welsh life.[9]

At no time did I regard my exit from the *Western Mail* as 'a grievous national loss', more a relief from the unceasing grind. Gwynfor Evans's generous valediction did, however, vindicate the stance the paper had taken on the key Welsh issues during my five years in charge. Top of the list was our campaign for a Welsh Assembly and, as a step in that direction, a Standing Conference on the Constitution. Not only did we want a new Welsh Language Act, but also Welsh-language education for all. In the democratic vacuum since the referendum, the *Western Mail* advocated investing the Welsh Economic Council with some form of elective control. Having witnessed the value of representation at the heart of the European Union in Brussels, an independent Welsh presence was an absolute necessity. The Valleys would continue to be among the most deprived parts of Europe without their very own Development Corporation to give them a bunk-up over the wall. They still are a painful monument to political betrayal, testifying to the failure of successive governments to close the economic and social divide existing between England and Wales. Besides a fast dual carriageway linking north and south Wales as a focus for development, special measures are as necessary now as when I was editing the *Western Mail* in the 1990s to offset the disadvantages faced by rural Wales, so often the backbone of our cultural life. If the Severn Barrage had been built when the *Western Mail* first advocated it, besides generating 5 per cent of the UK's energy requirements, it would have created tens of thousands of jobs at a fraction of the cost likely when it is eventually built. Neither was water, the nation's last remaining natural resource, forgotten. The *Western Mail* argued that the 'no profit no loss' restriction on water exported to England penalised Welsh consumers, and should be removed.

As much as I appreciated Gwynfor Evans's sentiments, I was deeply disillusioned by Plaid's apparent renunciation of independence as its eventual objective. Without constitutional independence, it was foolish to think Wales could ever become a fully paid-up member of the European Union or sit between Cuba and China at the United Nations. To suggest otherwise was a betrayal of those for whom Tryweryn was a catalyst for a resurgent Wales. To pretend as Dafydd Wigley, his successor, did in a *Newsnight* interview that Plaid Cymru had 'never ever' supported independence was the tipping-point for many nationalists. For them, the only place to turn, as previously, was to the extremist fringe.

Gwynfor Evans's early political convictions had seemed to lose their inspirational force after he won the historic Carmarthen by-election and entered mainstream English politics. Before this his pacifism had not stood in the way of him applauding Owen Williams and Emyr Llewelyn Jones, even John Jenkins, as patriots who inspired the nation to realise its immense possibilities. Tryweryn was a watershed that proved that democracy in Wales had become 'an abominable farce', he once wrote in the *Western Mail*, describing Williams and Jones as:

> [M]en of fine character acting from the highest motives. I disapprove of the dynamite, but I admire the courage and the character, the selflessness and sincerity and the splendid patriotism, which shine amidst so much that is sordid, self-seeking and corrupt in local and national politics. If I did not express my approval of these qualities I would think myself contemptible.

> It is the injustice and iniquity of this situation, which has driven some of the finest of our youth to criminal enterprises. Our anger would be better

directed against the system, which makes criminals of our best young men. However much we condemn the use of violence, it is clear that in this case it spells the end of political humbug in Wales.[10]

Criticised then for glorifying nationalist violence, Gwynfor Evans, thereafter, retreated behind his pacifist shield, kicking Owen Williams out of Plaid three years later for refusing to renounce direct action. The Plaid leader's inherent pacifism was fundamentally incompatible with the struggle for Welsh freedom, which by its very nature might always spill over into violent confrontation with the Establishment he himself loathed. In trying to reconcile the two, his message became ambivalent, too equivocal for those drawn to Plaid when they believed it to be in the vanguard of the struggle for freedom.

Several years after leaving the *Western Mail*, I was introduced by an inter-mediary to Owen Williams, and from this meeting sprung Cymru Annibynnol/ Independent Wales Party, another of those fringe groups committed to an independent Wales. The new party sucked in disillusioned individuals from the shadows of MAC1 and 2, and most probably Meibion Glyndŵr. With them came the by then inevitable contingent from MI5 or Special Branch, gathering like moths around a flame at the mere mention of the 'I' word.

The party's formation coincided with preparations for the 2001 National Census. Browsing the Office for National Statistics website one evening I came across a sample census form including an ethnicity question, inviting respon-dents to tick the appropriate box. Whereas just about every other ethnic group was offered this facility, there was no box specifically for the Welsh. To make matters worse, the Scottish Parliament had amended the form for Scotland to include a 'Scottish' tick-box. Not only had Wales been given an Assembly with inferior powers to those devolved to Scotland, Welsh ethnicity was to be offi-cially erased, in a multi-million-pound exercise probing every corner of our lives.

The process of assimilating Wales into England that began in earnest with the Acts of Union in the sixteenth century was unremitting and, while at times it might have seemed imperceptible to those directly affected, it contrived successfully to substitute the amorphous notion of 'Britain' for Welsh national sentiment and aspirations. Two hundred years after the Acts of Union had created the 'Kingdom of England and Wales', the English Bill of Union in 1706 swept aside the Scottish parliament to form the 'United Kingdom of Great Britain', to which Ireland was added in 1800 when the Dublin and London parliaments were merged. Hitherto, the notion of 'Britishness' had no common currency and it never will, because it is an illusion invented by English military force and dynastic ambition to subjugate three disparate ethnic groups, the Welsh, Scottish and Irish. Perfidious Albion has always been a skilful propagan-dist, wilfully and wickedly presenting primarily English interests as 'British', a deception that has reduced Wales to an economic and social dependency.

Only the language has distinguished it from the most backward parts of colonial 'Britain', and even the language's finger-hold on Wales's glorious past seemed doomed by the latter part of the twentieth century.

As uncompromising as they have been, the processes of integration have failed, however, to kill resistance totally. Like a drowning man surfacing for a last gasp, the Welsh will continue to reassert themselves until finally exhausted. But the opportunities for this have become increasingly less frequent. Water, reservoirs and the Investiture, holiday cottages and bilingual road-signs and official forms, all have formed part of this campaign of resistance. For its part, the missing tick-box reminded the Welsh of their fragility, especially when told that if they failed to be counted as British 'Others' their handouts from central English government would be cut. Of course, this was not true, but symptomatic of English disdain for the Welsh.

The omission deeply wounded many people who considered it commensurable with past humiliations, such as the mid-nineteenth-century ban on children speaking Welsh at school (the 'Welsh Not') and the contempt with which Liverpool Corporation had treated the protest over Tryweryn. But what a powerful campaign for an infant political party! If the census went ahead in its existing form the choice for respondents in Wales was either to tick a box stating they were British – or to write 'Welsh' in a space reserved for those from 'any other White background'.

In January 2000, fifteen months *before* the census was due, Cymru Annibynnol launched a campaign for the inclusion of a Welsh tick-box. Until then, the omission had escaped everyone, including those involved in census rehearsals conducted by the ONS in Ceredigion and Gwynedd, as well as the Welsh MPs responsible for vetting the form. This staggering oversight would not have occurred had responsibility for the census been devolved to the Welsh Assembly, as it had been to the equivalent legislative bodies of Scotland and Northern Ireland.

Other political activists quickly jumped on the bandwagon, one of these Simon Thomas (Ceredigion), the Plaid Cymru MP in whose constituency a census rehearsal had taken place the previous year. The *Western Mail* also threw its substantial weight behind the campaign, although reluctant to give a fringe party, Cymru Annibynnol, credit for highlighting the insult. Very soon a national boycott was being widely advocated unless the Office for National Statistics amended the form. Plaid suggested a clip-on page or stick-on labels. Neither idea was acceptable, said the ONS, warning that any attempt to tamper with the official form would invalidate it. The failure of census refuseniks to participate, warned the ONS, could mean reduced resources being earmarked for Wales by Westminster, a threat repeated in the National Assembly by First Minister Rhodri Morgan. The ultimate weapon in the ONS armoury was the threat of prosecutions, including fines, even imprisonment, for those refusing to return a completed form. The census was the responsibility of the Chief

Statistician, Len Cook. A New Zealander, Cook had encountered a similar ethnicity problem with regard to Maoris when running a census in his home country.

Cymru Annibynnol ramped up its campaign at the 2000 National Eisteddfod in Llanelli with a petition to the National Assembly. For seven days members stood on the *maes* in the hot sun collecting more than 10,000 signatures. The party also opened a special book, 'Cofrestr Cywilydd', inviting the signatures, names and addresses of those intending not to complete their census form; the more people committed to a boycott, the less chance of prosecutions.

Insisting it was too late to change the form the ONS resorted to spin, with the slogan: 'Tell us you are Welsh and we'll count you as Welsh.' Few were convinced. Time after time the ONS and Welsh Assembly Government insisted the forms had already been printed, when in fact printing never started until 27 July 2000, seven months after the omission was spotted. As late as December that year, barely four months before the census was due to take place, Census Director Graham Jones was asked by his boss Len Cook to consider an eleventh-hour amendment to the form, after the National Assembly had, rather late in the day, unanimously supported a motion for a Welsh tick-box to be included 'to allow people to express their Welsh identity'.

In Wales, census staff were in revolt. All seven area managers backed the Wales Census Manager, Welsh-speaking Deryk Williams, a former S4C executive, who told his boss in a fax that they could no longer defend the official ONS line that it was too late to change the wording of the ethnic background question. From the fax it is clear that the initial decision not to change the form was that of the Labour government, not the ONS. Williams and his area managers asked Cook to use all his political leverage to persuade the government to alter its mind:

> Our jobs were difficult enough before the National Assembly's decision, now they will be nigh on impossible if [the] ONS attempts to maintain the status quo …

> If I may add a personal note. I find it increasingly difficult to explain to the media in Wales why it is that the most senior officials of the ONS are never available for interview on census issues in Wales. Frankly, I feel that [the] ONS are hanging me out to dry, and I have had a belly-full.[11]

Seeing that Deryk Williams was on the point of resignation, Cook released him from any obligation to defend the ONS position: he was allowed to publicly support those demanding a Welsh tick-box. The situation for the ONS was fraught. For the first time in its history a national census might be boycotted by a substantial minority of the population, this having the effect of producing a series of flawed results.[12]

Charged with ascertaining whether the form could still be changed, Graham Jones found that despite the ONS's earlier prevarications it *was* still possible to amend it without needing to delay the census. The legislative timetable for making the change was tight, but it could still be done, with three days to spare. But there was another problem. Tony Blair's first Labour government was preparing for a general election, and if that were held in the spring then Parliament would be dissolved and the legislative processes could not be completed. In the circumstances, Graham Jones advised against changing the form. As it happened, Parliament was not dissolved until two weeks *after* the census was held.

There were other reasons for the ONS not to amend the form, foremost of these the estimated £2 million additional cost of printing another two million forms in English and Welsh. Then there was the 'English question'. Jones believed that if a Welsh tick-box was added the English would want one as well, requiring the ONS to change the form in England, too. In the circumstances, he advised Cook against making any changes.[13]

The battle lost, its petition ignored, Cymru Annibynnol launched an all-party Welsh Identity Campaign in support of a national census boycott. The focus would be a coffin symbolising the death of Welsh identity, to be carried around Wales by groups of pallbearers as a receptacle for rejected census forms. Almost everywhere the coffin went, starting at Wrexham and finishing in

The mock coffin symbolising the death of Welsh identity carried around Wales by Cymru Annibynnol / Independent Wales Party to collect rejected Census forms in 2001 as a protest over the omission of a Welsh tick box. Copyright: Robert ap Steffan.

Cardiff a week later, its appearance was welcomed by protesters waving their wretched yellow census envelopes. By the time it was carried on to the fore-court of the National Assembly at Crickhowell House on the last Sunday before census day, the four pallbearers were buckling under the weight. For many, the boycott symbolised national pride. Gwynfor Evans, then eighty-nine, posted his census form into the coffin in a final act of defiance. Predictably, the only people waiting at the National Assembly were a couple of Special Branch men with clicking cameras, and a policeman who insisted on taking a peep inside to check for bodies or explosives before the coffin disappeared into the hills.

After this the refuseniks, believing there was safety in numbers, awaited developments. By the end of July, three months after the census, there was still no sign of anyone in Wales being prosecuted for failing to complete their form. But behind the scenes, the ONS was agonising over whether to pursue the census refuseniks, in particular John Humphries. As secretary of Cymru Annibynnol/Independent Wales Party – the organisation spearheading the protest – it was inevitable I would be the focus for official censure. Aware that any prosecution had to take place within six months of the census, I had stirred the pot by asking the ONS press office whether this was likely. On hearing of my inquiry, David Marder, senior press officer at the ONS, fired off an e-mail, subject 'John Humphries', to a senior member of the management team, Ian G. Scott, with copies to Graham Jones, Len Cook and eight others, urging that I should be pursued with total vigour, despite any media furore:

> Surely, we have an absolute duty to pursue these forms with total vigour. From a media point of view it will of course be a total nightmare but if they are illegally holding confidential census material we are in the same position as the St Hilda's bin bags. What do we do if in a year or so Mr Humphries and co start 'analysing' this material (using census material that should have been kept secret for 100 years)? The Welsh media will have a field day so we mustn't be half-hearted and must be absolutely tight and resolute on the legal side and swift and clear with the enforce-ment.[14]

On receiving this Scott immediately e-mailed Graham Jones, the Director for the 2001 Census, saying he was in two minds about pursuing Humphries for the contents of 'his wretched coffin'. But he wanted the views of the rest of the team, especially in the light of advice contained in another e-mail. Details of this have been withheld by the ONS under Section 36 of the Freedom of Information Act, the section that states disclosure would inhibit 'free and frank exchange of views' between officials. The ONS has also used Section 42 of the Act exempting disclosure of other e-mails on account of 'legal privilege'.[15]

After gathering together the views of senior executives, Graham Jones advised Cook that there was 'universal agreement – we must pursue'. A letter to

Humphries was drafted for Cook to sign after taking legal advice. 'Always nice to have a tough one', was the New Zealander's response to impending litigation. Since a high-profile prosecution was certain to have political implications, Cook alerted his senior press officer, Marder:

> There is no option but to pursue getting these forms back, with the help of the law if needed. I will want to agree on the tactics, because of the very political nature of this. Any decision on tactics will be taken with our legal advisers. What reservations do we have on this?[16]

During the following few days the management team waited for advice from solicitors with regard to potential penalties to be imposed on Cymru Annibynnol/Independent Wales Party if it refused to surrender census forms the ONS believed it held in the coffin. Marder observed: 'Humphries is telling all the media he hasn't got any forms but wouldn't give them back even if he had'.[17]

During the flurry of e-mails passing between ONS executives the question arose as to whether Humphries could be held collectively responsible for the actions of other individuals if personally he did not hold any material. Finally, the ONS got its act together and wrote me a letter.[18]

The first I knew something was stirring was on a hot Sunday afternoon in mid August. I remember it well. It was a beautiful day, and I was sitting in the garden under a blue umbrella writing my weekly gardening column for the *Western Mail*, based upon the garden I was creating in the Usk Valley, when a courier arrived with a special delivery, a hand-delivered letter from Len Cook. So important was it that the Chief Statistician dared not risk HM Royal Mail, not even registered post. At a cost of several hundred pounds, the ONS had hired a car and driver to deliver the letter to me in person. The thrust of it was that the ONS wanted any forms posted in the coffin handed over at a pre-arranged time and place, or else. Cook wrote:

> I understand that representatives of the Independent Wales Party currently have in their possession census forms, which had been delivered to households under the provisions of the Census Regulations 2000 and which were subsequently either sent to the Welsh Identity Campaign or otherwise collected by Campaign representatives. We believe that the forms held in this way include completed returns.
>
> The Census Regulations 2000 set out the statutory requirements for prescribed persons to return completed census forms, and the arrangements for me to collect such forms. Under these provisions I am authorised to collect all such forms that you or other representatives of the Welsh Independent Party or the Campaign organisers may have in your custody.

In the circumstances I must ask that all forms held by the Independent Wales Party or Campaign organisers, including any which are incomplete, be returned to this office within ten days of the date of this letter. I am happy to discuss how this may be conveniently achieved.[19]

Cymru Annibynnol's reply was that no member of the party knew what had happened to the coffin and its contents. This seemed to satisfy Cook, but not the press officer, Marder, for whose department the furore over the tick-box had been a public relations disaster. In an internal e-mail, from which seven paragraphs have been deleted from the copy released under the Freedom of Information Act, Marder refused to let the matter drop:

There was separate evidence that at least one completed form went in their 'coffin'. However, the assertion is that they do not hold census forms. Either Humphries is simply lying (as part of his civil disobedience campaign), or the form has been disposed of, or Humphries is playing semantics with the word 'holding' (in other words they know perfectly well where the forms are but they are not holding them at the moment).

Of course, if he denies ever possessing any material, his whole campaign is then debunked as a sham. If he says it has been destroyed, thrown away or buried, we have to consider further what we can do.[20]

This prompted Len Cook to write again asking me for clarification:

Thank you very much for your letter dated 21 August. I am very much reassured by your assertion that neither you nor any representatives of either the Independent Wales Party or the Welsh Identity Campaign are holding any census forms.

It would, however, help to resolve any further uncertainties that might remain over this matter if you could explain exactly what happened to the several forms which, it has been claimed in the Welsh press and via the Independent Wales Party's website, were collected by members of the Welsh identity Campaign and are currently held in the peripatetic 'coffin'.

In the circumstances, I would be grateful for any information that you may have in respect of this matter and I look forward to hearing from you shortly.[21]

By then, most of us in the opposing camp were feeling quite chummy towards our Kiwi pursuer. After discussing his letter at its next meeting, the party decided nothing could be added to its previous statement.[22] No more was heard from Len until about a year later, when the coffin suddenly reappeared at the National Eisteddfod at St David's in Pembrokeshire. On learning of this, and still searching for his precious census forms, the National Statistician wrote a third time asking whether any were languishing in the coffin, because if they were he was duty-bound to collect them. Once again, Cymru Annibynnol, by then tearing itself apart as a result of that age-old Welsh disease, factionalism, was unable to help. Soon both Owen Williams as leader and I as secretary would resign, before we were replaced.[23]

The threat of prosecutions evaporated in Wales, but not elsewhere. About seventy individuals in Britain were prosecuted by the ONS for refusing to complete their 2001 forms, including two in Wales, for a variety of reasons unconnected with the Welsh tick-box campaign. The general opinion was that political intervention stopped the ONS from proceeding against participants in what was a widely supported campaign of civil disobedience. Five years of persistent use of the FOI Act, including an appeal to the Information Ombudsman, has failed to persuade the ONS to release further information.

While no figure is available for the number who boycotted the census, the ONS has admitted that the extensive media and publicity campaign preceding it meant that 418,000, or 14 per cent, responded by writing 'Welsh' on the form. By way of compensating for its failure to provide a Welsh tick-box, the ONS included a national identity question in its Labour Force Survey later that same year. This showed that 67 per cent of adults considered their national identity to be wholly or partly Welsh.

# 18

# DRUMBEAT OF HOME RULE

Taken in isolation, the dispute over a Welsh tick-box on a census form is trivial and quite out of proportion to the public indignation it generated. Why the omission resonated so widely was that it was seen as another example in the long history of Anglo-Saxon disdain for Wales. That it was not noticed sooner testifies to the diminution of Welsh identity after centuries of assimilation, beginning with the Acts of Union. For the majority of the culturally dispossessed, Welshness had become a state of mind shored up only by slogans and flag-waving. Only the remarkable resilience of the language saved the heartlands from the same fate.

Owen Williams, John Jenkins and others saw Tryweryn as a totem to remind the governing class that because a nation was defeated did not mean it forfeited its rights. But, as with the burning-down of the RAF bombing school by Saunders Lewis thirty years earlier, on its own Tryweryn achieved nothing. More reservoirs would be built to supply the Midlands and Liverpool with cheaper water than that available to Welsh consumers. The importance of Tryweryn was that it unleashed a chain of events that extracted concessions from a government increasingly unreceptive to Welsh aspirations. It was also a defining moment for Plaid Cymru: should it become a red-blooded nationalist movement, accepting direct action as a necessary part of the struggle for independence, or should it settle for evolving constitutionally towards a lesser form of devolution? According to Emrys Roberts, who then ran Merthyr Tydfil Borough Council for Plaid, the debate was between revolution and evolution. While the party would opt for the latter, retreating behind a smokescreen of disingenuous protestations and condemnation, the background crackle of direct action produced results for Plaid Cymru by undermining English government intransigence.

The reservoir and pipeline bombings of the violent 1960s, the campaign to stop the Investiture, the cottage arsonists and Cymdeithas yr Iaith Gymraeg's crusade on behalf of the language were all part of Welsh resistance to English hegemony. Even Cayo Evans's imaginary world contributed to the insurrection by distracting attention from the greater threat posed by Mudiad Amddiffyn Cymru. Not dramatically, but bit by bit, the Westminster establishment surrendered control. Tryweryn was followed by the creation of a Welsh Office with the very first Secretary of State for Wales; Clywedog by Gwynfor Evans's historic victory at Carmarthen; the pipeline bombings and Investiture protests by the Kilbrandon Commission on the Constitution and the formation of the Welsh Water Authority. The cottage arson campaign was a reminder that devolution was not dead after the 1979 referendum defeat. How much of this can be attributed to constitutional evolution? How much change was prompted by violent direct action or the threat of it? If nothing else, Mudiad Amddiffyn Cymru kept the question of Welsh independence alive. The cancellation of the Investiture by Harold Wilson, as seemed likely at one stage, would almost certainly have precipitated a constitutional crisis; the attacks on pipelines and reservoirs could be seen as an expression of public resentment over the pillaging of Welsh water resources; the attraction of rural Wales for second-home owners waned during the arson campaign; and the jailing of Cymdeithas yr Iaith Gymraeg members helped force more language concessions from government. For his part, John Jenkins was airbrushed out of history, a renegade with nowhere to go.

That direct action has not intruded into the debate for more than a decade only means an armistice, not that there will be no future flashpoints. The democratic deficit may have been partly resolved by the 1997 devolution referendum – but only by 6,721 votes. Is it reasonable to assume from this narrowest of victories that some kind of correlation existed between the 552,698 who voted against devolution and the 580,000 members of the electorate then resident in Wales, but born in England? The margin of victory was even more wafer-thin when measured against the demographic changes that will continue to shift the balance of power sufficiently to jeopardise any further progress towards meaningful self-government. Members of the Westminster Parliament fearing the slippery slope need only delay the process until the population transfer produces a 'no' vote. Even if that were to happen, the enduring bond, shadowy and elusive as it might be, must eventually defeat those opposed to Wales the nation state.

Future flashpoints need not necessarily be different because older ones can reignite, among the most explosive of these the continuing pressure exerted by inward migration on affordable housing for locals and, as a consequence, the erosion of the cultural bedrock. With 34 per cent of the population of north Wales declaring itself English-born in the 2001 census, the threat to some of Wales's most fragile cultural enclaves is imminent and pressing.[1] It is not difficult to imagine the scenario if a referendum on legislative devolution is defeated by the preponderance of incomers. Racial tensions, never far from the surface in any society, could easily emerge at the sight of the English battalions denying the Welsh their human and ancestral rights. Blowing up water pipelines supplying consumers across the border and burning down their holiday homes were clear signals to the English that they were not welcomed by some, no matter how hard other nationalists tried to disguise the fact. The message in telephone warnings and anonymous letters to the media, and 'Cofiwch Dryweryn' (Remember Tryweryn) painted on road bridges, was unambiguous: 'English go home'.

But the big tipping-point between nationalist evolution and revolution will arise if there is another attempt to foist an Investiture upon Wales. Fortified by the strength of opposition in 1969, others with the same resolve as Owen Williams and John Jenkins will be waiting in the wings if ever it is announced that a new Prince of Wales will be anointed at Caernarfon. Even though the next generation of protesters face a stronger headwind because of increased security surveillance, is it feasible the Palace would expose another Prince of Wales to the vicissitudes of an enduring Welsh extremism? A deciding factor is whether the not-insignificant cultural pay-off for keeping the peace – the Welsh Language Board, Welsh Language Acts, Welsh-medium schools, S4C, even Labour/Plaid Cymru cooperation in the Assembly – remains strong enough to silence potential activists. At present it is.

Ironically, another flashpoint could be a direct consequence of the language revival. Agreeing to a Welsh-language channel was a strategic coup for Margaret Thatcher, although she probably never saw it like that. At a stroke, S4C and its programme-providers created outlets for Welsh-speakers whose frustrations might otherwise have been subverted. As a former Welsh chief constable observed in the aftermath of the cottage arson campaign, 'Young people in Wales today have legitimate outlets for their concerns and as long as there are these avenues to pursue there are unlikely to be further outbreaks of this sort.'[2] Without a new Welsh Language Act, stimulating the creation of additional opportunities in the private sector for those emerging from the expansion in bilingual education, the teaching of Welsh is in danger of becoming nothing more than a cultural sop. The language, and the extent to which it is used, will always be at the centre of Welsh national consciousness.

Water has always been a flashpoint, not because it is expensive but because it is yet another manifestation of the economic disparities between England and Wales, and as such is one of many indentations on an unequal playing-field. The deep-seated resentment is not about the price but about paying a higher one than the generally more affluent consumers across the border. Long before Tryweryn added a cultural dimension, water was regarded as a national resource in the same way as coal and iron ore. Like 'Scottish oil', 'Welsh water' has always been at the top of the nationalist wish-list. That Welsh consumers subsidise English households by supplying cheap water has created resentment certain to be exacerbated by future shortages and escalating prices. The tension will be relieved only if a means is found to renegotiate a contract imposed on the former publicly owned Welsh Water Authority by the Thatcher government in 1984, and inherited by Dŵr Cymru/Welsh Water (see Appendix B). Of machiavellian complexity, the contract requires Dŵr Cymru to supply neighbouring Severn Trent with up to 360 million litres of raw water daily from its Elan Valley reservoirs, at a fraction of its real worth. This is because the price of water sold from this massive reserve continues to be calculated according to the 'no profit no loss' formula abandoned elsewhere when the water industry was privatised in 1989: that is, at about 3p per 1,000 litres, compared to upwards of 20p per 1,000 litres for raw water sold to the company's other bulk-supply customers.

The agreement was imposed on Wales by the Welshman Michael Heseltine, as Secretary of State for the Environment, when Severn Trent refused to pay a penny more after the Welsh Water Authority, asking only a fair price, offered it a supply 10 per cent *below* the cheapest Severn Trent could obtain from an alternative source. Even the conservative *Western Mail* was appalled by Heseltine's imposed settlement, commenting,

> The fact that the Elan Valley reservoir was built by the 19th century forerunners of the present Midlands authority to supply water to its own ratepayers was at the very least a questionable precedent; yet it is now utilised by the present authority as a permanent entitlement to a system of pricing which is strictly subject to its approval. The Welsh authority whose running costs are far in excess of Severn Trent's because of geographical and population factors must operate a water rate poundage, which is much higher than Birmingham's. The situation is so anomalous that it cannot be neglected in terms of logic and precedent. That means that low cost authorities like Severn Trent and the north west should be obliged to help meet the balance of the extra costs incurred by authorities like Welsh Water with its special natural problems.[3]

At a time when Welsh consumers were paying one of the highest water-rates in Britain, the receipts from supplying Severn Trent with 130 million cubic metres in 2002 were barely £4 million.[4] To ensure this does not change, the government specifically retained control of water supplies when transferring further powers to the Welsh Assembly in the Government of Wales Act 2006. If England needed water, said the Secretary of State for Wales, Peter Hain, at the time, nothing would be permitted to interrupt the supply from Wales, thereby guaranteeing that like 'Scottish oil', 'Welsh water' will remain a flashpoint.

Despite employing the finest legal brains in the land, Dŵr Cymru has failed to unpick an agreement designed to last at least until 2073. By then, a special trust fund set up under the contract to partly compensate Welsh water consumers for subsidising those in the Midlands could be worth hundreds of millions of pounds – all of which will revert to Severn Trent if the supply contract is not renewed in 2073.[5] In 2007 this proscriptive supply agreement prevented Dŵr Cymru from accepting from another company, Albion Water, the offer of a *higher* price for providing a supply from the Elan Valley reservoirs.[6]

For how long will Welsh water consumers tolerate injustices that accentuate prevailing economic and social differences between the two sides of Offa's Dyke? Ironically, concessions to Wales aimed at eliminating the distinctions have fuelled national aspirations and increased pressure on the constitutional links. Regarded as flawed and unfair, the devolution settlement makes it difficult for the public to distinguish between the implementation and financing of policies for England and Wales. Not only has the material divide become more confused, the psychological differences between the two countries have deepened. The only certainty garnered from the plethora of England-only announcements emanating from government is that Wales has somehow been left with half a loaf. Consequently, lines have been drawn that never existed while Wales remained more firmly wedded to England, the ramifications spilling out far beyond the immediate impact of economic and social policy initiatives. Society is in fact being recast to reflect this new sense of Welshness. Independence, although not yet constitutionally ratified, has taken root.

For the moment, the drumbeat of devolution has replaced the background crackle of direct action. But if the rhythm is frustrated by vested interests at Westminster or those of population transfer, there will be only a pause in Wales's forgotten 'war'. Labelling future insurgents as terrorists rather than freedom fighters will not change what's inside the bottle. Disillusioned by devolution's false dawn, it is not inconceivable that a new generation of foot-soldiers could emerge from the shadows of Mudiad Amddiffyn Cymru to give the process another violent push.

# NOTES

## Chapter 1

1. John Jenkins to author, November 2005.
2. *Daily Post*, 9 March 1966.
3. The National Archives, BD 11/3947, letters 6, 12 April 1966 to R. B. Thomas, Chief Constable, Mid-Wales Constabulary, from Arthur Thomas (chairman), Mair Edwards (Secretary), Montgomeryshire branch of Plaid Cymru.
4. *Daily Post*, 7 March 1966.
5. Jenkins to author, November 2005.
6. TNA, BD 11/3947, Geoffrey Lloyd, MP Sutton Coldfield, House of Commons, questions, 6 May 1966.
7. TNA, BD 11/3947, minutes, meeting between Cledwyn Hughes, Secretary of State for Wales, and Water Resources Board, 3 May 1966.
8. TNA, BD 11/3947 224537, letter, J. Street, Ministry of Defence, to J. Siberry, Under-Secretary, Welsh Office, 17 March 1966, with annotation to Siberry 21 March 1966, signed Idris Davey, Establishment Officer, Welsh Office.
9. TNA, BD 11/3947, Geoffrey Lloyd, MP Sutton Coldfield, House of Commons, questions, 6 May 1966; TNA, BD 11/3947, minutes, meeting between Cledwyn Hughes and Clywedog Reservoir Joint Authority, 15 September 1966; *Western Mail*, 22 October 1965.

## Chapter 2

1. J. Jenkins, *Prison Letters* (Talybont: Y Lolfa, 1987), foreword, Rhodri Williams, p. 6; also TNA, PREM 13/2903, Prime Minister Harold Wilson to Home Secretary James Callaghan.
2. G. Evans, *Fighting for Wales* (Talybont: Y Lolfa, 1991), p. 84.
3. *Western Mail*, 22 December 1955.
4. *Daily Post*, 2 October 1967; Evans, *Fighting for Wales*, p. 89.
5. *Western Mail*, 7 January 1956.
6. Evans, *Fighting for Wales*, p. 95.
7. Ibid., p. 95; *Western Mail*, 23 May 1957.
8. *Western Mail*, 22 November 1956.
9. *Times*, 22 November 1956.

10. Evans, *Fighting for Wales*, p. 83.
11. *Western Mail*, 18 November 1962.
12. *Western Mail*, 11 February 1963.
13. Ibid.
14. *Western Mail*, 8 May 1963.
15. TNA, DPP 2/4471, transcript, Regina v Owen Williams and John Albert Jones, 14 June 1963, Shire Hall, Dolgellau, antecedents and mitigation, pp. 7, 8, 11, 12.
16. Gerald of Wales, *Journey through Wales and the Description of Wales* (London: Penguin, 1978).
17. R. R. Davies, *The Age of Conquest: Wales 1063–1415* (Oxford University Press, 1991), pp. 31–5, 134–5, 192–5, 100–1, 134–5, 158–9, 160–1, 170–1, 196–203, 224–5, 228–37, 256–57, 260–1, 291–3, 388–9, 454–5.
18. T. Matthews, *Welsh Records in Paris* (Cardiff, 1911), p. 3.
19. TNA, DPP 2/4471.

## Chapter 3

1. TNA, DPP 2/4471, statement with regard to Williams's antecedents from Detective Inspector R. G. Owen at Snowdon Country Club trial.
2. O. Williams, *Cysgod Tryweryn* (Llanwrst: Gwasg Carreg Gwalch, 1995); also *Western Mail*, 8 May 1963.
3. Williams, *Cysgol Tryweryn*.
4. *Western Mail*, 15 March 1963.
5. *Western Mail*, 8 May 1963.
6. John Jenkins to author, 5–12 November 2005.
7. *Western Mail*, 11 February; 22 February; 15, 16 March; 8, 9, 10 May; 15 June; 2 July 1963; also Williams, *Cysgod Tryweryn*.
8. John Jenkins to author, 5–12 November 2005.
9. *Western Mail*, 30 March 1963.
10. *Western Mail*, 13 February 1963.
11. *Western Mail*, 29 March 1963.
12. Ibid.
13. TNA, DPP 2/4471, Regina v Owen Williams and John Albert Jones, Dolgellau Assizes.
14. *Western Mail*, 2 April 1963.
15. TNA, DPP 2/4471, transcript, Regina v Owen Williams and John Albert Jones, Dolgellau Assizes, 14 June 1963; Williams, *Cysgod Tryweryn*.
16. *Western Mail*, 8 May 1963; also TNA, DPP 2/4471, transcript, Regina v Owen Williams and John Albert Jones, Dolgellau Assizes, 14 June 1963.

## Chapter 4

1. O. Williams, *Cysgod Tryweryn*, (Llanwrst: Gwasg Carreg Gwalch, 1995).
2. TNA, DPP 2/4471, official court transcript, Regina v Owen Williams and John Albert Jones, Merioneth Assizes, 14 June 1963.
3. Ibid.; also *Western Mail*, 15 June 1963; *Western Mail*, 2 July 1973.
4. *Daily Herald*, 15 June 1963.
5. TNA, DPP 2/4471, Merioneth Assizes, Assizes, Regina v Owen Williams and John Albert Jones, official court transcript, 14 June 1963.

6. Ibid.
7. *Western Mail*, 16 June 1963.
8. *Western Mail*, 2 July 1963.
9. Williams, *Cysgod Tryweryn*.

## Chapter 5

1. R. Clews, *To Dream of* Freedom (Talybont: Y Lolfa, 1980); FWA trial reports, *Western Mail*, 17, 22 April 1969.
2. TNA, Director for Public Prosecutions, DPP, 2/4455, report from Superintendent Vivian Fisher on Cayo Evans and other FWA members.
3. Ibid.; also *Western Mail*, 15 January 1969; National Eisteddfod, Dolgellau, August 1966.
4. TNA, DPP 2/4455, report from Superintendent Fisher.
5. FWA trial reports, *Herald of Wales*, *Western Mail*, 23 April 1969.
6. FWA trial reports, *Western Mail*, 20 June 1969; also *Western Mail*, 20 October 1969.
7. FWA trial reports, *Western Mail*, 29 April, 31 May, 4 June 1969.
8. FWA trial report, 25 April 1969.
9. TNA, DPP 2/4455, Free Wales Army, Special Branch report, Metropolitan Police, 11 December 1967.
10. *Town*, December 1967, pp. 44–50.
11. Ibid.
12. Ibid.
13. Ibid.
14. TNA, DPP 2/4455, memorandum by Director for Public Prosecutions on the account of the activities of the Free Wales Army published in the December 1967 issue of *Town* magazine, 25 January 1968.
15. TNA, DPP 2/4455, parliamentary question and answer.
16. *Daily Telegraph* colour supplement, 30 August 1968, pp. 14–21.
17. TNA, DDP 2/4455, report to DDP, 'John Owen Summers – Free Wales Army,' 20 September 1966.
18. FWA trial reports, *Western Mail*, 25 April, 21 June 1969.
19. TNA, DPP 2/4455, police report, 'John Summers, Free Lance Journalist, of Church View, Lulsgate, Somerset', from Kenneth Clark, Deputy Coordinator, No. 7 Regional Crime Squad, to Chief Constable, Somerset, 23 August 1966.
20. TNA, DPP 2/4455, report from P. S. Prescott, Senior Experimental Office, Home Office South Western Forensic Science Laboratory, to Mr Kenneth Clark, Deputy Coordinator, No. 7 Regional Crime Squad, 20 August 1966.
21. TNA, DPP 2/4455, report 'John Summers, Free Lance Journalist, of Church View, Lulsgate, Somerset'.
22. FWA trial report, *Western Mail*, 7 May 1969.

## Chapter 6

1. *Western Mail*, 21 April 1970.
2. *Western Mail*, 17 April 1970.
3. John Jenkins to author, 11 September 2007.
4. TNA, ASSI 84/577.

5. TNA, ASSI 84/577, witness statement, Harold Pendlebury, *Daily Mail*.

6. John Jenkins to author, 11 September 2007.

7. Ibid.

8. B. Dooley, *Choosing the Green: Second Generation Irish and the Cause of Ireland* (Dublin: Beyond the Pale Publications, 2004); also John Jenkins to author, 11 September 2007.

9. John Jenkins to author, 5–12 November 2005, 11 September 2007, 8 February 2008.

10. Ibid.

11. Ibid.

12. Ibid.

13. TNA, ASSI 84/577, witness statements, Frederick Ernest Alders, Ann Woodgate.

14. National Library of Wales, 'Cliff Bere Correspondence and Papers 1940–1995'.

15. National Library of Wales, 'Huw T. Edwards Papers', A2/144, 15 June 1962; A2/145, 6 October 1962.

16. Jenkins to author, 5–12 November 2005.

17. TNA, ASSI 84/577, witness statement, Frederick Ernest Alders.

18. Jenkins, 5–12 November 2005.

19. TNA, ASSI 84/577, witness statement, Alders.

20. TNA, ASSI 84/577, witness statement, Woodgate.

21. *Western Mail*, 17 April 1970.

## Chapter 7

1. *Western Mail*, 17 November 1967.

2. TNA, ASSI 84/577, witness statement, Major Clifton Jefferies, Royal Army Ordnance Corps, Western Command Ammunitions Inspectorate, Chester.

3. TNA, ASSI 84/577, trial of John Jenkins, witness statement, Harold Pendlebury, *Daily Mail*; John Jenkins to author, 5–12 November 2005.

4. TNA, CAB 164/389, letter, Sir Burke Trend, Secretary to the Cabinet Office, to Goronwy Daniel, Permanent Under-Secretary of State, Welsh Office, 10 November 1967.

5. S. Dorril and R. Ramsey, *Smear! Wilson and the Secret State* (London: Fourth Estate, 1991), pp. 113–49; J. Young, 'The Wilson government's reform of intelligence coordination, 1967–68', *Intelligence and National Security*, vol. 16, no. 2 (Summer, 2001), pp. 133–51.

6. T. Benn, *Diaries* (London: Arrow Books, 2005), vol. 1, p. 175; Dorril and Ramsey, *Smear! Wilson and the Secret State*, pp. 113–49; C. Pincher, *Inside Story: A Documentary of the Pursuit of Power* (London: Sidgwick and Jackson, 1978), p. 167.

7. Trend to Daniel, 10 November 1967.

8. TNA, CAB 164/389, Daniel to Trend, 'Welsh Extremists', *Subversion in the United Kingdom*, 20 November 1967.

9. *Western Mail*, 20 November 1967.

10. Ibid.

11. Ibid.

12. *Western Mail*, 22 November 1967.

13. John Jenkins to author, 5–12 November 2005.

14. TNA, CAB 164/389, Sir Burke Trend to Sir Martin Furnival Jones, Head of MI5, 27 November 1967; Jones to Trend, 30 November 1967.
15. TNA, ASSI 84/577, Jenkins trial, witness statement, Major Clifton Jefferies, Royal Army Ordnance Corps, Western Command Ammunitions Inspectorate, Chester.
16. TNA, DPP 2/4471, evidence file for Department for Public Prosecutions, prepared by Superintendent Islwyn Jones and Detective Sergeant R. G. Owen, Caernarfon, 18 January 1968, p. 9.
17. John Jenkins to author, 5–12 November 2005, 11 September 2007.
18. TNA, ASSI 84/577, witness statement, Alders.
19. Jenkins to author, 5–12 November; TNA, ASSI, 84/577, witness statement, Alders.
20. TNA, ASSI 84/577, witness statement, Capt. André Millorit, Royal Army Ordnance Corps, Western Command Ammunition Inspectorate (South), Hereford.
21. TNA, CAB 164/389, Sir Philip Allen, Permanent Under-Secretary, Home Office, to Sir Burke Trend, Cabinet Secretary, 13 December 1967.
22. TNA, CAB 164/389, Sir Philip Allen, Permanent Under-Secretary, Home Office, to Sir Elwyn Jones, QC, Attorney General.
23. TNA, CAB 164/389, Sir Philip Allen, Permanent Under-Secretary, Home Office, to Burke Trend, Cabinet Secretary, 26 February 1968.
24. TNA, CAB 164/389, Burke Trend to Prime Minister Harold Wilson, 29 February 1968.
25. TNA, HO 325/119, letter, Sir James Waddell, Deputy Under-Secretary, Home Office, to James Callaghan, Home Secretary, 10 June 1968.
26. TNA, HO 325/119, letter, Neil Galbraith, HM Inspector Constabulary Wales, to Sir Eric St Johnston, HM Chief Inspector of Constabulary, 17 June 1968.
27. TNA, ASSI 84/577, Jenkins trial, witness statement, Jefferies.
28. TNA, HO 325/119, Sir James Waddell, Deputy Under-Secretary, Home Office, to Sir Philip Allen, Permanent Under-Secretary, Home Office, 10 June 1968; also Waddell to Home Secretary Callaghan, 25 June 1968.
29. TNA, HO 325/119, Sir James Waddell, Deputy Under-Secretary, Home Office, to James Callaghan, Home Secretary, 28 June 1968.
30. TNA, HO 325/119, Sir James Waddell, Deputy Under-Secretary, Home Office, to Col. William Williams, Chief Constable of Gwynedd, 28 June 1968.
31. TNA, ASSI 84/577, witness statements, John Stilgoe, Liverpool City water engineer; Alan Thompson, Chief Chemist, North Western Forensic Science Laboratory, Preston; Clifford Lockett, security patrolman, British Insulated Callender Cables, Helsby, Cheshire; also *Western Mail*, 29 June 1968.
32. TNA, HO 325/119, Col. William Williams, Chief Constable of Gwynedd, to Sir James Waddell, Deputy Under-Secretary, Home Office, 3 July 1968.
33. TNA, HO 325/119, Frank Williamson, HM Inspector (Crime), to Waddell, 11 July 1968.
34. TNA, HO 325/119, Frank Williamson, HM Inspector (Crime), to Sir Eric St Johnston, HM Chief Inspector of Constabulary, 17 July 1968; Waddell to Home Secretary, 19 July 1968.

## Chapter 8

1. TNA, HO 325/119, Sir John Waldron, Commissioner, New Scotland Yard, to Sir James Waddell, Deputy Under-Secretary of State, Home Office, 24 July 1968.

2. TNA, HO 325/119, E. Brampton F2 (Home Office Police Division), to Frank Williamson, HM Inspector of Constabulary (Crime), 25 July 1968.
3. *Western Mail*, 10 November 1968.
4. TNA, DPP 2/4471, witness statements, Detective Constable Geoffrey Allman and Detective Superintendent James Cuthbert; Roy Clews, *To Dream of Freedom* (Talybont: Y Lolfa, 1980).
5. TNA, DPP 2/4471, witness statement, Detective Inspector Robert Gwynne Owen.
6. *Western Mail*, 14 September, 5–10 November 1968.
7. *Western Mail*, 10–18 September 1968; also John Jenkins to author, 5–12 November 2005.
8. *Western Mail*, 10–18 September 1968.
9. Ibid.
10. Ibid.
11. TNA, DPP 2/4455, E. Brampton (F2, Home Office Police Division), to J. F. Claxton, Department of the Director of Public Prosecutions, 10 September 1968.
12. *Western Mail*, Free Wales Army trial, 15 May 1969.
13. *Western Mail*, FWA trial, 1 May 1969.
14. *Western Mail*, FWA trial, 7 May 1969.
15. *Western Mail*, FWA trial, 6 June 1969.
16. *Western Mail*, FWA trial, 29 April 1969.
17. *Western Mail*, FWA trial, 6 June 1969.
18. *Western Mail*, FWA trial, 3, 10 May 1969.
19. *Western Mail*, 27 February 1969.
20. Letter to author from Legal Secretariat to the Law Officers, Attorney General's Chambers, 11 October 2005, requested under Freedom of Information Act.
21. *Western Mail*, FWA trial, 17 April 1969.
22. *Western Mail*, FWA trial, 30 April 1969; *Western Mail*, 2 May 1969; *Western Mail*, 30 June 1969.
23. *Western Mail*, FWA trial, 13 May 1969.
24. *Western Mail*, FWA trial, 14 May 1969.
25. Ibid.
26. *Western Mail*, FWA trial, 29 May 1969.
27. *Western Mail*, FWA trial, 17 June 1969.
28. *Western Mail*, FWA trial, 18 June 1969.
29. *Western Mail*, FWA trial, 19 June 1969.
30. *Western Mail*, FWA trial, 20 June 1969.
31. *Western Mail*, FWA trial, 24 June 1969.
32. *Western Mail*, FWA trial, 26 June 1969.
33. *Western Mail*, FWA trial, 2 July 1969.
34. *Western Mail*, FWA trial, 1, 2 July 1969.
35. Ibid.

## Chapter 9

1. TNA, ASSI 84/577, witness statements, Harold Pendlebury, Ian Skidmore.
2. Ibid.
3. Ibid.

4. *Western Mail*, 11 April 1970; also TNA, ASSI 84/577, witness statements, Harold Pendlebury, Ian Skidmore.
5. John Jenkins to author, 5–12 November 2005.
6. *Western Mail*, 27 May 1968; TNA, ASSI 84/577, witness statement, Major Clifton Jefferies, HQ Western Command Ammunition Inspectorate, Royal Army Ordnance Corps, Chester; also Jenkins to author, 5–12 November 2005.
7. *Western Mail*, 27, 28 May 1968.
8. *Western Mail*, 28 May 1968.

## Chapter 10

1. *Western Mail*, 3 December 1968; John Jenkins to author, 5–12 November 2005.
2. *Western Mail*, 16 April 1969, p. 9.
3. Reporter Patrick Hannan to author.
4. *Western Mail*, 25–9 July 1969.
5. *Western Mail*, 25 April 1969.
6. TNA, PREM 13/2505, transcript, BBC *24 Hours* programme, 28 February 1969.
7. TNA, PREM 13/2505, George Thomas, Secretary of State for Wales, to Lord Hill, Postmaster General, 13 March 1969.
8. TNA, BD 25/296, also BD 67/74, letter, J. Clements, Welsh Office, to J. Giddings, Editor, *Western Mail*.
9. TNA, PREM 13/2903, minute, Prime Minister Harold Wilson to Home Secretary James Callaghan, 16 April 1969; reply, Callaghan to Wilson, 16 April 1969.
10. TNA, PREM 13/2903, note, George Thomas, Secretary of State for Wales, to Wilson, 21 April 1969.
11. TNA, HO 325/122, report, Sir James Waddell, Deputy Under-Secretary of State, Home Office, to Sir Philip Allen, Permanent Under-Secretary of State, Home Office, 20 May 1969.
12. TNA, HO 325/122, Dennis Trevelyan, Home Office Division F2 (counter terrorism), 26 June 1969.
13. Letter to author from Gargi Banerjee, Information and Record Management Section, Home Office, London, 26 August 2005.
14. TNA, HO 325/124, memorandum, 'The Prince of Wales at Aberystwyth and Caernarfon', W. P. Nichol, Director of Telecommunications, 22 April 1969.
15. TNA, HO 325/122, letter, Ronald Mitchell, Director, Forensic Science Laboratory, Cardiff, to Frank Williamson, HM Inspectorate of Constabulary, 20 May 1969.

## Chapter 11

1. TNA, PREM 13/2903, letter, Brian Cubbon, Private Secretary to Home Secretary James Callaghan, to Michael Wells, Prime Minister's Principal Private Secretary, 26 June 1969.
2. TNA, PREM 13/2903, Wells to Cubbon, 27 June 1969.
3. TNA, PREM 13/2903, Cubbon to Wells, 27 June 1969.
4. TNA, PREM 13/2903, J. F. Mayne, Assistant Private Secretary to Denis Healey, Minister for Defence, to Wells, 27 June 1969.
5. *Western Mail*, 26 June 1969.
6. Ibid.

7. TNA, ASSI 84/577, witness statement, Major Clifton Jefferies, HQ Western Command Ammunition Inspectorate, Royal Army Ordnance Corps, Chester; also *Western Mail*, 26 June 1969.
8. *Western Mail*, 26 June 1969.
9. *Western Mail*, 10 October 1969.
10. Ibid.
11. *Western Mail*, Taylor/Jones inquest, 15 October 1969.
12. Jenkins to author, 5–12 November 2005.
13. Ibid.
14. Ibid.
15. *Western Mail*, 30 June 1969.
16. *Western Mail*, 5 March 1969.
17. *Western Mail*, 28 June 1969.
18. Ibid.

## Chapter 12

1. *Western Mail*, 2 July 1969.
2. Ibid.; also inquest at Caernarfon, 29 July 1969.
3. TNA, HO 325/124, Frank Williamson report to Sir James Waddell, Home Office, on extremist bombings, 16 July 1969.
4. Ibid.
5. TNA, HO 325/124, Williamson to Waddell, Home Office, 16 July 1969.
6. Ibid.
7. Ibid.; also note by Sir Brian Cubbon, Private Secretary to Home Secretary James Callaghan, of meeting between Commissioner Metropolitan Police and Home Secretary, 29 July 1969.
8. *Western Mail*, 2 July 1969.
9. TNA, HO 325/124, letter, William Farley, chairman/secretary, Committee of Chief Constables, to Sir Philip Allen, Permanent Under-Secretary of State, Home Office, 10 January 1970.
10. TNA, 325/124, letter, R. G. Fenwick, HM Inspector of Constabulary, Birmingham, to R. A. James, Deputy Receiver, Metropolitan Police District, undated.
11. TNA, HO 325/124, Dennis Trevelyan, Home Office F2 Division, to Sir James Wardell, Deputy Permanent Under-Secretary, Home Office, 30 January 1970.
12. T. Emyr Pritchard, *Barn*, 'The political police at Shrewsbury' (December 1969); a copy was sent to the Home Secretary by Eirene White, Minister of State, Welsh Office.

## Chapter 13

1. *Western Mail*, Jenkins/Alders trial, 10–21 April 1970.
2. TNA, ASSI 84/577, witness statement, Mary Jones, Holyhead.
3. TNA, ASSI 84/577, witness statement, Gordon Wynne Jones, Holyhead.
4. Ibid.; also TNA, ASSI 84/577, police statement, Alders.
5. John Jenkins to author, 5–12 November 2005.
6. Ibid.
7. Ibid.

8. *Western Mail*, Jenkins trial, 10–21 April 1970.
9. Jenkins to author, 5–12 November 2005.
10. *Western Mail*, Jenkins trial, 10–21 April 1970.
11. *Evening News*, Manchester, 9 July 1966.
12. Jenkins to author, 5–12 November 2005.

## Chapter 14

1. J. Jenkins, *Prison Letters* (Y Lolfa, 1981), p. 32; also Eileen Beasley, 9 February 2008.
2. John Jenkins to author, 5–12 November 2005.
3. Jenkins, *Prison Letters*, p. 16.
4. Ibid., p. 64.
5. Ibid., pp. 73, 117.
6. Ibid., p. 32.
7. *Western Mail*, 21 April 1970.
8. Jenkins, *Prison Letters*, p. 118.
9. Ibid., pp. 99, 102.
10. *Western Mail*, 15, 16 November 1983
11. Ibid.
12. Jenkins to author, 5–12 November 2005.
13. Ibid.; also *Western Mail*, 17 October 1974.
14. Ibid.
15. Jenkins to author 5–12 November 2005, 11 September 2007.

## Chapter 15

1. J. Jenkins, *Prison Letters* (Talybont: Y Lolfa, 1981), p. 41; Rhys Evans, *Rhag pob Brad* (Talybont: Y Lolfa, 2005).
2. Jenkins to author, 5–12 November 2005.
3. Ray White to author, 14 November 2006.
4. R. Geary, 'The Dragon and the Flame: an analysis of the Welsh arson campaign', *Oxford Contemporary Review* (January 1994); E. Hobsbawm, *Bandits* (London: Weidenfeld and Nicolson, 1969); *Bangor and Anglesey Mail*, 19 October 1988.
5. *Western Mail*, 14, 17 December 1979.
6. Dyfed-Powys and North Wales police reports released to author under Freedom of Information Act.
7. *Western Mail*, 27 December 1979.
8. *Western Mail*, 29 December 1979.
9. BBC *Nationwide*, 12 March 1980.
10. *Western Mail*, 20 January, 4 February 1980.
11. *Western Mail*, 22 March 1980.
12. S4C, *Taro Naw*, 15 March 1980.
13. *Fire/Tân*, report sponsored by the Welsh Campaign for Civil and Political Liberties, 30 April 1980.
14. Ibid.
15. Ibid.
16. Ibid.
17. Ibid.
18. *Western Mail*, 15–16 November 1983.

## Chapter 16

1. M. Thatcher, *The Downing Street Years* (London: HarperCollins, 1993), pp. 214–16.

## Chapter 17

1. *Western Mail*, 15, 29 February, 9 May, 3 October, 28, 29 November, 1988; *The Times*, 28 November, 1988.
2. *Western Mail*, 19 October 1988.
3. Denis Balsom, *Western Mail*, 18 October 1988; also Ray White to author 14 November 2005.
4. A. Gruffydd, *Mae Rhywun yn Gwybod* (Dyffryn Conwy: Gwasg Carreg Gwalch, 2004), pp. 105–9.
5. *Western Mail*, 21 January 1993.
6. *Western Mail*, 27 March 1993.
7. North Wales Police: list of incidents of Arson/Attempted Arson deemed to be part of the Cottage Arson Campaign in North Wales. See Appendix A.
8. *Taro Naw*, 9 March 2004.
9. Letter, Gwynfor Evans to author, 23 August 1992.
10. Gwynfor Evans, 'Should direct action be condemned?', *Western Mail*, 10 July 1963.
11. Office for National Statistics, fax, D. Williams to Len Cooke, 7 December 2000.
12. ONS, letter, Len Cook to Deryk Williams, 19 December 2000.
13. ONS, e-mail, Graham Jones, Director Census, to Len Cook/John Pullinger, subject 'John Humphries', 13 December 2000.
14. ONS, e-mail, David Marder to Ian G. Scott, subject 'John Humphries', 25 July 2001.
15. ONS, e-mail, Ian G. Scott to Graham Jones, subject 'John Humphries', 25 July 2001; Freedom of Information Act 2000 (Section 50), Decision Notice, 11 June 2007.
16. ONS, e-mail, Graham Jones to Len Cook, subject 'John Humphries', 25 July 2001; ONS, e-mail, Len Cook to David Marder, subject 'John Humphries', 25 July 2001; ONS, e-mail, Len Cook to Graham Jones, subject 'John Humphries', 26 July 2001.
17. ONS, e-mail, Marder to Ian White, subject 'Census coffin: response on penalties', undated.
18. ONS, e-mail, Marder to Ian White, subject 'Census coffin: response on penalties', 22 August 2001.
19. Letter, Len Cook, ONS, to John Humphries, Chief Executive, Cymru Annibynnol/ Independent Wales Party, 15 August 2001.
20. ONS, Marder to Graham Jones, c/c National Statistician/Senior Management, subject 'John Humphries', 22 August 2001.
21. Letter, Len Cook, ONS, to John Humphries, 31 August 2001.
22. Letter, Humphries to Cook, 10 September 2001.
23. Letter, Cook to Humphries, with copy to Office of the Solicitor, 29 August 2002.

## Chapter 18

1. Office for National Statistics, Census 2001, 'Key Statistics from Assembly Constituencies and Assembly electoral regions for the National Assembly for Wales', Tables K505, K506.
2. Ray White, former Chief Constable, Dyfed-Powys, to author, 14 November 2005.
3. *Western Mail*, 14, 17 December 1979.
4. Ofwat, 2006–2007 Special Agreement Register, WSHBSE6, Dŵr Cymru/Welsh Water.

5. Nigel Arnett, Chief Executive, Dŵr Cymru, to author, April 2007; privatisation offer prospectuses, Severn Trent and Dŵr Cymru (6) Material Operating Agreements, 1989; letter to author from M. R. Knight, Company Solicitor, Severn Trent Water, 12 September 2000; letters to author from T. T. J. Ashcroft, Chief Solicitor, Dŵr Cymru, 23 August, 1 September, 9 October 2000; Ofwat, 2006–2007 Special Agreement Register, WSHBSE6, Dŵr Cymru/Welsh Water; also see Appendix B for details of water-supply contract.
6. Letter to Dŵr Cymru from Dr Jerry Bryan, Chief Executive, Albany Water, February 2007.

# SELECT BIBLIOGRAPHY

Anderson, Benedict, *Imagined Communities: Reflections on the Origin and Spread of Nationalism* (London: Verso, 1983).

Adamson, D., *Class, Ideology and the Nation: A Theory of Welsh Nationalism* (Cardiff: University of Wales Press, 1991).

Clews, Roy, *To Dream of Freedom* (Talybont: Y Lolfa, 1980).

Davies, R. R., *The Age of Conquest: Wales 1063–1415* (Oxford: Oxford University Press, 1991).

Davies, D. Hywel, *Welsh Nationalist Party 1925–1945* (Cardiff: University of Wales Press, 1983).

Evans, Gwynfor, *Fighting for Wales* (Talybont: Y Lolfa, 1991).

Evans, Gwynfor, *For the Sake of Wales* (Cardiff: Welsh Academic Press, 1996, 2001).

Evans, Gwynfor, *Land of My Fathers: 100 Years of Welsh History* (Swansea: John Penry Press, 1974).

Evans, Rhys, *Rhag pob Brad* (Talybont: Y Lolfa, 2005).

Fevre, Ralph and Thompson, Andrew (eds), *Nation, Identity and Social Theory: Perspectives from Wales* (Cardiff: University of Wales Press, 1999).

Geary, R, 'The Dragon and the Flame: an analysis of the Welsh arson campaign', *Oxford Contemporary Review* (January, 1994).

Gerald of Wales/Giraldus Cambrensis, *The Journey through Wales and the Description of Wales* (London: Penguin, 1978).

Gellner, Ernest, *Nations and Nationalism* (Oxford: Blackwell, 1983).

Gruffydd, Alwyn, *Mae Rhywun yn Gwybod* (Duffryn Conwy: Gwasg Carreg Gwalch, 2004).

Hobsbawm, E. J., *Nations and Nationalism since 1780* (Cambridge: Cambridge University Press, 1990).

Hobsbawm, E. J. and Ranger, Terence (eds), *The Invention of Tradition* (Cambridge: Cambridge University Press, 1983).

Hobsbawm, E. J., *Bandits* (London: Weidenfeld and Nicolson, 1969).

Hutchinson, J. and Smith, Anthony D. (eds), *Nationalism* (Oxford: Oxford University Press, 1994).

Jenkins, John, *Prison Letters* (Talybont: Y Lolfa, 1981).

Knowles, Dudley, *Hegel and the Philosophy of Right (1821)* (London: Routledge, 2002).

Matthews, T., *Welsh Records in Paris* (Carmarthen, 1911).

Morgan, K. O., *The Rebirth of a Nation: Wales 1880–1980* (Oxford and Cardiff: OUP, 1981).

Nairn, T., 'Culture and politics in Wales', in Hume, I. and Pryce, W. T. R. (eds), *The Welsh and Their Country* (Llandysul: Gomer, 1986).

Nairn, Tom, *The Break-Up of Britain: Crisis and Neo-Nationalism* (London: Verso, 1981).

Smith, A. D., *Theories of Nationalism* (London: Duckworth, 1971).

Smith, A. D., 'The nation: invented, imagined, reconstructed', *Millennium, Journal of International Studies,* 20/3 (1991), 353–68.

Smith, A. D., 'Chosen peoples: why ethnic groups survive', *Ethnic and Racial Studies*, 15/3 (1992), 436–56.

Smith, A. D., *Wales! Wales?* (London: Allen and Unwin, 1984).

Thomas, Ned, *The Welsh Extremist: A Culture in Crisis* (Talybont: Y Lolfa, 1991).

Williams, Gwyn A., *When Was Wales? A History of the Welsh* (London: Pelican, 1985).

Williams, Owen, *Cysgod Tryweryn* (Llanwrst: Gwasg Carreg Gwalch, 1995).

# APPENDIX A

List of incidents of arson/attempted arson deemed to be part of the Cottage Arson Campaign in north Wales. Supplied by Gwynedd Police under Freedom of Information Act.

1. 13 December 1979, arson, residential property, Pwllheli.
2. 13 December 1979, arson, residential property, Pwllheli.
3. 14 December 1979, arson, residential property, Blaenau Ffestiniog
4. 14 December 1979, arson, residential property, Blaenau Ffestiniog.
5. 15 December 1979, arson, residential property, Blaenau Ffestiniog.
6. 27 December 1979, attempted arson, residential property, Pwllheli.
7. 9 January 1980, attempted arson, residential property, Rhosygwalia, Bala.
8. 15 January 1980, arson, residential property, Llanbedrgoch.
9. 16 January 1980, arson, residential property, Brynsiencyn.
10. 25 January 1980, arson, residential property, Penrhyndeudraeth.
11. 31 January 1980, attempted arson, residential property, Bontddu.
12. 1 February 1980, arson, residential property, Mochnant.
13. 10 February 1980, arson, residential property, Bangor.
14. 16 February 1980, arson, residential property, Anglesey.
15. 18 February 1980, arson, residential property, Newborough.
16. 18 February 1980, arson, residential property, Llan Ffestiniog.
17. 28 February 1980, arson, residential property, Llan Ffestiniog.
18. 29 February 1980, attempted arson, St Mary's hut, Drws y Coed, Nanlle, Gwynedd.
19. 2 March 1980, arson, residential property, Corris.
20. 6 March 1980, arson, residential property, Denbigh.
21. 17 March 1980, arson, residential property, Dyserth.
22. 19 March 1980, attempted arson, Ffestiniog Railway, Porthmadoc.
23. 21 March 1980, arson, residential property, Aberdaron.
24. 27 March 1980, arson, residential property, Dinas Mawddwy.
25. 27 March 1980 and 17 July 1982, arson, residential property, Ffynongroew.*
26. 5 April 1980, arson, residential property, Beddgelert.
27. 8 April 1980, arson, residential property, Llandonna.
28. 17 April 1980, attempted arson, residential property, Dolgellau.

29. 17 April 1980, attempted arson, residential property, Dolgellau.
30. 2 May 1980, arson, residential property, Penymynydd.
31. 16 September 1980, arson, residential property, Tanygrisiau.
32. 31 October 1980, arson, residential property, Pwllheli.
33. 31 October 1980, attempted arson, residential property, Pwllheli.
34. 9 November 1980, arson, residential property Criccieth.
35. 1 February 1981, arson, residential property, Caernarfon.
36. 2 February 1981, attempted arson, residential property, Capel Garmon.
37. 3 February, 1981, arson to boat at Gwnhinhar Farm, Boduan, Pwllheli.
38. 1 March 1981, arson, residential property, Caernarfon.
39. 20 October 1981, arson, residential property, Llanberis.
40. 21 October 1981 and 22 February 1985, arson, residential property, Llandyfrydog.*
41. 21 October 1981, arson, residential property, Bodorgan.
42. 8 November 1981, arson, residential property, Amlwch.
43. 8 November 1981, arson, residential property, Amlwch.
44. 11 November 1981, arson, residential property, Bodorgan.
45. 15 November 1981, arson, residential property, Bodedern.
46. 1 December 1981, attempted arson, residential property, Cable Bay.
47. 5 December 1981, attempted arson, residential property, Aberffraw.
48. 5 January 1982, arson, residential property, Pwllheli.
49. 26 January 1982 and 3 March 1982, attempted arson, residential property, Mynydd Llandegai.*
50. 25 February 1982, arson, residential property, Pwllheli.
51. 6 March 1982, arson, residential property, Newborough.
52. 6 March 1982, arson, residential property, Abergele.
53. 23 March 1982, attempted arson, residential property, Hermon.
54. 27 March 1982, arson, residential property, Caernarfon.
55. 17 July 1982, arson, residential property, Ffynongroew.
56. 4 January 1983, attempted arson, Tŷ Gerrig, Boduan.
57. 20 January 1983, arson, residential property, Deiniolen.
58. 14 March 1983, attempted arson, residential property, Llanfihangel.
59. 8 April 1983, arson, residential property, Gronant.
60. 9 April 1983, arson, residential property, Lloc.
61. 29 April 1983, arson, residential property, Mostyn.
62. 16 July 1983, attempted arson, residential property, Llandudno.
63. 10 November 1983, arson, residential property, Aberffraw.
64. 3 November 1983, arson, residential property, Pwllheli.
65. 30 November 1983, arson, residential property, Bodorgan.
66. 15 January 1984, arson, residential property, Blaenau Ffestiniog.
67. 21 January 1984, arson chalet, Bronaber holiday complex, Trawsfynydd.
68. 23 January 1984, arson, residential property, Harlech.
69. 6 February 1984, attempted arson, The Show Bungalow, Fron Haul Estate, Rhyl.
70. 7 February 1984, arson, residential property, Trawsfynydd.
71. 22 March 1984, attempted arson, residential property, Cwmystradllyn.
72. 19 February 1985, arson, residential property, Porthmadoc.
73. 16 April 1985, attempted arson, residential property, Llanerchymedd.

74. 20 November 1985, arson, residential property, Penisarwaen.
75. 22 November 1985, arson, residential property, Aberdaron.
76. 24 November 1985, arson, residential property, Aberdaron.
77. 13 January 1986, arson, residential property, Llanuwchlyn.
78. 27 January 1986, arson, residential property, Caernarfon.
79. 19 March 1986, arson, residential property, Rhosgadfan.
80. 2 April 1986, attempted arson, residential property, Ruthin.
81. 26 September 1986, arson, residential property, Dolgellau.
82. 26 September 1986, arson, residential property, Deiniolen.
83. 26 September 1986, arson, residential property, Deiniolen.
84. 26 September 1986, arson, residential property, Penal.
85. 17 October 1986, arson, residential property, Pwllheli.
86. 17 October 1986, arson, residential property, Rhoslan.
87. 15 November 1986, arson at chalet, The Warren, Abersoch.
88. 16 November 1986, arson, residential property, Pwllheli.
89. 22 December 1986, arson, residential property, Conwy.
90. 23 February 1987, arson, residential property, Llanrwst.
91. 23 February 1987, arson, residential property, Abergele.
92. 15 June 1987, attempted arson, residential property, Abersoch.
93. 28 June 1987, attempted arson at Tax Offices, Porthmadoc.
94. 28 June 1987, attempted arson, The Show House, Welmar Estate, Abergele.
95. 16 September 1987, arson, residential property, Penisarwaen.
96. 9 October 1987, attempted arson, Bala Sailing Club.
97. 23 November 1987, attempted arson, residential property, Dolgellau.
98. 25 November 1987, attempted arson, harbour offices, Portdinorwig.
99. 2 January 1988, attempted arson, residential property, Aberdyfi.
100. 14 February 1988, arson, residential property, Bethesda.
101. 18 March 1988, arson, residential property, Betws y Coed.
102. 7 May 1988, arson, Prudential Property Estate Agents, 16 Church Street, Llangefni.
103. 17 October 1988, arson, Odds and Rods, Church Street, Beaumaris.
104. 17 October 1988, attempted arson, Watersports Centre, High Street, Bala.
105. 24 February 1989, arson, Meirionydd Yacht Club, Barmouth.
106. 24 February 1989, attempted arson, Moelfre Drug Store, Moelfre.
107. 27 February 1989, attempted arson, Padarn Stores, 58 High Street, Llanberis.
108. 18 April 1989, arson Bretell Architects, 7 Dale Street, Menai Bridge.
109. 22 June 1989, attempted arson, Dickies Boatyard, Beach Road, Bangor.
110. 23 July 1989, arson to Mercedes car, Pen y Cei, Harbour Road, Abersoch.
111. 10 August 1989, arson, Cooke, Wood and Caird Estate Agents, 154 High Street, Bangor.
112. 22 October 1989, arson, residential property, Dolgellau.
113. 9 November 1989, attempted arson to JCB, David MeLean site, Llanfair PG.
114. 25 November 1989, arson, *Kasia* Yacht, Greaves Wharf, Porthmadoc.
115. 30 November 1989, attempted arson *Syrena* Yacht, Marine Walk, Conwy.
116. 30 November 1989, attempted arson, *Barbara Allen* Yacht, Slate Quay, Caernarfon.
117. 30 November 1989, attempted arson, Plas y Brenin Outdoor Centre, Capel Curig.

118. 20 June 1990, attempted grievous bodily harm by letter-bomb, Land and Sea, Abersoch.
119. 20 June 1990, attempted grievous bodily harm by letter-bomb, Allo, Allo, Dolgellau.
120. 25 November 1990, attempted arson at The Chalet, Pentfadarch Holiday Complex, Holyhead.
121. 30 December 1990, attempted arson, Siop Gwyled, Rhostryfan, Caernarfon.
122. 28 March 1991, arson Conservative Club, King Edward Street, Shotton.
123. 6 July 1991, attempted arson, residential property, Abersoch.
124. 6 August 1991, attempted arson, Conservative Club, High Street, Bangor.
125. 6 August 1991, attempted arson at Army Careers Office, Glynne Road, Bangor.
126. 7 September 1991, attempted arson at Tourist Information Office, Llangefni.
127. 7 September 1991, arson, residential property, Capel Celyn, Bala.
128. 19 September 1991, attempted arson, Jodies Wine Bar, Telford Road, Menai Bridge.
129. 17 October 1991, attempted arson to Ford Fiesta at Shire Hall car park, Glan Nwyfa Road, Llangefni.
130. 18 November 1991, arson, residential property, Blaenau Ffestiniog.
131. 19 November 1991, postal device, sorting office, Betws y Coed.
132. 31 October 1992, arson, residential property, Capel Celyn, Bala.
133. 1 November 1992, arson, Towyn Camp, Penrhos, Pwllheli.
134. 1 November 1992, arson at DSS Offices, Llangefni.
* These properties were attacked twice.

Location of cottage arson incidents in Dyfed-Powys 1979–89:

1. 13 December 1979, Bickney, Llanrhian.
2. 13 December 1979, Parc y West, Llanrhian.
3. 30 December 1979, Penfeidr, Croesgoch.
4. 20 January 1980, Lock Cottage, Abermule.
5. 29 January 1980, Brynmilwch, Gwynfe.
6. 11 February 1980, Glan y Mor, Cenarth.
7. 17 February 1980, Llwyn y Rhun, Llangynidr.
8. 24 February 1980, Tanscawen, Llanllwni.
9. 24 February 1980, Pentwyn, Pontsticill.
10. 21 March 1980, Tŷ Newydd, Cenarth.
11. 30 March 1980, Anglers Retreat, Talybont.
12. 31 December 1980, Pencaegarw, Gwynfe.
13. 6 February 1981, Yr Hafod, Newport.
14. 6 February 1981, Siop Fach, Newport.
15. 2 March 1981, Pantyfedwen, Llanfynydd.
16. 18 March 1981, Blaenpant, Moylegrove.
17. 9 April 1981, Maesteg, Brynhoffnant.
18. 10 April 1981, Glanrafon, Llanfihangel y Creuddyn.
19. 25 April 1981, Lleithr Farm, St David's.
20. 26 April 1981, Bryneirin, Sarnau.
21. 5 January 1983, Penpegws, Rhydyfelin.
22. 15 February 1983, Pant y Cerrig, Brechfa.

23. 24 February 1984, Maglona, Llangrannog.
24. 24 February 1984, Llainwhip, Tanygroes.
25. 20 November 1985, Brynawelon, Tanygroes.
26. 20 November 1985, Cross Hill, Bangor Teifi.
27. 5 December 1985, Ceunant, Mynachlogddu.
28. 28 February 1986, Rhos y Maen, Bethania.
29. 27 February 1987, Aberhosan, Machynlleth.
30. 27 March 1987, Cefn Bach, Manordeilo.
31. 27 March 1987, Brynerddil, Manordeilo.
32. 14 February 1988, smallholding centre, Brongest.
33. 28 March 1988, Talog Mill, New Inn.
34. 20 April 1988, Allt Forgan, Llanwddyn.
35. 17 October 1988, Christie and Co., Carmarthen.
36. 18 October 1988, John Francis and Son, Carmarthen.
37. 26 October 1988, Lowgate, Sarnau.
38. 12 December 1988, John Francis and Son, Llandeilo.
39. 16 December 1988, Llechwedd, Llanwddyn.
40. 24 February 1989, Craft and Coffee Shop, Aberaeron.
41. 18 March 1989, Lees and Thomas, Haverfordwest.
42. 26 April 1989, Cawdor Farm Development, Llandeilo.
43. 30 July 1989, J. J. Morris, Haverfordwest.

Location of arson attacks outside Wales:

1. 27 February 1988, Prudential Estate Agency, Chester.
2. 27 February 1988, Beresford Adams Estate Agency, Chester.
3. 27 February 1988, Jordans Estate Agency, Chester.
4. 27 February 1988, Jackson-Stops Estate Agency, Chester.
5. 6 May 1988, Prudential Property Services, Liverpool.
6. 6 May 1988, Sykes, Waterhouse and Company, Liverpool.
7. 6 May 1988, John German Estate Agents, Shrewsbury.
8. 1 October 1988, Davies, Brown and Jennings Estate Agents, Wellington, Shropshire.
9. 1 October 1988, Prudential Property Services, Wellington.
10. 1 October 1988, Jones, Chapman and Harland, West Kirby.
11. 1 October 1988, Jackson-Stops and Staff, Chipping Campden.
12. 1 October 1988, Jones, Chapman and Harland, Neston, Wirral.
13. 1 October 1988, Prudential Property Services, Worcester.
14. 1 October 1988, Prudential Property Services, Clifton, Bristol.
15. 27 November 1988, Strutt and Parker, Hill Street, Mayfair, London.
16. 27 November 1988, Anscombe and Ringland, Notting Hill Gate, London.
17. 27 November 1988, Savills, Grosvenor Hill, London.
18. 27 November 1988, Black Horse Agencies/Gascoigne Pees, Lower Sloane Street, London.
19. 27 November 1988, Jackson-Stops and Staff, Milner Street, London.
20. 27 November 1988, John D. Wood, Kensington, London.

# APPENDIX B

Extract from the privatisation prospectus issued in November 1989, describing the arrangements entered into between the former Severn Trent and Welsh Water authorities relating to payment for water supplied from the Elan Reservoirs:

'MATERIAL OPERATING AGREEMENTS AND OTHER SIGNIFICANT ARRANGEMENTS

Dŵr Cymru's principal operating agreement relates to the bulk supply of water to Severn Trent Water from the Elan Valley Reservoirs.

The Elan Valley reservoirs were originally built by Birmingham Corporation and have supplied water to Birmingham since 1904. The ownership of the reservoirs and treatment works has changed through successive periods of water industry reorganisation. The present arrangements are designed to pass eventual ownership of the Elan Valley aqueduct and treatment works to Severn Trent Water, which is responsible for their operation and maintenance.

In 1984, Welsh Water Authority and Severn Trent Water Authority entered into a number of agreements constituting one arrangement relating to the supply of water from the Elan Valley Reservoirs to Severn Trent Water. This arrangement was intended to assure Welsh Water Authority an acceptable income and ensure continuity of supply to Severn Trent Water Authority.

The principal terms of the bulk supply agreement are that Dŵr Cymru is required to supply up to approximately 360 ml/d of untreated water from the Elan Valley Reservoirs to Severn Trent Water, at an annual charge, which varies from year to year by reference to the average of the water supply unit costs of Dŵr Cymru and Severn Trent Water. The agreement is for an initial term, which is expected to expire on 31 March 2073, and is renewable at Severn Trent Water's option for a further 99 years. If the bulk supply agreement is not renewed, or is terminated, the Director General could make an order under the Water Act requiring supply to be continued as explained in chapter 11 of the general section.

Simultaneously, with the execution of the bulk supply agreement, Severn Trent Water Authority entered into a conditional sale and purchase agreement for the sale to it by Welsh Water Authority of the Elan Valley aqueduct and connected land and buildings used for the distribution and treatment of water from the Elan Valley Reservoirs (the "Elan Valley Assets"). Completion of the sale is deferred until the earlier of the 31st March 2073 and the expiration of 21 years after the death of the last survivor of the issue of the late King George V (whether children or more remote) actually born before the date of his death.

The consideration for the sale (amounting to £31.7 million) was paid into a trust fund, of which part of the income (amounting to some £1.1 million in the year ended 31st March 1989) is paid to Dŵr Cymru augmenting its annual income from the Elan Valley arrangements. The remainder of the income is retained as an addition to the fund although there are provisions for distribution of part of any excess if the fund achieves growth substantially in excess of inflation. On completion of the sale all the trust fund will pass to Dŵr Cymru absolutely.

If the supply agreement becomes subject to renegotiation (including in circumstances where Severn Trent Water gives notice that it intends to renew the agreement for a further 99 years) there are various arbitration provisions. If the trust fund has not already vested in Dŵr Cymru, Severn Trent Water will be entitled to the income from the trust fund during any period of renegotiation or arbitration. If the renegotiation or arbitration does not produce a satisfactory conclusion then the contract for the sale of the Elan Valley Assets will lapse, with the result that they will remain owned by Dŵr Cymru; and the trust fund will by then have passed to Severn Trent absolutely.

Pending completion or failure of the conditional sale and purchase agreement Severn Trent is licensed to use the Elan Valley Assets (including the water treatment works) and is obliged to maintain them and meet all costs and liabilities (including rates) relating to them.'[1]

1. Author's note: The trustees of the trust fund in 2000 were Kleinwort Benson Trustees Ltd. Dŵr Cymru and Severn Trent have both refused the author's request for (1) details of the current size of the trust fund; and (2) distribution of income between the various beneficiaries. The only details in the public domain are those

contained in the 1989 prospectus. The only mention of the trust fund in Dŵr Cymru's annual report and accounts is to the effect that the proceeds are not included for accounting purposes. In 1998–9 proceeds to Dŵr Cymru from these arrangements (including the sale of the water to Severn Trent) amounted to £10.4 million. More recently, Dŵr Cymru's share of revenue accruing from the investment of the trust fund has been in the order of £2–4 million. At no time has Dŵr Cymru explained how these revenues are used specifically to benefit Welsh water consumers through a direct reduction in water bills. Revenue received by Dŵr Cymru from Severn Trent for the sale of water from the Elan Valley Reservoirs has been approximately £4 million annually since 2004.

# TIMELINE

**1962**

*July*: Sir Keith Joseph appointed Minister for Housing and Local Government, and also Minister for Welsh Affairs in Harold Macmillan Government.

*September*: Dai Pritchard (New Tredegar) and Dave Walters (Bargoed) release oil from transformer at Tryweryn in attempt to cause an explosion. Each fined £40.

*October 15*: Owen Williams (Nefyn), Robert Williams (Criccieth) and Edwin Prichard (Nefyn) raid quarry at Llithfaen and steal detonators for attack on Tryweryn.

*November*: Pritchard and Walters each fined £40 for releasing oil from transformer.

**1963**

*10 February*: Owen Williams, Emyr Llewelyn Jones and John Albert Jones plant bomb beneath transformer at Tryweryn.

*22 February*: Harold Wilson pledges leasehold reform if Labour party wins the general election.

*2 March*: Roderic Bowen QC, MP(Lib. Cardigan), says Plaid Cymru undecided whether to fight 'by the bomb or the ballot box'.

*30 March*: Emyr Llewelyn Jones jailed for 12 months at Carmarthen Assizes

*31 March*: Owen Williams and John Albert Jones place bomb beneath power pylon at Gellilydan, near Trawsfynydd Power Station site.

*14 June*: John Albert Jones placed on probation for three years at Dolgellau Assizes.

*1 July*: Owen Williams jailed for twelve months at Denbighshire Assizes.

## 1964

*18 October*: James Griffiths appointed first Secretary of State for Wales (until 5 April 1966).

*18 October*: Sir Frank Soskice, MP (Newport) appointed Home Secretary (until 23 December 1965)

*26 October*: Hughes-Parry Report proposes equal status for Welsh and English in legal, business and administrative affairs of Wales.

## 1965

*23 December*: Roy Jenkins appointed Home Secretary (until 30 November 1967).

## 1966

*6 March*: Sabotage causes £30,000 damage at Clywedog Reservoir construction site; delays project by six months.

*5 April*: Cledwyn Hughes appointed Secretary of State for Wales (until 5 April 1968).

*8 July*: Marcus Gale (Llangollen) and Harry Jones (Cefn Mawr, near Wrexham) given probation for offences concerning explosives.

*14 July*: Gwynfor Evans. President of Plaid Cymru wins by-election at Carmarthen to become his party's first member of the House of Commons.

*21 October*: Aberfan Disaster kills 144, including 116 children.

## 1967

*27 February*: Free Wales Army given inner-tube bomb to plant in Birmingham City aqueduct at Cefn Penarth, Crossgates, near Llandudno; first Welsh Language Act extended use of Welsh to some legal proceedings.

*30 September*: Hole blown in 42-inch diameter Liverpool Corporation pipeline at Llanrhaeadr-ym-Mochnant.

*17 November*: Large bomb explodes on lintel above entrance to Temple of Peace, Cardiff.

*30 November*: James Callaghan appointed Home Secretary (until 19 June 1972)

## 1968

*5 January*: Four-foot hole blown in breeze-block wall of Snowdonia Country Club, Penisarwaun, near Caernarfon.

*24 January*: Hafod Colliery, Wrexham, explosives magazine broken and 300 lbs of explosives stolen.

*28 February*: Robert Griffith Jones (Groeslon) and Edward Wilkinson (Llanllyfni) given one year's suspended sentence for unlawful possession of explosives in connection Snowdonia Country Club explosion.

*6 March*: Owen Williams fails to answer bail on charges of being in unlawful possession of explosives in connection Snowdonia Country Club explosion.

Flees to Ireland.

*24 March*: Walls blown down, windows smashed in explosion at Inland Revenue Offices, Tŷ Glas Road, Llanishen, Cardiff.

*5 April*: George Thomas appointed Secretary of State for Wales (until 20 June 1970).

*2 May*: John Jenkins and Ernest Alders, members of MAC2 hold secret press conference near Chester to explain their objectives.

*25 May*: Explosion blows out windows at Welsh Office in Cathays Park, Cardiff.

*27 May*: Bomb damages pipeline and fractures concrete sill at Lake Vyrnwy, Montgomeryshire.

*27 June*: Major damage caused to Liverpool Corporation aqueduct crossing Chester–Warrington Railway line, water flooding road and undermining railway embankment.

*9 September*: RAF Warrant Officer seriously injured by bomb planted in control tower at Pembrey.

*9 November*: Owen Williams not guilty of unlawful possession of explosives.

*2 December*: Bomb damages pipeline at West Hagley supplying water to Birmingham from the Elan Valley.

*17 December*: Queen opens Royal Mint at Llantrisant, Pontypridd.

## 1969

*1 March*: Owen Williams addresses Anti-Investiture rally in Caernarfon.

*April*: Prime Minister Harold Wilson appoints Kilbrandon Commission on the Constitution.

*10 April*: Inland Revenue Office, Hamilton House, Chester damaged by bomb. Blast blows in hospital windows.

*15 April*: Minor damage caused by explosion outside Cardiff's new police head-quarters.

*23 April*: Booking clerk finds bomb in luggage locker at Cardiff Queen Street Station.

*28 April*: Bomb blast outside Central Electricity Generating Board offices at Gabalfa, Cardiff.

*2 May*: Parcel bomb addressed to Detective Sergeant Lavery intercepted at police headquarters, Cardiff.

*25 June*: Time bomb defused on McKenzie Pier, Holyhead, close to where Royal Yacht *Britannia* due to dock on day of Investiture.

*30 June*: Letterbox bomb at postal sorting office Victoria Park, Cardiff.

*30 June*: George Taylor and Alwyn Jones killed while assembling bomb near railway line along which Royal Train due to pass.

*1 July*: Investiture of Prince of Wales at Caernarfon Castle.

*1 July*: Bomb explodes at Love Lane, Caernarfon near the bottom of Chief Constable of Gwynedd's garden.

*2 July*: Free Wales Army trial ends with the jailing of Cayo Evans (15 months), Dennis Coslett (15 months), and Keith Griffiths (9 months).

*5 July*: Boy maimed at Caernarfon by extremist bomb while retrieving football from ironmonger's yard.

*14 August*: South Stack Relay Station damaged by explosion.

*17 August*: Explosive device left on steps outside St Martin's County Health offices, Chester, fails to explode.

*9 October*: Glyn Jones and Dewi Jones jailed for 18 months for assembling McKenzie Pier bomb, and Allan Jones for six months suspended for two years for offences connected with petrol bomb experiments.

*5 November*: Last of MAC2 munitions destroyed in explosion in Holyhead Park.

## 1970
*20 April*: At Flintshire Assizes, Mold, John Jenkins, Director of Operations for MAC, jailed (10 years) and Ernest Alders (6 years) after admitting eight offences linked to the bombing campaign.

## 1971
Kilbrandon Commission recommends devolution for Wales and Scotland.

Welsh Water Authority created by Peter Thomas, Conservative Secretary of State for Wales, after Council for Wales recommends formation of Water Development Authority for Wales to regulate water supply and protect Welsh interests.

## 1974

Dafydd Elis-Thomas elected Member of Parliament for Meirionnydd (until 1992, when elevated to House of Lords).

Dafydd Wigley elected Member of Parliament for Caernarfon (until 2001).

## 1979

*1 March*: Referendum on granting devolution to Wales is defeated.

*13 December*: Start of cottage arson campaign with fires at Pwllheli (2), Llanrhian, Pembrokeshire (2).

## 1980

Cottage arson incidents, North Wales (28), Dyfed-Powys (9).

## 1981

Cottage arson incidents, North Wales (12), Dyfed-Powys (9).

Gwynfor Evans retires as president of Plaid Cymru (since 1945).

## 1982

Cottage arson incidents, North Wales (8), none in Dyfed-Powys.

*1 November*: S4C, the Welsh-language television channel, starts broadcasting.

## 1983

Cottage arson incidents, North Wales (10), Dyfed-Powys (2).

## 1984

Cottage arson incidents, North Wales (6), Dyfed-Powys (2).

Dafydd Elis-Thomas elected President of Plaid Cymru (until 1991).

## 1985

Cottage arson incidents, North Wales (5), Dyfed-Powys (3).

## 1986

Cottage arson incidents, North Wales (13), Dyfed-Powys (1).

## 1987

Cottage arson incidents, North Wales (9), Dyfed-Powys (3).

## 1988

Arson campaign escalates with attacks on 20 estate agents in England; also 6 in North Wales, 8 in Dyfed-Powys.

**1989**

Cottage arson incidents, North Wales (13), Dyfed-Powys (4).

**1990**

Cottage arson incidents, North Wales (4).

**1991**

Cottage arson incidents, North Wales (10).

Dafydd Wigley elected President of Plaid Cymru (until 2000).

**1992**

Cottage arson incidents, North Wales (3).

**1993**

*26 March*: Sion Aubrey Roberts jailed for 12 years for sending incendiary devices through the post to police detectives and politicians.

New Welsh Language Act gives Welsh equal status with English with regard to the public sector; Welsh Language Board formed.

# INDEX